Republican Jesus

Republican Jesus

*How the Right
Has Rewritten the Gospels*

TONY KEDDIE

UNIVERSITY OF CALIFORNIA PRESS

University of California Press
Oakland, California

© 2020 by Tony Keddie

Cataloging-in-Publication Data is on file at the Library
of Congress.

ISBN 978-0-520-35623-8 (cloth : alk. paper)
ISBN 978-0-520-97602-3 (ebook)

Manufactured in the United States of America

28   27   26   25   24   23   22   21   20
10   9   8   7   6   5   4   3   2   1

For my dad

Contents

Illustrations

Acknowledgments

I owe profuse thanks to my wife, Becky, for encouraging me to write this book, for sharing her wisdom with me, for reading and debating every little detail with me, and for being a true partner in all things.

Many thanks to the University of British Columbia for research support; to Doug and Brent for advice; to LM for inspiration, prudent suggestions, and timely encouragement; to Ben and Pat for incisive feedback on early drafts; to Sara, Toph, Steve, Kurtis, Rob, and Gregg for helpful and challenging comments on chapters; to Lara for top-notch research assistance; to Dora for help with proofreading; to those UBC grad students who workshopped a chapter with me; to past and present students, from whom I have learned so much; to my agent, John Butman, for seeing potential in this project and providing abundant encouragement prior to his tragic passing; to Lucy Cleland, for her support ever since; to my anonymous reviewers for providing such helpful and constructive feedback; to Eric Schmidt, Austin Lim, Alex Dahne, Dore Brown, Elisabeth Magnus,

Cindy Fulton, and the rest of the terrific team at the University of California Press for their unflagging dedication to this project; and to the many family, friends, and colleagues who've entertained my ramblings about Republican Jesus along the way.

I think it's unfortunate that more authors don't acknowledge the importance of good mental health when writing a book, especially a book on challenging topics. My therapist, John, has been a huge help, and I'm grateful that I don't have to pay for his care.

I lovingly dedicate this book to my dad with thanks for teaching me compassion through important lessons, spoken and unspoken.

A Note to Readers

Except when otherwise noted, quotations of the Bible are taken from the New Revised Standard Version (NRSV), quotations of the Greek translation of the Hebrew Bible (the Septuagint) are taken from *A New English Translation of the Septuagint* (NETS), and quotations of Greek and Latin texts are from the Loeb Classical Library translation series.

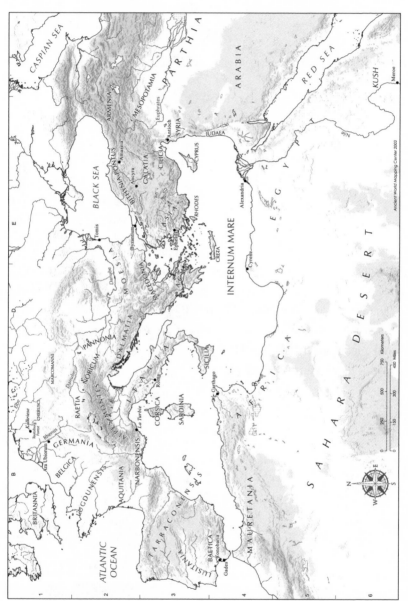

Map 1. Map of the Roman Empire after the conquests of Augustus. Credit: Ancient World Mapping Center, University of North Carolina at Chapel Hill (www.awmc.unc.edu).

Map 2. Map of Palestine during Jesus's lifetime, showing the division of Herod's kingdom between his sons and Roman officials. Credit: Ancient World Mapping Center, University of North Carolina at Chapel Hill (www. awmc.unc.edu).

Introduction

Jesus to me is somebody I can think about for security
and confidence. Somebody I can revere in terms of
bravery and in terms of courage and, because I
consider the Christian religion so important,
somebody I can totally rely on in my own mind.

No one reads the Bible more than me.

—President Donald J. Trump

Republican Jesus is the most powerful man in America. He died
more than two thousand years ago, but even an insubstantial
statement of praise directed toward him can win a presidential
election in the United States today.

So, who is he?

Republican Jesus is a Christian, white, working-class carpenter who was born in Israel a long, long time ago. His mom wasn't
ready to have a baby, but she was prolife and had a good, hardworking man by her side, so it turned out just fine. After legally
immigrating to Egypt for a short time, Republican Jesus and his
parents pulled themselves up by their sandal-straps in the rural
heartland of northern Israel. By his early thirties, Republican
Jesus had become an aspiring religious reformer with a clear

set of positions: the poor are already blessed, weapons protect people from weapons, free health care comes only in the form of miracles, and there's no sense in saving the earth, since God will destroy it soon anyway. Most of all, Republican Jesus opposed Big Government with all of its taxes and regulations. This struggle against Big Government ended in his crucifixion—a great irony since Republican Jesus was prolife but not opposed to capital punishment.

According to prominent Republican Christian influencers, including politicians, media pundits, and corporate lobbyists, Jesus's death and resurrection marked not the end, but the beginning, of a Christian crusade against Big Government. Appealing to the Bible as the constitution for their right-wing movement, these Republican influencers have duped millions of Christians into believing that their nefarious interpretations of the Bible not only are factual but are God's own Word. Politically conservative believers, as a result, hold their distinct political views in part because they think the Bible tells them so.

I'm not buying it. As a professional historian and university professor whose expertise is politics and economics in the world of Jesus and the gospel writers, I feel obliged to denounce the Republican Jesus as a tool designed and wielded for political gain. This Jesus has no place in the ancient world. He was manufactured by right-wing politicians and their corporate bedfellows in the midst of American cultural and political contests over the last century. Republican Jesus is by no means the only interpretation of Jesus's politics and ethics with currency in American culture, but it is by far the most consequential interpretation.

This book identifies and discredits the insidious, cherry-picked biblical interpretations that serve as the foundation for the Republican Jesus. Republican Christian influencers have created a gospel for themselves that is very unlike the ones written by Matthew, Mark, Luke, and John. It is a gospel of limited government—a gospel that rejects government regulations benefiting the poor and marginalized—and it serves as the framework for most modern Republican interpretations of Jesus's politics. According to this gospel, Jesus was clearly opposed to forms of government intervention ranging from taxation and welfare to universal health care and the legalization of same-sex marriage.

Republican Christian influencers interpret the biblical actions and sayings of Jesus through the lens of their Small Government politics and then claim the Bible is the basis of their Small Government politics. Through this faulty feedback loop, Republicans have discovered a "biblical" Jesus whose political opinions are the mirror image of their own.

TOUGH QUESTIONS

I've wanted to write a book about the Republican Jesus for quite some time, but I finally felt compelled to start when a student at the Canadian university where I teach asked me—the proud American professor who delights in anecdotes about the Philly sports theodicy and Texan barbecue cults—why the Americans who seem to love Jesus the most are the ones who use him in the most hateful ways.

It was an unsettling question.

It happened as we were discussing the birth narratives about Jesus in the New Testament gospels of Matthew and Luke. An American student had already brought up Rev. Paula White-Cain's claim that Jesus was not, in fact, a refugee but instead had traveled legally to Egypt with his family shortly after his birth—

as if it had been just a nice family vacation to Disney World instead of a life-or-death struggle to escape King Herod's violent "massacre of the innocents."

We had spent much of the class discussing how the story of the holy family going to Egypt, which appears only in the Gospel of Matthew, is historically problematic. It is, as I discuss in chapter 8, part of Matthew's artistic choice to portray Jesus as a New Moses. But even if it were historically reliable, the text itself refutes White-Cain's claim: it is a story of a persecuted family seeking refuge from a tyrant by crossing the border into a safer land. But the border was a border between Roman provinces (like a border between US states) and crossing it required no special documentation. Crossing that border would have involved paying tolls, but it wouldn't have involved scaling a wall, fording a river, or being separated from your family and thrown into a harsh detention center by enforcement officers.

White-Cain, a champion of the Prosperity Gospel and the chairwoman of President Trump's Evangelical Advisory Board, discussed Jesus in a way that pretended to be historical but made no sense of either the story of Jesus in the Gospel of Matthew or the historical situation of Jews like Jesus and his disciples in the Roman Empire. It was the first time that I came up against a version of the Republican Jesus that I couldn't understand in any way other than as a hateful fiction spun to gain political traction. I couldn't recognize her interpretation of the Bible as anything other than fiction—not "alternative facts," but 100 percent fiction.

The best impromptu response that I could give the student who asked why Americans use Jesus in this way was that not *all* American Christians use Jesus in this way (just as, by the same token, conservative Christians in other countries have been known to whip out their handy Jesus references when convenient too). But my student's question and our discussion of White-Cain's comments really got under my skin. How was it that conservatives like White-Cain had developed an understanding of Jesus that was so far removed from the original texts and historical contexts of the New Testament? Somehow, the Republican Jesus had taken on a life of his own.

I conceived this book as an attempt to answer my students' questions more fully—to explain how methodologically flawed and ideologically motivated Republican interpretations transformed the Jewish leader of an apocalyptic movement on the margins of the Roman Empire into the mouthpiece for modern phenomena like free-market capitalism, fetal personhood, gun rights, and the separation of church and state.

HERMENEUTICS OF HATE

When I was a graduate student at Yale Divinity School, I worked as an assistant in the institution's world-renowned library of rare books and archives on American Christianity. For a historian-in-training with a Roman Catholic background, archival work in this library was an immersive introduction to the full range of Protestant thought, from the practical concerns of Christian missionaries in the so-called Third World to the hair-splitting debates of erudite theologians over the interpretation of the Bible (a discipline known as "hermeneutics").

I spent many coffee-fueled days organizing the yellowing personal papers of George Lindbeck, a Lutheran professor from Yale who is widely revered as one of the most important theologians of the twentieth century. Lindbeck was one of the founders of an approach known as "postliberal theology." I came to learn that the "liberal theology" this approach follows doesn't refer to progressive God-talk with leftish politics and a hippie Jesus. It's called "liberal," from the Latin *liber* (free), because it bases Christian thought and practice in the Enlightenment notion of a freethinking individual: interpretation entails an autonomous freethinking modern interpreter determining the true meaning of biblical texts by reconstructing what ancient freethinking authors originally intended these texts to mean. It's an approach to scripture that developed in the nineteenth century and added an important dimension to the role of the believer in the understanding of scripture.

The postliberal approach emerged as a response to this, asserting the significance of community, culture, and language in shaping the ways that individuals think. For postliberal theologians, every interpretation of the Bible is influenced by the doctrines and practices of a Christian community, which are in turn shaped by the history of biblical interpretation (this is sometimes called a "hermeneutic circle"). In other words, truth doesn't come from the original meaning of texts but through the dynamic ways that Christians interpret these texts in light of their own communal contexts, language, culture, and experiences.

Both liberal and postliberal approaches reject the traditional position established during the Protestant Reformation that any given scriptural text has a single, clear, plain-sense meaning that was directly inspired by God.

Thumbing through Lindbeck's letters, articles, and speeches, I became captivated by the field of hermeneutics. Derived from the Greek verb *hermēneuō*, which means both "translate" and "interpret," hermeneutics is the study of the theory and methods of biblical interpretation.[1] Its practitioners recognize that every understanding of a text is a conscious or unconscious interpretation that brings with it certain presuppositions, or prejudices. Understanding—or finding meaning in—a text is thus a process in which interpreters integrate the text into their own predetermined way of seeing the world.

This philosophical and theological discipline raises a dizzying set of questions about the meaning and authority of the Bible: Who is the source of the meaning of a biblical text—God, the original authors, church authorities, individual interpreters, communities of interpreters, or some combination of these? Were the biblical authors inspired by God, and if so, did God inspire the words they wrote or only their intentions in writing? Were the biblical authors infallible? Do biblical texts record history? Are translations of the authors' Hebrew, Aramaic, and Greek words into English and other languages able to convey the texts' original meanings, whether they are considered inspired or not? Can a biblical text have more than one meaning, and if so, is every meaning equally valid?

I didn't fully appreciate the ethical importance of reflecting on these questions about how we interpret texts until I began teaching the New Testament at a large public university in Texas, where Christian fundamentalism is such a mainstay that the state is sometimes declared the "buckle of the Bible Belt." Here I encountered students who were fierce defenders of the idea that the Bible is the inerrant or inspired word of God but were incapable of articulating their positions clearly, let alone defending their positions with any of the subtlety or consistency of theologians.

When exposed to evidence of contradictions and errors within the gospels, problematic translations of the ancient languages in English Bibles, or variant texts in our ancient Greek manuscripts of the gospels, some conservative students admirably invested themselves in refining, reframing, or revising their positions on inerrancy or inspiration. Others retreated into robotic mantras: "The Bible is the Word of God, the Bible is the Word of God, the Bible is the Word of God ..."

My first experiences presenting a historical approach to the New Testament to conservative students were as encouraging as they were frustrating. I was encouraged by those students who, like theologians engaged in hermeneutics, were inquisitive and eager to learn about historical, literary, and sociological approaches to the Bible that could complicate and enrich their understanding of biblical texts. But I was—and remain—frustrated with students whose deeply ingrained dogmatism is an impediment to learning or even arriving at a mutual understanding. Instead of engaging with the texts for themselves and entering into dialogue with their peers, some students stubbornly refuse to relinquish the "clear" meanings they have learned from their pastors and parents.

I believe religion, and especially religious texts, can serve as a powerful medium for engaging with the world. Though I am no longer a practicing Roman Catholic, I have no interest in using historical inquiry to diminish anyone else's faith. I recognize that a biblical text may be valuably interpreted in many different ways that foster learning and compassion.

As a scholar of the humanities, however, I feel that I have a right and responsibility to apply my historical training to invalidate biblical interpretations that encourage marginalization and oppression. When a modern community fixes the meaning of a biblical text as a basis for discrimination on the grounds of religion, race, ethnicity, sexuality, gender, class, citizenship, or ability, I view this as a hermeneutic of hate. It is a hermeneutic because it is an individual or communal interpretation and, in many cases, not a plain-sense reading or historical fact, despite claims to the contrary. There are many biblical texts, to be sure, that historical analysis should expose as endorsing hate, whether in the form of rape, conquest, slavery, genocide, or some other atrocity. What I call hermeneutics of hate encompass instances in which these "texts of terror," as one feminist theologian famously called them, are interpreted as the authoritative basis for modern forms of hate as well as instances in which modern forms of hate are imposed onto biblical texts where they have no clear historical basis.[2]

These are hermeneutics *of hate* because they are used to classify certain humans as inferior to others. They are a class of oppressive language. As Toni Morrison observed in her visionary 1993 Nobel Prize lecture, "Oppressive language does more than represent violence; it is violence, does more than represent the limits of knowledge; it limits knowledge."[3] Hate is part of an often-unconscious process of interpretation that integrates the text into a prejudicial worldview that fosters violence and limits knowledge.

Republican influencers' hermeneutics of hate are a particular cause of alarm when they are deployed to produce harmful laws that legitimate discriminatory politics. By interrogating the flawed logic of those Christians who articulate hermeneutics of hate, I join forces not only with progressive Christians but also with a growing number of Christians from traditionally conservative churches who are speaking out against abuses of the Bible by Republican influencers. These influencers, it is worth noting, are overwhelmingly those who enjoy privilege in our society—namely, wealthy, white, heterosexual men.[4]

Republican influencers, who disseminate their discriminatory biblical interpretations to Christian voters through television, the internet, and the pulpit, use three strategies in particular: they *garble* the text by mistranslating or limiting the meaning of its words (whether in the ancient languages or English translation); they *omit* relevant parts of the text by extracting a verse from its literary context and sometimes cutting out sections of verses; and they *patch* this cut-up text together with other cut-up texts into the framework of a carefully designed quilt that's backed by ignorance, stuffed with hatred, and sewn with self-interest. When Republican influencers interpret the Bible in this way, they manipulate the ancient texts to promote modern Republican political positions. For this reason, I like to call their garble-omit-patch approach the "GOP method." To be clear, many religious leaders and writers have taken similarly misleading and ahistorical approaches to scripture—even the gospel writers treat the Hebrew scriptures in this way—so this method should be understood as an approach that Republican influencers often use but did not invent.

This GOP approach involves concealing the circular process of interpretation by "prooftexting" biblical verses—that is, by citing these texts as the authoritative proof of the exact modern values and behaviors that influence how these texts are understood. To be sure, some conservative intellectuals do pay careful attention to the original language, literary context, and historical context of a given text and develop complicated arguments to support their interpretations, but the method I've described remains prevalent among contemporary Republican influencers.

I present this book as a challenge to politically conservative Christians to recognize that hermeneutics of hate are by-products of distinctly modern, American political discourses that adherents are complicit in reproducing. It doesn't have to be this way. If conservatives can make the choice to reject ancient institutions like slavery and polygyny, which are explicitly endorsed by some biblical texts, then surely they can forsake harmful interpretations that aren't even warranted by the texts themselves.

BEYOND THE BATTLE OF THE VERSES

In one of the most memorable scenes in Aaron Sorkin's *The West Wing*, the Catholic Democratic president Josiah Bartlett holds an audience captive while he indicts Dr. Jenna Jacobs, a conservative pundit who uses the Bible to condemn homosexuality. The president's monologue, though fictional, is a brilliant example of how many progressive Christians respond—or would love to respond—to Republican hermeneutics of hate.

President Bartlett, skillfully acted by Martin Sheen, addresses Jacobs with the cool conviction of someone who knows he's getting the last word: "I'm interested in selling my youngest daughter into slavery as sanctioned in Exodus 21:7. She's a Georgetown sophomore, speaks fluent Italian, always cleared the table when it was her turn.... What would a good price for her be?"

Then the President really takes her to task. "While thinking about that, can I ask another?" he continued. "My chief of staff Leo McGarry insists on working on the Sabbath. Exodus 35:2 clearly says he should be put to death. Am I morally obligated to kill him myself or is it okay to call the police? Here's one that's really important because we've got a lot of sports fans in this town. Touching the skin of a dead pig makes one unclean (Leviticus 11:7). If they promise to wear gloves, can the Washington Redskins still play football? Can Notre Dame? Can West Point? Does the whole town really have to be together to stone my brother John for planting different crops side by side? Can I burn my mother in a small family gathering for wearing garments made from two different threads? Think about those questions, would you?"⁵

The president's point is that the Bible was written in an ancient world that maintained many customs that we would consider appalling in modern democratic societies. Therefore, he implies, it can't be interpreted literally as a guide to modern ethics. When conservatives treat the Bible this way, they are necessarily being selective, picking and choosing which scripturally mandated behaviors they wish to keep and which they wish to discard. They are drawing their interpretations from a history of practice in order to establish what they understand to be meaningful and consistent hermeneutics.

President Bartlett modeled two methods that liberals regularly use to criticize conservative interpretations: *disputing the relevance* of these ancient writings to modern ethics and *identifying inconsistencies* in Republican treatments of the Bible.

A third common method is *deflection*. A debate between a Republican Christian and a Democratic Christian over the Bible is very likely to devolve into a Battle of the Verses. Take, for example, a debate that emerged during a House Committee on Agriculture session in 2013 over proposed cuts to the Supplemental Nutrition Assistance Program (SNAP). In response to long-standing Republican appeals to 2 Thessalonians 3:10 as proof of God's directive that "anyone unwilling to work should not eat," a Democratic representative cited Jesus's command to care for "the least of these" in Matthew 25:40, which prompted a Republican to return with Matthew 26:11, "For you always have the poor with you."⁶

It makes sense that progressive Christians who take the Bible seriously would decide to respond in kind to Republican proof-texting, especially in a heated debate. But this reproduces a problematic usage of texts while leaving Republican interpretations intact. A Battle of the Verses is a one-upmanship contest with no winners.

This book is a call to action for political moderates and progressives, whether Christian or not, to tackle Republican hermeneutics of hate head-on by restoring conservatives' isolated prooftexts to their historical and literary contexts. In the face of the current epidemic of malignant misinformation, it is vital that we call out irresponsible invocations of texts for what they garble, omit, and patch together. More often than not, a contextualized prooftext does not appear to discriminate in the same ways as its contemporary Republican interpretation, although sometimes it is no less morally disturbing.

A HISTORICAL RECKONING

I am committed to deciphering what the New Testament and other ancient sources can tell us about who Jesus was or might have been, as well as why each gospel writer told Jesus's story the way he did. This approach, known as "historical criticism" or the "historical-critical method," is one of the predominant methods of interpretation used today by Bible scholars of all backgrounds and religious affiliations. *Critical* here implies disciplined investigation, as in *critical thinking*, not *critical* in the sense of being disparaging.

Like liberal theology, the historical approach anchors the meaning of texts to their original contexts. As one leading historical critic explains, the historical focus "appeals to criteria of language and history that are not derived from or beholden to modern faith commitments and ideologies, and this gives it at least a qualified objectivity in assessing issues in dispute."[7] *Qualified* is an important word here because it acknowledges, following the lead of postliberal theologians and postmodernists in general, that every interpretation is biased to some degree by the interpreter's identity, language, culture, and experiences.

It's impossible to read a text without imposing some of our own expectations onto it. I suspect that my privileged position as a white, cisgender man has shaped my understanding of these texts in ways that I will never fully understand. Nevertheless, I am confident that historical methods and some awareness of the hermeneutical process help to prevent the most egregious misuses of the Bible. When I consider Jesus's position on a political issue, I interpret every source text as part of its broader literary and historical contexts. How, I ask, does this passage fit with the theological and literary themes of the book from which it came? How do other texts written in the same time and place use this language or approach this issue? If the Jesus that is found turns out to be totally unique in an ancient context but perfectly aligned with a modern political perspective, there's a good chance that this Jesus is a modern political fantasy.

Throughout this book, I interpret Jesus and the earliest stories about him as products of a distinctive, if geographically and chronologically varied, ancient Mediterranean context. I call this context "the New Testament world."

Our earliest stories about Jesus's life and teachings, the gospels, derive from Jewish and mixed Jewish-Gentile communities before there was a religion known as Christianity.[8] The title *Christian* didn't come into use until the late first or early second centuries CE.[9] Before this time, there were people whom we may simply call "followers of Jesus" or "Christ followers," and some of them identified more closely with Judaism than others. There were no standardized doctrines or creeds. There was no Trinity or Original Sin or even a clear idea of exactly how divine

Jesus was. There was no organized church and no standard and authoritative version of the New Testament.

A major challenge for historians using the New Testament gospels as sources for the life and teachings of Jesus is that these books were written more than a generation after Jesus's death.[10] Certain clues in each of the canonical gospels—Matthew, Mark, Luke, and John—reveal that they were composed after the Jerusalem Temple was destroyed by the Romans in 70 CE. As the tragic climax of the First Jewish Revolt against Rome, which began in 66 CE, the Temple destruction had social and religious consequences for Jews and followers of Jesus across the empire.[11] Responding to these repercussions, the authors of the New Testament gospels carefully crafted Jesus's story so as to distinguish Jesus and his followers from the Jewish rebels involved in the First Revolt. Jesus was a Judaean who was crucified by the Romans as a criminal, the gospel writers conceded, but he was by no means one of those seditious revolutionaries!

The First Jewish Revolt and the destruction of the Temple were so consequential as stimuli for the formation of group boundaries between followers of Jesus and other Jewish groups that I would wager that Christianity would look very different today had these traumatic events never transpired. Regardless, it is important to recognize that these events became the prism through which the gospel writers interpreted the meaning of Jesus's words, actions, and death.

How well do you remember the words, actions, and assassination of Martin Luther King Jr., or Bobby Kennedy? Chances are that, if you were even alive at the time, you remember the highlights but not the details, and you have come to understand their speeches and actions as they've been interpreted since that time—as removed from their original historical contexts. Now consider that these were major figures in an age of newspapers, radios, and televisions, and that we are living in an age of unprecedented information availability. Without that technology to aid their memories, the gospel writers knew about Jesus only through literary texts and, more importantly, by word of mouth.

It is, as specialists on the science of memory explain, impossible to remember the past without interpreting it in light of one's present conditions and one's hope for the future.[12] Would you tell the story of Martin Luther King Jr. without linking it, whether intentionally or unintentionally, to the subsequent civil rights struggles and the Black Lives Matter movement? Would you tell the story of Bobby Kennedy without expressing some despair about how much longer the Vietnam War dragged on without him as president?

Because of the time lapse between Jesus's life and when the gospels were written, most professional historians acknowledge that it is very unlikely that the disciples who are the namesakes of the gospels actually wrote these texts. Hailing from a region with a literacy rate of perhaps as little as 3 percent of the population, the disciples of Jesus, whose first language was Aramaic, would not have been able to write books in Greek, the original language of the gospels.[13] The author who wrote the Gospel of Luke and its sequel, Acts of the Apostles, even mentions that the apostles John and Peter were "unlettered," or "illiterate" (Acts 4:13). He also explains that he was not himself an eyewitness to the events in Jesus's life (Luke 1:2).

We do not know who wrote the gospels. The authors of these books, or their early readers, would have attributed them to famous disciples—a form of false attribution of authorship that was common in antiquity—as a way to honor their legacies and crib their authority.[14] For the sake of convenience, biblical scholars still refer to these unknown authors by the traditional names of their gospels.

Even if the authors of the gospels were all eyewitnesses to the events of Jesus's life, we wouldn't expect them to interpret these events in the same way. In modern court cases, it's typical for eyewitnesses to register very different interpretations of what they saw. Because the gospel writers were *not* eyewitnesses, though, and they wrote for different audiences in different times and places, their stories diverge even more than eyewitness accounts. Each gospel depicts Jesus in a slightly different way— Matthew's Jesus, for instance, resembles a Jewish rabbi, while Luke's Jesus appears like a Cynic philosopher.[15]

The authors of our earliest surviving books about Jesus remembered what mattered most to them and told the story of Jesus as it was meaningful to them in their particular postwar contexts. By patching together these different gospel accounts and disregarding the profound divergences between the New Testament world and modern America, Republican Christian influencers have created an anachronistic and internally contra- dictory story of Jesus tailored to address the concerns and anxi- eties of modern conservatives.

. . .

Making sense of our ancient sources for early Christianity is no simple task, and it certainly isn't as easy as opening a Bible to find a clear and unambiguous historical record. But this is no reason to shy away from a historical approach to Jesus and the ancient gospels that were written about him.

My aim in this book is to use historical methods to show where some of the dominant Republican interpretations of Jesus came from and to show why, on the basis of ancient historical evidence and careful attention to the texts, they are often just plain wrong. This book does not attempt a comprehensive historical analysis of the origins and development of Republican biblical interpretations, with all of their theological variants. Instead, it identifies a selection of especially noteworthy facets of the modern contexts and motivations of right-wing interpretations of the gospels.

I do not intend to use historical methods to conjure up a Democratic Jesus. Even though I think that progressive Christians have generally interpreted Jesus's life and teachings in more historically defensible ways, I will note regularly that progressive interpretations of Jesus can also be problematic. I identify as a progressive Democrat, to be sure, but in my published scholarly work I have not shied away from critiquing the biases of leftist interpretations that imagine Jesus and other ancient Jews as opponents of modern capitalism.[16]

Unlike some progressive Christians, I don't mind if the historical evidence points me toward a reconstruction of the historical Jesus that clashes with my own politics. At the same time, I care deeply when problematic interpretations of the Bible are used to persuade people to buy into modern political platforms. Both Democrats and Republicans are guilty of this, but Republicans rely much more heavily on their interpretations of the Bible to exclude and harm those in marginal positions in our contemporary society.

When we divorce ancient writings entirely from their historical contexts, it is too easy to interpret them in irresponsible ways—ways that not only obscure the voices and experiences of the persons who lived in those times but also allow for appropriations that vilify contemporary groups. Jews, Muslims, Native Americans, African Americans, women, the LGBTQ+

community, immigrants, and the poor are frequently victims of methodologically flawed biblical interpretations that are presented as historical facts.

This book is written for anyone who is fed up with the Republican Jesus. Since Republican influencers' beliefs and actions affect all Americans regardless of their political or religious convictions, Republican Jesus affects all Americans. He's all of our problem.

I have written this book as an American in diaspora, gazing across a border—the "nicer" Canadian-American border—at the political maelstrom of Trump's administration. I have written it with the conviction that sound historical knowledge is not only politically expedient but also crucial for clarity and progress amid the post-truth haze of Trump's propaganda. I have also written this book because I can no longer stand idly by and watch as hatred and exploitation are normalized, legalized, and sanctified in the name of Jesus.

That's not the historical Jesus or the gospel writers' Jesus. It's the Republican Jesus, and he's out of control. But it's not too late to stop him.

PART ONE

Who Is Republican Jesus?

CHAPTER ONE

A Portrait of
Republican Jesus

"You can safely assume you've created God in your own image," the progressive born-again Christian novelist Anne Lamott has written, "when it turns out that God hates all the same people you do."[1] The same can be said for Jesus Christ, but the difference is that Jesus was also a human man whose terrestrial words and deeds have been written down and treated as history. For someone to create a Jesus who hates all the same people as them, they need to rewrite the history of the human Jesus by interpreting the New Testament gospels to reflect their prejudices and fulfill their desires.

Just as readers identify with the protagonist of a novel, believers envision the gospels' Jesus in their own image. As a result, countless Jesuses populate our world, and each one's appearance and teachings suit the particular community envisioning him. There are Protestant and Catholic versions of Jesus, of course, but there are also Greek Orthodox and Coptic Orthodox Jesuses, Buddhist and Muslim Jesuses, Black and Asian Jesuses, and so on.[2] In his book *American Jesus,* Boston University professor

Stephen Prothero has likened Jesus to a chameleon because his color often changes, literally and metaphorically, so that he matches his varied communal settings.[3]

One variable that can yield very different Jesuses, even within the same denomination, is politics. When I was a believer, I encountered entirely different Jesuses in two churches that were both Roman Catholic.[4] As a boy growing up in Levittown, Pennsylvania, a predominantly white, working-class town spiraling downward from deindustrialization, I encountered a white, working-class Jesus who bootstrapped his way to economic survival. Not insignificantly, my church was called St. Joseph the Worker and it leaned right politically. I have fond childhood memories of staring at the church's statue of St. Joseph holding a handsaw and seeing in him the type of man that I aspired to be—an industrious man like my father, a welder who worked hard to protect his family.

My sentiment of admiration, however appropriate and deserved, was shaped by a conservative political framework. For its struggling working-class parishioners, the church espoused a gospel in which individuals' hard work pays off without any need for intervention by the government. Even while advancing the Catholic legacy of supporting unions, the church still indirectly encouraged voters to support many of the conservative, limited-government political positions of Republicans.

When I moved to a politically moderate and firmly middle-class church in New Haven, Connecticut, I found absolutely no trace of the working-class Jesus of my childhood. I also couldn't get away with wearing jeans and a T-shirt to Mass anymore, but that's a different story. In place of emphasizing the work ethic of individuals, this increasingly diverse church's Jesus was enamored with cultural inclusivity and charity.

It's not that these two churches promoted contradictory Jesuses, but that the ways they interpreted Jesus's life and teachings varied in emphasis. These differences, which were often subtle, corresponded to the divergent politics of the two communities.

Political interpretations of Jesus transcend denominations and have power even beyond Christian circles. These interpretations influence people's lifestyle and politics, whom they love and whom they hate. But what's dangerous about them is that they usually aren't recognized as interpretations; they're accepted as sacred truths.

While any interpretation can sow the seeds of prejudice and exclusion, Republican interpretations of Jesus have proven especially successful at this in recent history and in our current political moment. It is crucial, for this reason, that we expose the ways that Republican Jesus functions as a tool of hatred and marginalization.

WHO IS REPUBLICAN JESUS?

Republican Jesus is the metaphor I use to encompass Republican interpretations of Jesus that have been widespread and politically significant in the last century of American history. As an investigative lens, Republican Jesus helps us recognize patterns in the political assumptions of leading figures of the Christian Right. This metaphor is set at a level of resolution that allows analysis of common political assumptions among Republican Christians without getting caught up in more minute theological differences between denominations or individual churches.

It might appear, as a result, that Republican Jesus is a brainchild of Evangelicals rather than a product of other conservative Christians like right-wing Roman Catholics or members of the

Church of Jesus Christ of Latter-day Saints. This impression would be partially warranted, not because Evangelicals are the only contributors to prevailing understandings of Republican Jesus, but because the widespread culture of Evangelicalism has played a dominant role in shaping broader Republican interpretations of Jesus's politics. As one leading scholar of American religion has explained, Evangelicalism is not simply a subculture; it has achieved the status of a sociocultural majority through its imprint on American civil religion, popular piety, and pop culture—and, for our purposes, on Republican Jesus.[5]

Not every Republican interpretation of Jesus is the same, but most have one thing in common: they imagine Jesus as a proponent of limited government (aka Small Government). The Republican Jesus opposes government spending and regulations and calls on his followers to put their faith in the free market rather than the government.[6] He promotes individual prosperity over human equality and social welfare.

Republican Jesus's hostility toward Big Government is the hinge on which all of his social positions turn. Republicans have interpreted Jesus as opposed to taxation, welfare programs, universal health care, abortion, gun control, immigration, and climate change. In every case, Republican influencers present their partisan interpretations of Jesus as biblical and historical truth.

To better understand the Republican Jesus, in this chapter I critically examine a recent and widely influential version of Republican Jesus that has more currency than ever in the post-truth age of Trump. A *New York Times* best seller, *Killing Jesus: A History* was published by the Fox News conservative pundit Bill O'Reilly and the sports writer Martin Dugard in 2013 and was made into a National Geographic movie produced by Sir Ridley Scott in 2015. This well-timed book and film developed long-standing conservative interpretations of Jesus's Small Government politics in concert with the rising tide of resentment politics that carried Trump into the White House. *Killing Jesus* provides an excellent window into prevalent Republican understandings of Jesus as a proponent of limited government.

KILLING JESUS: A "FACT-BASED" HISTORY?

Not only do many Republican Christians believe that their interpretations of the Bible are God's inerrant or inspired words, but they also consider the Bible an accurate and straightforward source of history. America's Christian Right has gone to great lengths over the years to produce and promote a flawed version of history that supports its politics. Most familiar, perhaps, is the "historical" claim that America's founding fathers were Christians and that the country was formed as a Christian nation.[7]

Whereas professional historians have been quick to debunk these falsifications of American history, they've been more reticent to acknowledge Republican interpretations of the Bible as part of the Christian Right's political enterprise in rewriting history. Yet these biblical interpretations are forged by means of the same flawed methods—cherry-picking sources, ignoring the biases of ancient authors, not analyzing sources in their original languages, and neglecting broader historical contexts. The Republican Jesus is the very definition of fake history.

The contrived nature of this history is evident in *Killing Jesus*. O'Reilly and Dugard are self-identifying "historians," but they don't have training in historical methods and ancient languages. In place of professional training, they assure readers that they "know much" about Jesus.[8] The authors protest too much when they use ancient vocabulary and ornamental footnotes to give readers the impression that their "fact-based book" is a thoroughly researched history based on careful study of historical sources in their original languages.[9] On the contrary, there's not a single footnote or non-English term that the authors needed to include to support their argument.

"Putting together *Killing Jesus* was exceedingly difficult," O'Reilly and Dugard proclaim. "We had to separate fact from myth based upon a variety of sources, some of which had their own agendas. But we believe we have brought you an accurate account."[10] On the contrary, there's no instance in the book where the authors have separated "fact from myth," and there's no evidence that they've taken the ancient authors' agendas into account. In fact, because they've consistently accepted the ancient authors—both Christian and non-Christian—at their word, their book is replete with historical errors and misrepresentations.

O'Reilly and Dugard's history of Jesus suffers from grave methodological flaws. Most jarringly, the authors never discuss how they sort their sources. Which are more or less reliable? Actually, the book rarely discusses the ancient sources. It presents a story of Jesus that harmonizes all four canonical gospels without dealing with their discrepancies.[11] Likewise, O'Reilly and Dugard often rely on other ancient authors such as Josephus, Philo, and Suetonius, but, as the University of Birmingham New Testament scholar Candida Moss has observed, they accept their accounts as factual without considering these ancient authors' own agendas.[12]

Killing Jesus is not a history, and its authors are not professional historians.[13] O'Reilly revels in fake histories that portray America as a Christian nation that fulfills working-class hopes of prosperity. Incidentally, O'Reilly makes a lot of noise about being from my working-class hometown's counterpart—Levittown, New

York—even though he is a millionaire whose affection for the working class is a ploy to secure support for political positions that benefit the wealthy. Together with his fellow Roman Catholic, Dugard, O'Reilly has written a whole series of "Killing" books about subjects known, unlike Jesus, from a full range of documentary sources like letters and diaries—books like *Killing Lincoln, Killing Kennedy,* and *Killing Reagan.* The authors' primary interest in American history is evident in the postscript to *Killing Jesus,* where they unnecessarily stress the importance of Jesus to George Washington in support of the Christian Right's tendentious history of the founding fathers as Christians.[14]

O'Reilly and Dugard's book is hagiography, or, as Moss puts it, "historical fan fiction." Its authors aren't just uncritical fanboys of Jesus, though; they're calculating fabricators of a version of Jesus that endorses Republican politics. O'Reilly was, after all, one of the most esteemed political commentators on Fox News— a longtime propaganda machine for Republicans and currently Trump's personal state media—before he was kicked out amid a scandal that exposed him as a serial sexual harasser who had paid millions for the silence of his victims.[15] He's a conservative, but he prefers not to commit to any single variety of conservatism.

O'Reilly has at times been critical of the Tea Party, but he has more often espoused Tea Party positions and supported their initiatives.[16] With strong backing from the leading correspondents at Fox News, the Tea Party began as a Far Right movement but garnered wide-ranging appeal among Republicans in the run-up to the 2012 election. The Tea Party, which protested taxation and called for Small Government, often appealed to fake histories of America's founding (including its namesake movement, the Boston Tea Party) and the Civil War to legitimate its "reactionary Republicanism"—that is, the politics of religious, fiscal, and racial conservatism that Trump invoked during his presidential campaign.

Armed with O'Reilly and Dugard's 2013 book and its 2015 movie adaptation, Republicans caught up by the Tea Party's surge of resentment found a historical precedent in a Jesus who shares their hostility toward Big Government.

JESUS VERSUS BIG GOVERNMENT IN *KILLING JESUS*

In my line of work, I've read quite a few books about Jesus, but rarely have I come across one that uses the words *taxes, money, expensive,* and *wealthy* as frequently as O'Reilly and Dugard's *Killing Jesus.* These words are all used to depict the Roman Empire, Herodian kings of Judaea, and the Jewish priests as a corrupt ruling class colluding to exploit rural working-class folks—that is, respectable bootstrappers like Jesus. *Killing Jesus* should be called *Killing Taxes.* It's a Republican gospel of limited government disguised as a "history" of Jesus.

Even though it happened more than half a century before Jesus's ministry, the demise of the Roman Republic and beginning of the Roman Empire in 27 BCE receives unwarranted attention in *Killing Jesus.* Rome, in the authors' view, became especially oppressive when it transitioned from republic to empire: "While the Roman Republic kept its distance from Judaean politics during the reign of Julius Caesar, the Roman *Empire* rules the Jews in an increasingly oppressive fashion."[17] By this logic, the empire was a Big Government comprising invasive institutions like taxation at the command of the emperor, who had absolute power, whereas the *Republicans* of the earlier era had had a fairer government overseen by the Senate.

O'Reilly and Dugard conceive of the empire (but not the republic) in terms of modern empires. They explicitly liken the Roman Empire to the Nazis, who have often served alongside the Soviets as a convenient foil for the Republican Jesus's politics.[18] O'Reilly considers himself an expert on this topic. Everything he dislikes is susceptible to conflation with the Nazis. If Democrats had a nickel for every time O'Reilly likened Big Government policies to the Nazis on *The O'Reilly Factor,* they could afford universal health care.[19]

Under O'Reilly and Dugard's Roman Empire, the Jewish people "have been levied with tax after tax after tax."[20] According to the authors, these taxes were administered by Jewish tax collectors, but they diverted most of the money to Rome; the emperors "got the first cut of all tax proceeds."[21] This created a hostile environment in which Galilean peasants like Judas of Gamala, known from the first-century Jewish historian Josephus, were constantly on the brink of revolt. These Tea Party–like tax rebels wanted a "Galilee ruled by Israelites instead of Roman puppets who crippled the people with unbearable taxes."[22] In this book, Jesus was killed by the Romans and their Jewish conspirators for pursuing limited government for his nation.

There are several problems with the authors' portrait of the relationship between the Roman Empire and the Jews. Most glaringly, they fail to mention that the Roman general Pompey brutally conquered Judaea for the "Republic" in 63 BCE and that the Judaeans were financially exploited more in the ensuing two decades than at any point under the empire.[23] O'Reilly and Dugard's statement that the Roman Empire increasingly oppressed the Jews also relies on their understanding of Herod "the Great" (nobody called him "the Great" while he was alive) and his sons, especially Antipas, who ruled Galilee during Jesus's lifetime, as "puppet kings" of Rome who were "nonpracticing" or "marginally faithful."[24] Here, the authors relay an ancient prejudice against the Herods as not being authentically Jewish because their family was recently converted, though this occurred before Herod was even born.[25]

There's no reason for us to doubt the faith of Herod, who married into the priestly Hasmonean family that had previously ruled Judaea, or his sons. Herod rebuilt the Jerusalem Temple on a massive platform that made it one of the grandest temples in the world. Archaeological remains, moreover, reveal Jewish ritual baths in Herodian palaces. Unlike Roman emperors and other client-kings, Herod and Antipas also didn't have their portraits engraved on their coins out of respect for Jewish laws prohibiting figural images.[26]

O'Reilly and Dugard are right that the Herods participated in aspects of Roman culture, but they neglect to acknowledge that the Herods consistently adapted Roman culture to fit their own Jewish cultural templates.[27] The Jew-versus-Roman opposition O'Reilly and Dugard have used to frame their fake history makes little sense of these Jewish kings.

According to O'Reilly and Dugard, Roman culture is perverse and exploitative, marked by violence, greed, homosexuality, and other forms of hedonism. The authors supply prolonged descriptions of Emperor Tiberius's lascivious sexual acts with young boys and girls at drunken orgies in his palace on Capri, not to be outdone by his lust for torture and murder.[28] They paint a picture outlined by Suetonius, an author who wasn't even born until more than twenty years after Tiberius's death. While there's no reason to doubt that Rome's political elites sometimes engaged in same-sex sexual activities, Suetonius's account, which the authors certify as history, hurls accusations of sexual deviance as a means of slander. Suetonius crafted the scene to legitimate the sitting emperor Hadrian's new moral propaganda by coloring earlier emperors as licentious tyrants.[29]

Since O'Reilly and Dugard's approach to history relies on black-and-white binaries without nuance, they do not allow for hybrid, or multiple, identities. With specific reference to Fox News, the progressive Christian minister Robin Meyers has referred to this reductionist logic as an epidemic of "media-induced terminal false dichotomies."[30] Conservative political pundits like O'Reilly don't believe in complications, uncertainties, and gray areas. For him and Dugard, the Romans are bad, rich, greedy, violent, and oppressive while Jews like Jesus are good, poor, selfless, nonviolent, and oppressed. Is there any place in this series of false dichotomies, we should wonder, for Jews who aren't in communion with Jesus?

KILLING JESUS AS A POLITICAL ALLEGORY

In *Killing Jesus*, there are good working-class Jews like Jesus and there are bad, wealthy Jews who are like the Romans. On a quick read, the Catholic authors' recognition of Jesus as a Jew appears progressive. But on closer inspection, there is more to the authors' biases than meets the eye. *Killing Jesus* is a political allegory in which ancient characters and events are used to express the authors' modern political views on class, race, and religion. In O'Reilly and Dugard's allegory, working-class Jews like Jesus represent modern Christians and wealthy Roman-like Jews stand in for modern Jews. Decoding the allegory of *Killing Jesus* reveals a gospel of limited government marked by anti-Semitism, white nationalism, and Christian supremacism.

Killing Jesus depicts the high priests, Sadducees, and Pharisees as corrupt and powerful leaders of the Jewish religion centered on the Temple in Jerusalem. Where professional historians would stress that the gospels' negative depiction of these groups reflects both bias and hindsight (since the gospels were written after the Temple was destroyed by the Romans), O'Reilly and Dugard double down on the gospels' polemics. These men are taken as representatives of the Jewish religion, which becomes a religion of wealth rather than faith. In the authors' rendering, the high priest Annas's *"entire life* has revolved around procuring wealth and power."[31] Nowhere do they acknowledge that the high priests consistently maintained the worship of God at the Temple. Instead, anti-Semitic stereotypes about Jewish greed abound in their conflation of Jewishness with the pursuit of wealth. The Passover holiday commemorating the liberation of the Hebrews from slavery in Egypt, for the authors, is merely a "ritual of money changing."[32]

The Jewish sects known as the Sadducees and Pharisees fare no better. O'Reilly and Dugard describe the Sadducees as "a wealthy and more liberal Temple sect who count Caiaphas among their number" (the high priest Caiaphas is the archvillain throughout *Killing Jesus*).[33] Note the words "more liberal" here. The authors seem to use this language because they conflate the Sadducees with Roman culture, which they perceive as pro–Big Government and prohomosexuality like modern American liberals.

By this logic, the Pharisees—the group that gave rise to the rabbinic movement that produced the Mishnah and Talmud— are more conservative than the Sadducees. Such an assessment fits with traditional Christian stereotypes of the Pharisees as legal rigorists. Yet the ancient evidence suggests that the Pharisees were actually more liberal, or flexible, when it came to the interpretation of law than the Sadducees and other Jews.[34] Descriptors like "liberal" are ultimately misleading, but they contribute to the authors' political allegory. Part of the reason that O'Reilly and Dugard would call the Sadducees "more liberal" is that they were closely tied to the Jerusalem Temple, which they consider an outpost of Roman Big Government. The Pharisees, on the other hand, also lived and worked in the Galilee, in what the authors envisage as the more conservative north.[35]

O'Reilly and Dugard present the avaricious Judaism of the Judaean south as utterly unlike the pious, working-class Judaism of the Galilean north—the true Judaism that would give rise to Christianity. During Jesus's lifetime, the region of Judaea (including Jerusalem) was under the direct rule of Roman governors like Pontius Pilate, while the Galilee (where Jesus's ministry began) was subject to the client-ruler Herod Antipas. This geopolitical division has enabled many modern Christian interpreters to conceive of the people of Galilee as fundamentally different than those of Judaea (map 2).

Geographic determinism undergirds O'Reilly and Dugard's segregation of Jesus and his disciples from mainstream Judaism. The authors draw a stark contrast between synagogue worship and Temple religion that ironically echoes the anti-Catholic biases of traditional Protestant interpreters: "In the synagogue, there are no high priests or clergy, no standard liturgy, and anyone is allowed to play the part of rabbi, or 'teacher.' Also, there is no money on the tables."[36] In Galilean villages like Nazareth, according to the authors, religion was pure, uncorrupted by ritual and the pursuit of wealth.

This geographical distinction does not stand up to ancient evidence.[37] Synagogues were as common in Galilee as they were in Judaea, and as common in cities like Tiberias (in Galilee) and Jerusalem as they were in villages like Nazareth. Synagogues in this period were community centers where some prayer and teaching happened, but they were not sacred centers of worship like modern synagogues and churches. Jews who worshipped in synagogues, whether in Galilee or elsewhere, still revered the Jerusalem Temple as the center of their religious worship—as the one and only house of God.[38]

Ignoring these nuances, O'Reilly and Dugard throughout their book call Jesus "the Nazarene"—a clever nickname that reminds readers that, though Jewish, Jesus is different than *those Jews* who worship at the Temple.

O'Reilly and Dugard's Jesus also shares the same class interests as Galilean villagers. The authors emphasize that Jesus was working class. When Joseph died, he left Jesus "the family business," carpentry.[39] Since carpentry is a skilled profession, Joseph was "able to pay his taxes. And, indeed, most people in Galilee can do the same—but just barely."[40] The authors take care to describe Joseph and Jesus as meritorious working-class men whose economic success was impeded only by Big Government—by taxes imposed by the Romans and their Jewish henchmen.

As a working-class man, O'Reilly and Dugard's Jesus looks different from the wealthy Jews and Romans. "From his Galilean accent and simple robes to his workingman's physique, it is clear that Jesus is one of them"—a part of the masses of overtaxed Galilean pilgrims.[41] Jesus's disciples also share this working-class physiognomy. "The fishermen themselves are even sturdier, with thick hands and forearms heavily callused from a lifetime of working the nets. The sun has made their faces leathery and deeply tanned. It is a tan that extends over the entire body."[42] Their appearance is totally unlike that of the leaders of the Jewish religion. O'Reilly and Dugard explain that "these simple artisans and fishermen look poor and tattered in comparison with the Pharisees."[43]

It is in O'Reilly and Dugard's geographical determination of the bodily appearance of Jesus and his disciples that we can begin to detect insidious elements of white nationalist ideology. The segregation of Galilean Judaism from Judaean Judaism has been repeatedly discredited by New Testament scholars in recent decades. It was once, however, a quite common assumption among theologians that had its origins in nineteenth-century European nationalism.

One of the earliest and most influential authors to use a geographical definition of racial origins to distance Jesus from Judaism was the French Catholic philosopher Ernest Renan (1823–92). Renan is best known for his theory of race as geographically determined. He was one of the first philosophers to formulate the ideas of the Aryan race that Hitler took as the basis of his odious nationalism. In 1855, Renan even declared himself "the first to recognize that the Semitic race compared to the Indo-European race represents in reality an inferior composition of human nature."[44]

Renan's *Life of Jesus* (1863) spins these racist views into a history of Jesus that shares a lot in common with *Killing Jesus*. Renan describes Galilee as a beautiful, romantic landscape—"charming and idyllic"—in contrast to the region around Jerusalem to the south, which is the "saddest country in the world."[45] Whereas Renan's Galilee is a verdant "terrestrial paradise," Jerusalem is barren, parched, and stony. "The North," Renan remarks about Galilee, "alone has made Christianity: Jerusalem, on the contrary, is the true home of that obstinate Judaism which founded by the Pharisees, and fixed by the Talmud, has traversed the Middle Ages and come down to us."[46]

Renan cast doubt on the idea that Jesus, raised in the glorious Galilee, was himself a Semite. "It is impossible," he resolved, "to raise here any question of race, and to seek to ascertain what blood flowed into the veins of him who has contributed most to efface the distinction of blood in humanity."[47] He was, however, willing to admit that Jesus was raised within the Jewish religion because this set into relief his greatest accomplishment—transcending his Jewishness. According to Renan's interpretation of the gospels, as soon as Jesus protested at the Temple in Jerusalem, he "appears ... as a destroyer of Judaism.... Jesus was no longer a Jew."[48]

O'Reilly and Dugard prime readers to think of Jesus as racially superior to Jews from their description of his first encounter with Jerusalem's Jewish leaders as a young boy (an account that appears only in Luke 2:41–52 and is considered fanciful by most historians). "If anyone thinks it odd that a smooth-cheeked, simply dressed child from rural Galilee should be sitting alone among these gray-bearded rabbis, with their flowing robes and encyclopedic knowledge of Jewish history, they are not saying. In fact the opposite is true: Jesus's understanding of complex spiritual concepts has astonished the priests and teachers. They listen to his words as he speaks and treat him like a savant."[49]

Aside from furnishing this patronizing depiction of Jewish leaders seeking knowledge from the young Jesus, the authors carefully distinguish Jesus's appearance from that of the Jewish leaders. From their prose, the difference would appear to be a matter of distinctions of class and age. On this page of their book, though, the authors provide a picture of a famous painting to flesh out, quite literally, their description of appearances. Heinrich Hofmann's 1881 painting *Christ in the Temple* (figure 1) depicts the Christ child in white garments with a glowing, white, European face. Meanwhile, it portrays the Jewish leaders surrounding Jesus as big-nosed, bearded men in exotic, Oriental robes.[50]

The combination of this image with the book's persistent descriptions of distinctions between Jesus's Galilean movement and his Judaean opponents encourages readers to think of "the

Figure 1. Heinrich Hofmann's *Christ in the Temple* (1881). Credit: Wikimedia Commons (photographer: Elke Walford).

Nazarene" as a white, European destroyer of Judaism rather than as a Middle Eastern Jew. For an American audience, portraying Jesus as white resonates with the racist Jim Crow invective of the decades following the Civil War, in which Christians sometimes cited Jesus's supposed whiteness as proof that whites were superior to Negroes (figures 2 and 3).[51]

O'Reilly and Dugard's racialization of Jesus compounds white Christian nationalism with anti-Semitism. As in Renan's book, Jesus's confrontation with the money changers in Jerusalem is a climactic moment in *Killing Jesus*. The "Cleansing of the Temple" episode (this modern title already has Christian supremacy baked into it) occurs in the lead-up to Jesus's arrest in the Synoptic gospels (Mark, Matthew, and Luke) but at the beginning of his ministry in John.[52] Consistent with their patchwork approach, O'Reilly and Dugard have Jesus make a scene at the Temple twice—once at the beginning of his career and once

The VIRGIN MARY and the CHILD CHRIST.
Could the Child Christ possibly be of the same flesh as the **Negro?**

Figure 2. White supremacist drawing showing Mary with infant Jesus and comparing a black and a white child, from the Missouri minister Charles Carroll's book *The Negro: A Beast, or In the Image of God* (1900).

in the final days of his life.[53] They devote more space to the earlier instance and faithfully follow the Gospel of John—the most anti-Jewish and least historically reliable of the gospels—but with a nonbiblical emphasis on Jesus as a tax protester.

According to John, an irate Jesus flipped the tables of the money changers and drove out those selling at the Temple while saying, "Stop making my Father's house a marketplace!"[54] O'Reilly and Dugard call the money changers by the Hebrew term *shulhanim* in their account. The transliteration of this term, which appears in centuries-later Jewish texts like the Mishnah and Tosefta but is not used in the Greek gospels and probably wouldn't have been used by Aramaic-speaking pilgrims like Jesus, serves no purpose other than to emphasize the Jewishness of the money changers.[55] According to O'Reilly and Dugard, after all, the Passover holiday that brought Jesus to Jerusalem "might be ... about faith and piety," but "it is also about money."[56]

Figure 3. White supremacist drawing showing Jesus and comparing a black and a white man, from Carroll, *The Negro: A Beast, or In the Image of God* (1900).

O'Reilly and Dugard turn the scene into a conflict between Galileans and the Judaean Temple establishment in a way that it is not in any of the gospels. Jesus is provoked to action only when he "sees the people of Galilee standing helpless before these greedy money-changers and the haughty high priests overseeing them."[57] The reasons the authors give for the presence of money at the Temple are the collection of taxes for the Temple-Empire establishment and the repayment of high-interest loans dispensed by the Temple.[58]

The authors' illustration of the economic situation here is suspiciously reminiscent of the American Recession and housing crisis of 2007–10, which instigated the Tea Party movement among Republicans. Whereas the ancient sources make no mention of a housing crisis, *Killing Jesus* blames the Temple authorities for subprime lending practices that result in "the loss of a home, the loss of land and livestock, and eventually life as a debt slave or membership in the 'unclean' class."[59]

The historical Jesus might have opposed the collection of the annual half-shekel Temple taxes, as we'll see in chapter 7, but we have no reason to think he was opposed to any other taxes. We also have no evidence that he condemned the Temple's lending practices. He probably opposed the purchase of animals for sacrifice, but not because he rejected Temple sacrifice or the economic role of the Temple. Like other Jews whose writings have survived from this period, Jesus most probably resented the priestly elites' corporate monopoly over commerce in Jerusalem.[60]

O'Reilly and Dugard's portrait of a Jesus opposed to the Big Government of the Roman Empire and Jerusalem Temple is a political allegory that makes little sense of the ancient evidence. *Killing Jesus*'s gospel of limited government features a Republican Jesus who is Christian, European, and working class and stands in solidarity with his Galilean people against Big Government. Once the veil is lifted from O'Reilly and Dugard's "history," its conservative project can easily be broken down into a set of false dichotomies that transect the book:

Good	Bad
Galilean Jews (read: Christians)	Judaean Jews and Romans
Nonviolent	Violent
Traditional values	Homosexual culture
Tax protesters	Big Government
Working class	Corrupt ruling class
Rural	Urban
Pious religion of faith	Ritualistic, profit-driven religion
European, white (except for Italian emperors and governors)	Semitic

Killing Jesus combines a mainstream Republican distaste for Big Government with Far Right ideologies of anti-Semitism, white nationalism, and Christian supremacism. These biases are nowhere more evident than in the final paragraphs of the book's afterword, where the authors lament the centuries-long occupation of Jerusalem by violent Muslim Arabs and express relief that Jerusalem has been back in Jewish hands since the 1967 Six-Day War.[61] These brief remarks betray a Christian brand of Zionism that appeals to the Christian Bible as divine justification for Jewish sovereignty over Jerusalem while portraying Muslims as enemies and infidels.

O'Reilly and Dugard's book isn't a history about a Jewish man from the Middle East in ancient times; it's a political allegory designed to grant biblical legitimation to the desires of white Christian Republicans in contemporary America.

KILLING JESUS THROUGH RIDLEY
SCOTT'S RACIAL LENS

Through visual representation, Ridley Scott's film adaptation of *Killing Jesus* transforms the book's politics into something subtler but just as disturbing. By faithfully preserving the book's Small Government politics (taxes and tax collectors are reviled throughout) but changing its representation of race, Scott's film presents a tale in which Jesus denounces Big Government for oppressing people of color.

It might be surprising to think of National Geographic and Sir Ridley Scott, one of the most celebrated filmmakers of all time, teaming up to make a Bill O'Reilly book into a TV movie. But Fox purchased National Geographic in 2015 after years of gradual absorption; ever since, its status as a leader in science education has eroded like the Arctic coasts in a world that ignores climate change.[62] Thanks to the celebrity power of Scott and the abundant resources of Fox/National Geographic, O'Reilly and Dugard's Republican gospel has now reached an even wider and more diverse audience.

American Christians love movies about Jesus, especially when they're broadcast on cable television during Holy Week. *Killing Jesus* attracted 3.8 million viewers with its first airing on Palm Sunday in 2015 alone, and it was even nominated for Primetime Emmy and Critics' Choice awards in that same year. Thanks to the National Geographic branding and a historical narration at its conclusion, the movie appears to its viewers as a legitimate scientific inquiry into the history of Jesus.

Christopher Menaul served as the movie's director, with Scott and O'Reilly acting as executive producers. In his "Behind the Scenes" remarks on costumes, Menaul leaves little doubt that his vision for the film aligned with the book's class politics. The production crew went to great efforts, he explains, to make Jesus and his disciples look poor by dressing them in simple, ragged garments with a muted color palette. They intended for this to contrast sharply with the "opulence of the priests and of the regal power of the Herodian family and indeed of the Roman imperial occupying force."[63] As in the book, then, Jesus and his working-class Galilean supporters are lined up against a wealthy and corrupt coalition consisting of the Romans, the Herodian kings, and the Jewish priests.

The film's geographical and class distinctions translate into racial differences, but in a much different way than in O'Reilly and Dugard's book. After causing a stir by hiring white actors to play Egyptians for its 2014 blockbuster *Exodus: Gods and Kings*, Scott's production company was careful not to repeat this mistake with *Killing Jesus*.[64] They hired people of color—actors of Middle Eastern, African, and Indian descent. But they hired them only to play Jesus and his disciples (figures 4 and 5).

Ever since a University of Manchester medical artist named Richard Neave used ancient forensic evidence to reconstruct Jesus's face in 2002, filmmakers have paid more attention to Christ's racial appearance.[65] Neave's widely publicized reconstruction (figure 6) depicted Jesus with light brown skin and curly hair in stark contrast to the typical European images of Christ like the one by Hofmann in O'Reilly and Dugard's book.[66]

Still, it was a provocative move for Scott's company to hire a Lebanese American Muslim actor, Haaz Sleiman, for the role of Jesus. He's not the tanned white man that a reader of O'Reilly and Dugard's book would expect. Though Sleiman was cast for the leading role of the film, his name does not appear on the cover of the DVD case alongside the names of the white actors

Figure 4. Still from National Geographic's *Killing Jesus* movie, showing Jesus (Haaz Sleiman) surrounded by other Galileans. Credit: MovieStillsDB.

playing Pontius Pilate, Caiaphas, Herodias, and Herod (the *Frasier* star Kelsey Grammer)—our first clue that this decision wasn't so progressive.[67]

Whereas Jesus and his disciples are almost all played by actors of Middle Eastern, African, and Indian descent, the Roman authorities and the Jewish leaders are all played by actors of European—mostly English and Irish—descent. And while the actors playing Jesus and his disciples speak with fake accents, the white actors do not.

A key to deciphering how the film relies on a dichotomous representation of good characters as people of color and bad characters as white people is the casting of Joe Doyle as the traitor Judas Iscariot. The white-skinned, light-eyed, English actor even acknowledges in his "Behind the Scenes" interview that the producers paid special attention to making Judas appear

Figure 5. Still from National Geographic's *Killing Jesus* movie, showing Herod the Great (Kelsey Grammer), left, and his son Herod Antipas (Eoin Macken), right. Credit: MovieStillsDB.

different than Jesus and his disciples. Whereas the Galilean followers of Christ wear costumes that make them look poor, Judas's garments are more ornate, "which would suggest that he's slightly more well-off than the others."[68] Judas isn't a true follower of Christ, so, through both race and costume, the film

Figure 6. Richard Neave's anthropological reconstruction of the face of Jesus, which first appeared on the cover of *Popular Mechanics* in December 2002. Credit: Getty Images.

represents him more like the Roman-Jewish establishment than Jesus's crew.

Picturing the good guys as non-European and bad guys as white seems like the type of subversive move that a filmmaker with radical racial politics would make. In this case, however, racial representation is serving the interests of O'Reilly's conservative political allegory, which segregates the Galilean Christ followers from other Jews.[69]

Scott similarly relied on race to serve a political allegory about the joint threats of scientific innovation and globalization in one of his earliest films, *Blade Runner* (1982, with a director's cut in 1992). A loose adaptation of Philip Dick's science fiction novel *Do Androids Dream of Electric Sheep?* (1968), *Blade Runner* revolves around the enslavement of bioengineered humans in a dystopian Los Angeles of the future (2019 was the future then!). The film's synthetic humans are all white, while the majority population of the city is Asian. Meanwhile, black people are nowhere to be found. As Brian Locke, a leading scholar of racial representation in film, explains, "The film reinscribes white supremacy by displacing the historical tension between white and black onto another type of racial body, namely, the figure of the Asian."[70]

Scott's *Killing Jesus* does something comparable: it displaces the historical tension between Christian and Jew onto nonwhite bodies. *Killing Jesus* does not appeal to white fears of globalization by portraying white people as victims like *Blade Runner,* but it does exploit the bodies of people of color to promote the exact Small Government politics that marginalize minorities. Through Scott's lens, *Killing Jesus* conveys pervasive Republican ideas of race and class by reconfiguring the racial codes of O'Reilly and Dugard's political allegory. Instead of white, working-class Christians resisting Big Government as in the book, the movie shows poor minorities like Jesus and his disciples blaming Big Government for their marginalization. Paradoxically, the good guys being racial minorities actually encourages viewers to think that people of color believe that Big Government is the cause of their oppression, not the solution.

For viewers who accept the message of National Geographic's Jesus, the gospel of limited government helps minorities. Jesus himself, so it goes, was a man of color who wanted nothing to do with government welfare programs. He worked hard to support his family. All that got in his way were the high taxes and regulations of the fascist Roman government and its greedy Jewish conspirators.

Even with very different racial codes than the book, the *Killing Jesus* movie advances a distinctly Republican Jesus.

. . .

This is why the Republican Jesus is so seductive: he doesn't seem like a bad guy. Like most versions of Jesus, he wants to help the poor and oppressed. Nearly all interpreters of the gospels—Democrats and Republicans, Christians and non-Christians—agree that Jesus sought to help the oppressed. But the gospels raise some important questions that have been the subject of very different interpretations: Who counts as the oppressed? What is the cause of their oppression? And how does Jesus think their oppression should be overcome?

For most Republicans, the answer to all of these questions may be found in Jesus's alleged opposition to Big Government. This is a matter of politics (How much should a government regulate?), but it has repercussions for economics (How much and for what causes should a government tax its subjects? Are there ways in which a government should support the poor?), civil rights, and moral ethics (Should all citizens have the right to bear arms? Should governments provide access to birth control and abortion clinics? Should all subjects of a government have equal access to health care? How should governments define marriage? Is the government responsible for addressing climate change?).

The book and movie *Killing Jesus* is just one example of how Jesus is presented by Republican influencers, and one that skews libertarian. Other versions of the Republican Jesus, as we'll see, are more probusiness than libertarian. I've put *Killing Jesus* under the microscope because of how widely influential it has been in recent years and how blatantly it uses the pretense of history to make Jesus support Small Government. This point is the nexus at which all of the variants of the Republican Jesus in historical and contemporary discourse converge.

O'Reilly and Dugard's book isn't based on recent historical scholarship, but its interpretation of Jesus also didn't fall down from heaven.[71] In the following chapters, I trace the origins and development of the Republican interpretation of Jesus that plagues American politics today. Where does this Republican Jesus come from?

PART TWO

Where Does Republican Jesus Come From?

CHAPTER TWO

Early Modern Heralds

The Republican Jesus's gospel of Small Government places faith in free markets and the free will and uninhibited ability of individuals to pursue their own prosperity. O'Reilly and Dugard's version of Republican Jesus promotes this faith by protesting Big Government taxes as an impediment to the economic success of fishers, farmers, and carpenters. By this logic, Big Government is a threat to the free market, which grants all free individuals the same opportunities to succeed. Anyone who isn't successful, as a result, must not have worked hard enough.

Since Jesus's death, Christians have fought over the social and political implications of his words and deeds. Around the turn of the fifth century, wealthy Christian leaders such as Augustine and Ambrose struggled with how to justify their immense wealth, and that of other Christian leaders, with the emphasis in the gospels on selling property and renouncing wealth to achieve salvation. As Jesus tells a rich young man in the Synoptic gospels, "It is easier for a camel to go through the eye of a needle than for someone who is rich to enter the kingdom of God."[1] So many Christian leaders had become very wealthy by late antiquity, when the Roman Empire was transformed into a Christian empire, that the Princeton historian Peter Brown refers to this as the "Age of the Camels."[2] The bishops' usual solution to the eye of the needle dilemma was that wealth itself was acceptable but unchecked desire for wealth could keep a person from heaven.[3] Other Christian groups, such as the followers of Pelagius and certain monastic communities, maintained that Jesus called for wealth to be renounced and inheritances given away.

The ancient debates over Jesus's ethics didn't focus on the question of government intervention like modern debates. This is because the preindustrial economies of the ancient and medieval worlds did not revolve around the "free" market as in modern capitalism. In these imperial economies, which were heavily dependent on agricultural labor performed by slaves and peasants, capital investments and trade in commodities were much more limited.

Republican influencers' interpretations of Jesus as a proponent of Small Government depend on ways of thinking about the government's relation to the economy and free individuals that didn't fully develop until the early modern period (ca. 1500– ca. 1800). In concert with the advent of capitalism, two ways of thinking emerged in Europe in this period that are fundamental to later interpretations of Jesus by Christian Republicans in America, Protestantism and classical liberalism.

Republican Jesus is American through and through, born in the aftermath of the Great Depression as the Religious Right became organized around opposition to Big Government. We can't fully understand this Republican Jesus, though, without first understanding what he inherited from Protestantism and classical liberalism. From these interrelated early modern ideologies, the Republican Jesus inherited his antiauthoritarian attitude, his affection for Small Government, and his interest in the advancement of bootstrapping individuals.

REPUBLICAN JESUS'S
PROTESTANT INHERITANCE

As the redeemer of an individual's liberty from the stranglehold of authoritative institutions, the Republican Jesus owes a great debt to the cantankerous German monk Martin Luther, the celebrated father of the Protestant Reformation.

Luther gets a lot of the credit for igniting the sixteenth-century Protestant Reformation, but it was already in the air, so to speak. The Holy Roman Empire was slowly disintegrating as the budding nation-states in England, Spain, and France challenged the power of the Italian Papal States. Germany was still part of the empire the church had inherited from classical Rome, but popular resentment against the church's financial corruption was starting to boil over. Believers in some parts increasingly resented the clergy and especially the pope.[4]

Luther quickly became one of the leading representatives of a new form of Christianity rooted in political opposition to the governmental authority of the church—to the church as Big Government, so to speak.[5] Against the rampant corruption of the money-mongering Roman Catholic Church, Luther sought to give the masses more direct access to God. In the early 1500s, Catholic clergy were offering salvation at a price: a person could purchase "indulgences," the name for remissions that reduced some of the penalties for their sins. Without these indulgences, they would need to account for their sins in purgatory, an intermediate state or place in which the souls of the deceased had to purify themselves of their sins. "When coin in the coffer rang," one of Luther's indulgence-peddling opponents allegedly proclaimed, "the soul from purgatory sprang."[6]

The German monk didn't reject either indulgences or purgatory outright, but he was adamant that salvation couldn't be bought.[7] Instead, he began his famous Ninety-Five Theses—a long series of early modern tweets he posted on the door of his church in Wittenberg in 1517—by quoting Jesus: "Our Lord and Master Jesus Christ, in saying '*Poenitentiam agite . . .*,' wanted the entire life of the faithful to be one of penitence."[8] The Latin *poenitentiam agite* means "Do penance" or "repent" and is a citation of the standard Latin version of Matthew 4:17: "*Repent:* the Kingdom of Heaven is at hand." For Luther, Jesus clearly stated that penance requires individuals to turn personally toward God rather than slip some bills into their local priest's cincture.

Luther transferred control over knowledge of salvation from the clergy to the masses, "the priesthood of all believers." He relied on new technology—the printing press—to spread his views and to displace the established Latin version of the Bible, which was comprehensible only to the clergy, with his own German translations of the Bible, which could be expounded during worship or consulted on an individual basis.[9]

Luther was careful, however, not to grant too much freedom to every Christ-loving Hans the plumber in the haunted backwoods of north central Germany. The limits of his aversion to government power are clearest in his decision to side with the princes against the peasant rebels during the German Peasants' War (1524–26)—a position he promoted through his bluntly titled treatise *Against the Murderous, Thieving Hordes of Peasants.*[10] He may have resisted the Roman Catholic Church, but he had no interest in becoming the hero of a peasant revolt.

Theologically, Luther limited the freedoms of individuals through his doctrine of predestination, the belief that God predetermines all things, including the salvation of some but not others. Luther's theology of predestination severely curtailed the freedom of individuals to work out their own salvation. He insisted that an individual is justified—and hence saved—through faith alone, by God's grace alone. Faith is a prerequisite for salvation, but God has predetermined that the faithful will be justified.[11] Luther's emphasis on an individual's faith corresponded to his argument—based on his interpretation of the apostle Paul's letters—that works of the law didn't afford salvation. By downplaying "works" as the cause of salvation, Luther denounced both Catholic rituals and the Jewish law (over the course of his career, Luther's anti-Judaism became increasingly acute, culminating in his publication of *On the Jews and Their Lies*).

This populist, Bible-thumping, faith-based refutation of both the Jewish law and Catholic clerical authority over state affairs would eventually become the basis for the Republican Jesus's rejection of Big Government. Luther's view of free will, on the other hand, proved too pessimistic to support the notions of individual merit and self-interest that have been erected as the pillars of free-market capitalism. Luther's book on this topic, *The Bondage of the Will*, maintains that the will is entirely incapacitated by sin, so that humans cannot attain their own salvation. Only through the grace of God's redemption is the will liberated.

Instead, Republican Jesus's principles of religious and economic free will derive from the theology of Jacob Arminius, a Dutch theologian who was active in the late sixteenth and early seventeenth centuries. Arminius was schooled in the so-called Reformed theology of the French reformer John Calvin, who was an even stronger proponent of absolute predestination than Luther. But Arminius refused the full-blown Reformed denial of free will. Even though his opponents cast him as a new Pelagius, Arminius was no champion of free will. Pelagius had made waves in the turn-of-the-fifth-century church by declaring that individuals had the free will to choose good works and faith over sin.[12] The official position of the Catholic Church follows the strong theology of predestination in the works of Augustine, Pelagius's illustrious opponent.[13] In practice, though, most ordinary Catholics in Luther's day and today assume a more or less "semi-Pelagian" position in which human free will cooperates with God's grace in the attainment of eternal life.

Arminius's views were more complicated and, on the whole, closely aligned with Calvin's Reformed theology.[14] His sticking point was conditional predestination: God has foreknowledge of who will be saved and who will be damned, but he still "decided graciously to accept those who repent and believe in Christ."[15] Arminius's idea that anyone who by grace believes will be saved, while still asserting divine foreknowledge, allowed that individuals can improve their position through faith. Arminian theology therefore attributes some responsibility to individuals for overcoming the plight of Original Sin to receive the reward of salvation.

While this may not seem like a big deal now, it was a major contribution to Christian thought at this time. Against the dominant theologies of his day, Arminius claimed that ordinary people had (some) agency over their salvation.

If that sounds familiar to you, that's because it is: Arminian ideas have remained a part of Protestant thinking since the Reformation, especially in American contexts, and they are now one of the most prominent components of Republican interpretations of Jesus's politics. If we translate Arminius's theology into economics, we have the Republican Jesus's social program: individuals have the power to improve their position by God's grace; they don't need the government's help.

According to one historian, economic Arminianism has been one of the most widespread "class theologies" in American history.[16] Even though it was officially rejected by the Dutch Reformed Church at the Synod of Dort in 1618–19, Arminianism continued to spread throughout Europe in direct and indirect ways. It has been especially influential among Methodists and the Holiness movement but has also found traction among Baptists, some circles of Presbyterians, and other Christian denominations.[17]

Theologically, Arminianism found its roots in America as European adherents of these religions immigrated in search of religious freedom. During the spirited mid-nineteenth-century religious revivals known as the Second Great Awakening, evangelical Arminianism spread quickly among the working classes as a way to relieve the anxieties caused by industrialization and urbanization.[18]

People today often joke about a hardworking penny-pincher's "Protestant work ethic." This expression comes from the famous sociologist Max Weber's argument in *The Protestant Ethic and the Spirit of Capitalism* that Protestants (especially Calvinists) work hard as an expression of their self-confidence in being predestined to salvation; as a result, they accumulate wealth that they are taught not to spend on the corrupting possessions of this world.[19] It would be more precise in both European and North American contexts, though, to speak of the "Arminian work ethic," for the business-owning and political elites who shaped industrial class relations have held fast to the idea of the free individual who overcomes adversity.[20]

REPUBLICAN JESUS'S
CLASSICAL LIBERAL INHERITANCE

Whereas Protestantism emerged in political opposition to the church acting as Big Government, classical liberalism emerged in the attempt to establish nation-state governments that competed with one another for land and money on the rapidly expanding world stage. From its origins, classical liberalism was a very close friend of capitalism and colonialism.

Classical liberalism is an economic perspective that individuals' freedom and private property are secured by limiting the power of the government. Not to be confused with our contemporary connotations of "liberals" as left-of-center Democrats, classical liberalism comes closer to what we in America today would call libertarianism. The classical liberal understanding of economics is usually called laissez-faire, which in French means "let (them) do"—that is, let businesses and markets act freely, without constraint by governments (with the assumption that then any individual can succeed by merit). In certain circles of right-wing American English, this political-economic perspective has been reduced to a "lazy-fair" philosophy: "the poor are lazy, so it's fair that they're poor."

The earliest proponents of classical liberalism were the shapers of capitalism, an economic system in which money is invested in the expectation of making a profit.[21] In its preindustrial adolescence, this system took the form of merchant capitalism, where wealthy investors sought profits from trade in far-flung regions and teamed up as corporations: the Dutch East India Company, the English East India Company, the Dutch West India Company (West India = the Americas), and so on.[22] These corporations exploited and gradually colonized their trading "partners," and one of their most sought-after commodities was slaves—that is, humans violently seized from their homelands and sold for profits. Liberalism supported this cause by providing a philosophical platform for reducing taxation and mitigating other forms of government intervention so that there would be no checks on the vicious zeal of free enterprise.

The dominant political framework for American capitalism today is "neoliberal," where "neo-" represents adherence to the elaborations of classical liberalism among theorists of "neoclassical" economics since the late nineteenth century.[23] Though political theorists developed neoliberalism as a "state-phobic" response to government interventionist theories that gained popularity after the Great Depression and undergirded FDR's New Deal, neoliberalism is most often associated with the 1980s deregulatory policies and "freedom" rhetoric of US president Ronald Reagan and UK prime minister Margaret Thatcher.[24] Most Republicans today are neoliberal in their political orientation because they believe that Small Government, secured through deregulatory and austerity measures, union-busting, and the privatization of public institutions like the military, public schools and universities, health care, and prisons, grants individuals the "freedom" to prosper (though usually at the expense of other people and their freedoms).[25]

From this neoliberal perspective, the government, just like God, should not hand out anything other than the sheer possibility to succeed.[26] This position assumes that what is possible for one person is the same as what is possible for every other, overlooking institutional variables such as racism, sexism, classism, ableism, and gerrymandering. It's a theological recipe for economic success: rags to riches by grace through faith.

Arminian and other non-Calvinist philosophies of the individual's will are the basis of classical liberalism and neoliberalism.

One of the architects of modern international law's foundation in liberalism, the Dutch jurist Hugo Grotius, was imprisoned in 1619 following the Synod of Dort for disturbing the public order by acting in the interests of adherents of Arminianism, known as the Remonstrants. Grotius is as notorious for his brazen escape from prison in a book chest as he is for formulating the principle of the freedom of the seas in order to protect the corporate ambitions of the Dutch commercial empire in Southeast Asia and elsewhere.[27] Grotius became embroiled in the dispute between Calvinists and Remonstrants by advocating the authority of the government to appoint Arminius and his Remonstrant successor Conrad Vorstius as professors at the University of Leiden.[28] In this instance, he was not defending Big Government as much as he was protesting Big Church acting as Big Government.[29]

It was precisely as a defender of Arminianism that Grotius developed his influential ideas about individual liberty, private property, the separation of church and state, and religious toleration by the government—that is, toleration of theological differences among believers in God (but not toleration for atheists).[30]

Grotius's liberal political ideas flowed directly from his Arminian theology.[31] He smacks us in the face with this connection in his *Commentary on the Law of Prize and Booty* (of the pirate sort, that is):

> God created man *autexousion* [Greek for "of one's own power"], "free and *sui iuris* [Latin for 'of one's own law or right']," so that the actions of each individual and the use of his possessions were made subject not to another's will but to his own. Moreover, this view is sanctioned by the common consent of all nations. For what is that well-known concept, "natural liberty," other than the power of the individual to act in accordance with his own will? And liberty in

regard to actions is equivalent to ownership in regard to property. Hence the saying: "every man is the governor and arbiter of affairs relative to his own property."[32]

Grotius's Arminian stance towards free will holds that it is the right and responsibility of each individual, not the government, to incline his will and orient his actions for his own good.

Grotius fashioned his Arminian liberalism in support of the colonial interests of a profit-hungry megacorporation known as the Dutch East India Company. In addition to making sure that Dutch ships were sailing on free international waters and invoking Jesus's words "My kingdom is not of this world" (John 18:36) to discredit the Catholic pope's donation of the East Indies to Portugal, Grotius fought for tax exemptions for the corporation.[33]

Taxes, for Grotius, should ensure liberties but not hinder free enterprise. When Haarlem and other Remonstrant towns refused to pay their taxes unless their religious liberty was protected, Grotius drafted the Declaration of Haarlem (1618) in defense of the Remonstrants—a move that his accusers used against him during his trial the following year.[34] Along the same lines, he believed that the East India Company should be free from federal tolls on the commodities they traded.[35]

It should come as no surprise, then, that Grotius—who was also an erudite biblical interpreter—notes in his commentary on Jesus's famous line "Render therefore unto Caesar the things which are Caesar's; and unto God the things that are God's" (Matt. 22:17) that Jesus specifically and only supported paying taxes on land and persons.[36] He doesn't even consider whether Jesus also referred to tolls and customs duties on commodities exchanged because that would mean Jesus endorsed taxing Grotius's beloved corporation and thereby impeding the free will of individuals (and, by extension, "corporate persons") to make profits from trade.

John Locke, who has stolen Grotius's thunder as the "father of liberalism," supported British colonialism in North America by taking cues from Grotius's model for colonial enterprise in the East Indies. Active in England in the mid- to late 1600s, Locke was an avid reader of Grotius and his disciples.[37] Whereas Grotius's colonial agenda involved facilitating overseas trade with the East Indies, Locke had America in his crosshairs: he was involved in the British administration of the American colonies as secretary to the lords proprietors of the colony of Carolina, secretary and treasurer of the Council for Trade and Foreign Plantations, secretary to the Board of Trade, and a stockholder in slave-trading companies.[38] Locke fought in these capacities for a Small Government that would reduce the tax burdens of trade for the English just as Grotius had done for the Dutch.[39] More than Grotius, though, Locke invested himself in efforts to shape the British occupation of the American colonies in order to produce huge profits for aristocrats like himself.

Like Grotius, Locke was a non-Calvinist Protestant who used the Bible as a prooftext for his colonial, capitalist agenda. Raised as a Puritan in predominantly Anglican England, Locke's Arminian-influenced, yet eclectic theology was consistent on one front: it affirmed free will as the basis of individual responsibility.[40]

The biblical story of the "fall" of Adam and Eve was crucial to Locke's thought on liberty, property, labor, and government. For Locke, Paradise prior to the Fall was the human state of nature that should serve as the basis for understanding human rights. The fruit-lust of Adam and Eve didn't introduce the genetic infection of Original Sin into the world as Catholics and Calvinists believed; their actions didn't cause utter human depravity.[41] Instead, the Fall changed very little.[42] In his published writings, Locke shrewdly dodges the fact that Genesis

3:17–19 describes hard agricultural labor as God's curse against humans for their disobedience.[43] He emphasizes, instead, that the curse of Adam was mortality.

For Locke, God created Adam—man in his bare-naked natural state—as a self-interested being. This self-interested individual voluntarily entered into society when consenting to the creation of Eve. Subsequently, the individuals within this primitive society took possession of private property through appropriation and use.

To avoid theological complications when explaining the formation of private property, Locke gives the example of a "wild Indian" in America gathering a piece of fruit as a stand-in for Adam and Eve's identical action in the garden.[44] The fruit becomes private property because its owner engaged in labor to take possession of it, increasing its value and saving its potential from going to waste (Locke, of course, deemed most of the ancestral lands of Indigenous peoples in the "New World" as going to waste because they were not in service of "civilized," Christian farmers).[45]

God, for Locke, had invested humans with freedom and responsibility even before the Fall. When God commanded Adam to "subdue" the earth in Genesis 1:28, he was commanding man to "improve it," Locke explains in his *Second Treatise of Government*, "for the benefit of life, and therein lay out something upon it that was his own, his labour."[46] Instead of self-interest and labor as the sin of humans and their penalty for it, then, Locke pronounces self-interest and labor as human nature, foreshadowing the liberal economist Adam Smith's claim that humans have a natural "propensity to truck, barter, and exchange."[47] In good Arminian fashion, Locke stresses the activity of human agents over God's grace.

Because Locke cast property as a natural and unalienable right, he thought that government shouldn't regulate it. In Locke's estimation, government existed for consenting citizens and should interfere in society only to keep individuals from entering into violent or fraudulent relations. Jesus (Matt. 22:17) and Paul (Rom. 13:1–7) commanded that people should pay taxes for exactly this purpose. "This is the reason," Locke notes in his paraphrase of the apostle Paul's call for obedience to authorities in Romans 13, "why also you pay tribute, which is due to the magistrates, because they employ their care, time and pains, for the publick weal [i.e., "well-being"], in punishing and restraining the wicked and vicious; and in countenancing and supporting the virtuous and good."[48]

Religion, too, should be an individual choice—so long as the chooser has a religion.[49] Like Grotius, Locke defended the separation of church from state because he maintained that belief in Christ as the Messiah relies on free will and cannot be forced.

Still, Locke argued that the principles of government should be based on the natural law that is revealed in the Old Testament and was republished by Christ.[50] Not only did Christ restore to humans the opportunity of immortality that was lost in the Fall, but he also gave them a perfect system of moral ethics: "Such a Body of Ethicks proved to be the Law of Nature, from the principles of Reason, and teaching all the Duties of Life; I think no body will say the World had before our Saviour's time."[51] God endowed humans with Reason—an Enlightenment catch-all term for humans' power to understand their place in the universe and how to improve it—but it was only through Jesus that this knowledge could be fully realized so that individuals could achieve victory over death.

As viewed through Locke's aristocratic Arminian looking glass, then, the Bible authorizes natural, God-given freedoms like property and Christianity. Government exists only to protect these liberties.

PROTESTANTISM AND CLASSICAL LIBERALISM AT AMERICA'S FOUNDING

For America's founders, Locke was a major influence. If he had still been alive and sided with the American colonials instead of their British colonizers, he might as well have written the American Declaration of Independence and Constitution himself. The principal architects of the American government were disciples of Locke's Arminian liberalism, although they were often more devoted to religious freedom than he was.[52]

While a delegate to the Virginia Assembly in 1776 and 1777, Thomas Jefferson burned through many candles reading Locke's writings (as well as Grotius's).[53] To make his case for a separation of church and state in the new nation, Jefferson depended heavily on Locke's *Letter concerning Toleration*. Speech notes that he had prepared outlined many merits of Locke's letter, such as the central principle that government should function only to protect life, liberty, and property, not the individual's soul or salvation. He would declare, however, that Locke was wrong not to extend religious freedom to Catholics and nonbelievers, saying that "where he stopped short, we may go on."[54] Jefferson was even a diligent reader of the Qur'an and an advocate, though prejudiced in certain ways, for the rights of Muslims in America (a fact that Republican influencers are eager to suppress).[55]

Jefferson, like many of the founding fathers, was a deist. In contrast to the conservative Christian fantasy that is still featured—to the chagrin of many professional historians—in standard history textbooks, America was no Christian nation at its founding.[56] In the late 1700s, about 15 percent of Americans belonged to a church.[57] Deists believed in the existence of God, but they rejected both the idea of a God who intervened in human affairs and the traditional Protestant emphases on God's grace, the Fall, the need for atonement, and the Trinity. They boasted, instead, a naturalistic religion in which God amounted to a supreme intelligence that created the world, but then—like a divine watchmaker—left humans to their own devices, to make use of their Reason.[58]

Jefferson condemned the Calvinist theology of predestination as a blasphemy against God. "It would be more pardonable," he stated, "to believe in no god at all, than to blaspheme Him by the atrocious attributes of Calvin."[59] This was as much a liberal dismissal of Calvinism as it was a denial of predestination in the Anglican tradition in which he had been raised.

Jefferson turned to Jesus to support both his liberalism and his deism. He developed some of his views on Jesus through his exchanges with Rev. Joseph Priestley. A politician and chemist, Priestley is best known for discovering oxygen and inventing the soft drink, but he was also a staunchly Unitarian advocate for Christian dissenters against the colonial Anglican Church. He was a big fan of the liberal economist Adam Smith's *Wealth of Nations,* published in 1776, and especially Smith's rejection of governmental restrictions on free trade.[60] Priestley, then, was on the same page as Jefferson when it came to economics, but he also influenced Jefferson's views on religion, and Jesus in particular. After reading Priestley's long-windedly titled 1786 book, *An History of Early Opinions concerning Jesus Christ, Compiled from Original Writers, Proving That the Christian Church Was at First Unitarian,* he said that he accepted Priestley's evidence "as the basis of my own faith."[61]

In a letter he wrote to Priestley in 1803, Jefferson elaborated on his distinctive convictions about Jesus:

> I should proceed to a view of the life, character, and doctrines of Jesus, who sensible of incorrectness of their ideas of the Deity, and of morality, endeavored to bring them to the principles of a pure deism, and juster notions of the attributes of God, to reform their moral doctrines to the standard of reason, justice and philanthropy, and to inculcate the belief of a future state. This view would purposely omit the question of his divinity, and even his inspiration. To do him justice, it would be necessary to remark the disadvantages his doctrines had to encounter, not having been committed to writing by himself, but by the most unlettered of men, by memory, long after they had heard them from him; when much was forgotten, much misunderstood, and presented in every paradoxical shape.[62]

Jefferson's deist perspective on Jesus is the basis of his treatise on *The Life and Morals of Jesus of Nazareth,* better known as the "Jefferson Bible." Using a razor and glue, Jefferson patched together the parts of the New Testament that he considered the original moral teachings of Jesus while omitting any miracles or supernatural events like Jesus's resurrection.[63] He agreed with Locke that Jesus was a teacher of moral laws that should inform government, but he cared little for the supernatural elements in which "the most unlettered" disciples had encased Jesus's moral principles.

When he drafted the Declaration of Independence in 1776, Jefferson based America's ethics in the "Laws of Nature and of Nature's God"—not in the trinitarian God of the dominant Christian tradition.[64] The Declaration states that "we hold all these truths to be self-evident, that all men are created equal, that they are endowed by their Creator with certain unalienable Rights, that among these are Life, Liberty and the pursuit of Happiness." This phrase simplifies the natural rights Locke sought to protect in his *Second Treatise of Government*—"life, liberty, and estate." George Mason had included these in the Virginia Declaration of Rights just a few weeks before Jefferson wrote the national Declaration of Independence. Although Jefferson collapsed Mason's "enjoyment of life and liberty, with the means of acquiring and possessing property, and pursuing and obtaining happiness and safety" into "Life, Liberty and the pursuit of Happiness," he undoubtedly imagined property as an expression of the natural right to pursue happiness that the Creator granted to humans.[65]

Whereas the Declaration of Independence had deism as its religious lowest common denominator, the Constitution was a godless document. The only place that religion appears in the Constitution of 1787 is Article VI: "No religious test shall ever be required as a qualification to any office or public trust under the United States." Catholics and Jews were among those who sought this protection from having to show affiliation with some brand of Protestantism to hold public office. It was the Quakers, though, with their pacifist and antislavery positions, who presented the biggest threat to those Protestants who opposed the inclusion of this article in the Constitution.[66] Even with this federal provision in place, many states continued to keep laws on the books that allowed tests of allegiance to Protestantism as a qualification for holding office. The Supreme Court didn't outlaw these tests at the state level until 1961.[67]

Many of the founding fathers followed Jefferson down the Lockean path toward Small Government, but there were also influential men who rallied for a stronger central government. A conflict broke out between Federalists, who wanted a strong central government that would force states to collect taxes the government needed in order to repay the debts accumulated during the war, and Anti-Federalists, who opposed Big Government.[68] Anti-Federalists like Jefferson fought for the amendment of a Bill of Rights to the Constitution, claiming that it would protect individuals from the monarchic trappings of Big Government. Federalists like Alexander Hamilton and John Adams (the second president) thought that outlining certain rights would give the false impression that these constituted the full extent of human rights protected by government. They were right. Many conservatives today continue to read the Constitution as complete, inerrant, and unchanging—exactly how they read the disparate texts compiled into the Christian Bible.

The Bill of Rights opens its First Amendment with the statement that "Congress shall make no law respecting an establishment of religion, or prohibiting the exercise thereof." This amendment was mired in controversy even among the ranks of Anti-Federalists. Jefferson, for instance, had strong disagreements with other Anti-Federalists about how much the government should intervene to protect the rights of Protestants. Foremost among his opponents was Patrick Henry, a former governor of Virginia known for the dramatic words he spoke in an oration that promoted revolution by preying on Virginians' fears of Indian and slave revolts: "Give me liberty or give me death!"[69] An aristocratic slave owner, Henry opposed the Constitution on the grounds that it didn't go far enough in protecting his liberties.

Although Henry also worked within the intellectual tradition of liberalism, he envisioned America as a Christian commonwealth. Jefferson wasn't amused by Henry's assault on his deist vision of a separation of church and state. "What we have to do," Jefferson encouraged his ally James Madison about Henry, "is devoutly pray for his death."[70]

In 1784, Jefferson was at loggerheads with Henry over Henry's proposal that the government should collect a tax to fund Christian denominations. Jefferson equated this taxation to the vampirish exactions of the colonial Anglican Church. He wrote that the dissenters had forgotten the Anglicans' "teeth and fangs."[71] With the help of Madison, Jefferson's Virginia Statute for Religious Freedom was passed in 1786. This statute served as the basis for the free-exercise clause in the First Amendment, which was approved in 1791.

Protestantism and liberalism were strong forces in the formation of the American government. Surprisingly, however, there often appeared to be some tension between them. The defenders of liberalism believed that freedom of economy and freedom of religion were two sides of the same coin. To become free from the shackles of the colonial economy, and especially its high tariffs that threatened American profits from the slave trade in which Jefferson and the other founding fathers indulged, Americans also had to free themselves from the church's nefarious influence over the government.[72]

Even for the proponents of Small Government and religious liberty, though, Protestant interpretation of the Bible remained the moral bedrock for this government born through a war of independence. It's no coincidence that Jefferson cut-and-pasted taxation into the very first line of his Bible: "And it came to pass in those days, that there went out a decree from Caesar Augustus, that all the world should be taxed."[73] Only the Gospel of Luke includes this census in its story of the birth of Jesus, and it doesn't appear until the second chapter of the gospel. Jefferson chose to begin his story of Jesus here not because it is an obvious starting point. A critic of the use of censuses to collect burdensome taxes during the nation's first censuses, he began his story of Jesus here because doing so casts the rest of Jesus's life and teachings as nothing less than a revolution against Big Government.[74]

.　　.　　.

Without Protestantism and classical liberalism, the Republican Jesus of today is unimaginable.

From Protestantism, the Republican Jesus received his antiauthoritarian, populist attitude and his interest in saving individuals instead of classes, communities, or all humankind. He even received a less typical feature of Protestant theology in the form of the Arminian belief that a human's free will is able to overcome great adversity. This brand of Protestant theology was in many ways bestowed on the Republican Jesus through the mediation of classical liberalism.

From classical liberalism, the Republican Jesus received his affection for Small Government and his habit of protecting individual rights to property and prosperity. He also inherited a talent for lining the pockets of aristocrats and their power-hungry corporations behind the mask of protecting free enterprise.

Together, Protestantism and classical liberalism were instrumental in colonialism and the development of capitalism. In the early stages, their proponents wielded these ideologies in ways that marginalized Indigenous communities and people of color who were taken in slavery. As they took shape during an era of industrialization and urbanization, proponents also used them to marginalize the working classes. After all, it's the poor's own problem if they don't take advantage of their right to the pursuit of happiness (the lazy-fair perspective).

Protestantism and classical liberalism are deeply entangled in the cultural fabric of American history. They have left an indelible mark on American popular piety and conservative politics. But in the wake of the Great Depression, the corporate proponents of classical liberalism began to lose their struggle against Big Government for the first time. The Republican Jesus was born because these corporate leaders needed a Savior.

CHAPTER THREE

A Corporate Assault on the New Deal

Fired up by populist zeal, nineteenth-century American Protestants advanced varieties of Christianity that reinforced the laissez-faire economics introduced into American politics by Anti-Federalists in the previous century. During the religious revivals known as the Second Great Awakening (1790s to mid-1800s), preachers blanketed the frontier lands, converting masses of farmers, merchants, artisans, and factory workers. In the wake of these revivals, Evangelicals came to constitute the vast majority of American Protestants.

The complex and dismal doctrines of mainstream Lutheranism and Calvinism weren't very attractive to potential converts, so the revivalists instead peddled what one historian has described as "a folk religion characterized by disdain for authority and tradition."[1] Baptists, Presbyterians, and especially Methodists made huge advances while a gamut of new grassroots churches emerged; the Seventh-Day Adventists, Disciples of Christ, the Church of Jesus Christ of Latter-day Saints (Mormons), and Pentecostals were among the most successful of the new movements. Regardless of their doctrinal and organizational differences, the new and renewed churches adopted a classical liberal notion of the individual's free will as a central tenet of their theologies.[2]

Today's Evangelical Protestants—the largest US religious demographic at a quarter of the population—trace their origins to these revivals and their precursors.[3] Evangelicals are united by the belief that the Bible is God's (more or less literal) revelation to humans, the belief in the centrality of conversion and especially the emotional act of choosing salvation by being "born again," and the belief in missionary responsibility for spreading the faith.[4] Although most Evangelicals are conservatives, they're not all conservatives, and the Christian Right that emerged in the twentieth century includes segments of mainline Protestants and Catholics along with Evangelicals.

Already during the Second Great Awakening, Evangelical revivalists were prophets for profits. Relying, when they could, on factories and shops as the venues for their revivals, they preached about conversion, accepting the spirit in one's heart, and individual self-discipline through hard work—all of which provided moral relief to the economically downtrodden while distracting the new converts from resisting the varied forms of exploitation that industrialization brought.[5] But eventually unchecked industrialization took its toll.

Whereas church membership surged between the nineteenth-century revivals and the years following World War I, it came to a screeching halt with the Great Depression, and the leading denominations experienced major losses.[6] The hope of faith, it turns out, couldn't ease the stinging wounds from layoffs, debts, foreclosures, bankruptcies, and persistent economic anxiety.

When President Franklin Delano Roosevelt initiated the New Deal, everything changed. Strong government programs offered economic salvation that flew in the face of the Christian churches' antiauthoritarian liberalism. The Christian Right emerged as conservatives reasserted their classical liberal heritage in response to this assumed threat of communism, a menace on the loose both in FDR's government and abroad. And when these conservative Christians began patching together texts from the New Testament to bolster their opposition to Big Government, the Republican Jesus was born.

JESUS'S NEW DEAL

In the 1933 epic film *King Kong,* a gigantic gorilla-like monster scales the corporate skyline of a bustling New York City to protect, however aggressively, a homeless and unemployed woman. We learn from one of the film's opening scenes that she resorted to stealing food because she couldn't survive on soup from charity kitchens alone. Like this film's menacing beast, FDR's New Deal was an enormous and fearsome government initiative that terrorized corporate businessmen to save the poor from the laissez-faire institutions of the Great Depression.

The New Deal was a sweeping series of government programs and projects that FDR initiated when he took office in 1933 to create jobs, alleviate poverty, and stabilize the economy.[7] Within the alphabet soup of new programs were the Civilian Conservation Corps (CCC), the Civil Works Administration (CWA), the Farm Security Administration (FSA), the Public Works Administration (PWA), and the Social Security Administration (SSA); of these, Social Security is the only survivor today, and barely.

"The only thing to fear is fear itself," FDR announced about his gargantuan reforms during his first inaugural speech. These memorable words were merely the garnish to a masterful oration that put Jesus at the center of decades of heated moral debates. "Practices of the unscrupulous money changers stand indicted in the court of public opinion, rejected by the hearts and minds of men," the wealthy Episcopalian president declared, referring to Jesus's "Cleansing of the Temple" in the gospels:[8]

> True, they have tried, but their efforts have been cast in the pattern of an outworn tradition. Faced by failure of credit, they have proposed only the lending of more money. Stripped of the lure of profit by which to induce our people to follow their false leadership, they have resorted to exhortations, pleading tearfully for restored confidence. They only know the rules of a generation of self-seekers. They have no vision, and when there is no vision the people perish. Yes, the money-changers have fled from their high seats in the temple of our civilization. We may now restore that temple to the ancient truths. The measure of that restoration lies in the extent to which we apply social values more noble than mere monetary profit.[9]

Jesus, in FDR's view, condemned big bankers and businessmen for impoverishing the people through their selfish pursuit of profits. In speeches and radio shows that sounded like sermons, FDR would often repeat this biblical indictment of money changers. Jesus corresponded to the president himself, of course, but FDR didn't emphasize this. Political cartoonists were quick to make this connection, however, whether by drawing FDR in front of the temple-ish neoclassical architecture of the New York Stock Exchange or portraying him chasing out the buyers and sellers with a whip, as in the Gospel of John's version of this episode (figure 7).

"—*To cast out them that sold and bought*—"
—St. Mark 11:15

Figure 7. Political cartoon showing FDR manhandling the money changers at the New York Stock Exchange. This cartoon, by Gregor Duncan, appeared in *Life* in May 1934.

Even though most American Christians at this time read the Bible through a lens of classical liberalism, FDR was by no means the first to interpret Jesus as a social prophet. Proponents of the so-called Social Gospel—a heterogeneous movement based on the radical notion that Christians should pursue political action to help the poor and combat other social crises—had turned to the gospels to support their cause for decades.[10] The socialist presidential candidate and pioneering union organizer Eugene V. Debs was called "our most Christlike character" by Social Gospel proponents, who lamented his suffering in prison (for giving an antiwar speech in 1918) and subsequent death.[11] Only the most progressive Christians viewed Debs and other founders of the American social democracy movement as martyrs, though, whereas FDR's less radical platform garnered broader appeal.

From his presidential pulpit, FDR broadcast his progressive reading of the gospels far and wide, restoring the faith of many down-on-their-luck George Baileys who had been bankrupted by the Great Depression. Progressive Catholics and Protestants rallied behind the president, proclaiming that the New Deal "incorporated into law some of the social ideas and principles for which our religious organizations have stood for many years." The New Deal, according to the head of the Federal Council of Churches, advanced the biblical "significance of daily bread, shelter, and security."[12]

The Mr. Potters of FDR's world, on the other hand, weren't happy, and they were quick to respond with their own Jesus, who would have no trouble foreclosing on the old Savings and Loan.

REPUBLICAN JESUS'S CORPORATE BEGINNINGS

"We must give more attention to those things more cherished than material wealth and physical security," proclaimed H. W. Prentis, president of the National Association of Manufacturers (NAM), at the influential business lobby's annual meeting in

1940. "We must give more attention to intellectual leadership and a strengthening of the spiritual concept that underlies our American way of life." About seven years into the New Deal, Prentis and America's other corporate leaders made a deliberate turn to Christian nationalism as "the only antidote" to the New Deal's "virus of collectivism."[13]

Corporate America's business lobbies recruited charismatic preachers who insisted that Jesus's teachings concerned the salvation of the individual. His "spiritual" teachings weren't sullied by political and economic positions, they'd claim: the Messiah was no social prophet! But if we translate his individualistic moral lessons into politics and economics, they'd shrewdly concede, Jesus would support a Small Government form of capitalism focused on individual freedoms over social welfare.[14] Together with the nation's leading bankers and industrialists, these conservative preachers erected a new Republican Jesus—a Jesus who, though composed of the European raw materials of Protestantism and classical liberalism, was proudly stamped *Made in America.*

NAM sought out Rev. James W. Fifield Jr. as the face of its campaign to have Republican Jesus save corporations from the evils of the welfare state—collective bargaining rights, Social Security, corporate taxation, and transparent business dealings. Originally from Chicago, Fifield took over the First Congregational Church in Los Angeles in 1935. Under his leadership, this elite congregation became a megachurch of its day with nearly four thousand members, including the mayor of L.A., a leading real estate speculator, the president of the California Institute of Technology, the celebrity filmmaker Cecil B. DeMille, and the presidents of mining, insurance, and chemical companies. Ironically, this church is one of the country's more progressive today.

Dubbed the "Apostle to the Millionaires" by his critics, Fifield's influence extended—like that of televangelists in more recent history—far beyond his L.A. congregation. He started an adult education series that had almost thirty thousand paying pupils, a Sunday Evening Club with nine hundred regularly in attendance, and five radio programs.

Still, Fifield's biggest initiative was cofounding Spiritual Mobilization, an organization whose mission statement was "to arouse the ministers of all denominations in America to check the trends towards pagan stateism [read: the New Deal], which would destroy our basic freedom and spiritual ideals."[15] Spiritual Mobilization interpreted the Bible in individualistic terms in order to proselytize Christian leaders to a form of Small Government capitalism. "The way for America is back," Fifield professed. "How far back? Back as far as the old Gospel which exalted individuals, which placed responsibility for thought on individuals, and which insisted that individuals should be free spirits under God."[16]

The Spiritual Mobilization organization's outreach campaign disseminated its anti–New Deal Jesus widely with the help of self-interested corporate patrons. Spiritual Mobilization served as a political lobby, networking center, and industrious clearinghouse for probusiness Christian media. The organization benefited from ongoing support from corporations like General Motors, Chrysler, DuPont, Republic Steel, National Steel, U.S. Steel, International Harvester, Firestone Tire and Rubber, Sun Oil, Gulf Oil, Standard Oil of New Jersey, Southern California Edison, Colgate-Palmolive-Peet, J.C. Penney, and the National Cash Register Company. Even more, the organization's advisory committee included presidents of the US Chamber of Commerce, presidents of prominent universities and seminaries, leading Wall Street analysts and economists, the founder of the National Small Businessmen's Association, and congressmen.[17] At its height, the organization enlisted about seventeen thousand clerical representatives around the country.[18] It's hard to overstate the influence of Fifield's anti–New Deal brand of Christianity and its portrait of Jesus, especially during and after World War II.

The corporate Spiritual Mobilization network explicitly opposed their Jesus to FDR's New Deal Jesus. When supporters of the New Deal quoted Jesus that you can't serve both God and mammon, those championing Fifield's Jesus struck back that you must make mammon serve you.[19] When the believers in Fifield's Jesus advanced private acts of charity, those supporting the New Deal Jesus countered that charity keeps the rich rich and the poor poor without providing long-term economic relief.[20] When the New Deal Jesus advocates spoke of Jesus driving out the big banker money changers, Spiritual Mobilization cried out, "Thou shalt not steal!" The eighth commandment (according to the numbering followed by most Protestants) was Spiritual Mobilization's favorite biblical jab because the organization accused FDR's government of stealing private property in its efforts to redistribute wealth.[21] In this contest, each side's Christian supporters became more enraptured by their icon.

Fifield and his Spiritual Mobilization organization were particularly influential in the creation of Republican Jesus, but countless other preachers and movements also contributed. The Baptist minister George D. Heaton, for example, brought the Republican Jesus into the daily lives of many working-class Americans by transforming workplace cultures. Heaton was active in the South beginning in the 1940s, when he delivered invited speeches at the Southern Industrial Relations Conference.

As an industrial chaplain, he focused much of his attention on "the miracles performed through supervision"—bringing the gospel of the Republican Jesus into factories by influencing the actions of supervisors.

The successful Christian supervisor, for Heaton, was someone who increased production, not someone who placed the needs and rights of workers first. Denouncing collective bargaining as a "fetish," Heaton declared that "people never become friends through bargaining." He considered industrial production "as miraculous a thing as modern life witnesses," maintaining that Jesus exemplified productivity when he turned water into wine at Cana. Republican Jesus apparently didn't tolerate any grapes of wrath.

Supervisors should heed the example of Jesus, Heaton asserted. Like Jesus healing the man with the withered hand because he "saw the opportunity to take this man and to alter his physical condition so that he could become productive," supervisors should alter the conditions of workers however they can to increase production.[22] Unions and institutional authority, so it goes, impede the ability of supervisors to follow the example of Christ the Good Supervisor—to impose on workers whatever conditions might increase productivity.

The efforts of Heaton and others to Christianize workplaces didn't cease after FDR's presidency. Instead, they served as the foundation for a mode of workplace discipline still embraced by Christian companies today. The best-known example is Walmart, whose conservative billionaire owners have for decades advanced a Christian model of "service leadership." By casting Christ as a "servant leader" and encouraging workers to think of their labor as "service to others," the corporation has made a fortune while not paying its servants a living wage or compensating them with appropriate benefits.[23] Walmart is the corporation of Fifield's and Heaton's dreams.

Starting in the 1930s, then, American industrialists responded to the Jesus promoted by FDR and Christian progressives by enlisting clergy like Fifield and Heaton to devise an anti–New Deal Jesus. In doing so, the corporate-sponsored Christian Right that was emerging started to shape a new self-image of America as a Christian nation.

REPUBLICAN JESUS VERSUS THE COMMIES

Between FDR's first inauguration and the decade following World War II, the budding Christian Right fervently prepared to redesign America as a Christian nation. Communism provided a perfect foil for their Christian nationalism: America should be everything that the Nazis and Soviets were not. For the Religious Right, this meant that America needed to embrace its Christian free market as the antidote to pagan communism.

Abraham Vereide was a power player in the Christianization of the American government at this time, so politically influential behind the scenes in the 1940s and '50s that he has been likened to a Mafia boss.[24] Two books by the investigative journalist Jeff Sharlet, recently turned into a Netflix documentary series, have exposed Vereide as one of the founders of a powerful secret network of male right-wing Christian lobbyists who call themselves "the Fellowship" and "the Family."[25] Still active today, this network promotes a right-wing Christian agenda through tax-free fund-raising and "backroom diplomacy."

A Methodist clergyman, Vereide ran the charity company Goodwill until he had a lazy-fair realization that "charity pauperizes," with the result that "the average person seeking aid ...

does not want to work for it." After resigning from Goodwill in the year of FDR's inauguration, Vereide took to supporting businessmen in their struggle against unions in Seattle. City Chapel, an organization he founded there, hosted regular non-denominational prayer breakfasts for businessmen. Vereide and his peers at City Chapel soon pursued the specific ambition "to foster and promote the advancement of Christianity and develop a Christian nation."[26]

Vereide's brand of Christian economic conservatism won support from corporate patrons as well as prominent politicians. By the early 1940s, Vereide's prayer breakfasts were no longer just for corporate leaders; in Washington, D.C., they infiltrated the House of Representatives and Senate. By 1946, the board of the National Council for Christian Leadership, the national version of City Chapel, included eight senators, ten US Representatives, and corporate titans like the president of the National Association of Manufacturers and leaders of the steel and timber industries.[27] Senator A. Willis Robertson—the father of the Christian Broadcasting Network's fierce Antichrist-watchdog, Pat Robertson—was one of the champions of Vereide's mission.

"The choice," Vereide urged members of his House breakfast group in 1949, "boils down to this: 'Christ or Communism.'" Uniting the Christian Right by fostering personal relationships with Jesus throughout the nation, he insisted, would create "a united front against the forces of the anti-Christ."[28] In the wake of World War II, communism served as a convenient foil for what one historian has described as the Christian Right's "spiritual-industrial complex."[29] No matter how much Che Guevara might look like Jesus, they insisted that Jesus was no Commie.

Communism in all its forms was equated with totalitarianism, fascism, and Nazism, but this imaginary Communazi bogeyman was just a cover for a conservative assault on American unions.[30] All supporters of social democracy, even Christian social democracy, were likened to the Nazis, Soviets, and Maoists. The House Committee on Un-American Activities (HUAC), which was first convened by Congress in 1938, waged an inquisition against prolabor groups like the Congress of Industrial Organizations, the Works Progress Administration's Federal Theater Project, the American Youth Congress, and the left-leaning National Council of Churches.[31] HUAC's persecution of suspected communists was a witch hunt based on flawed and misinterpreted information, as Arthur Miller laid bare in *The Crucible,* his incisive 1953 play on the Salem witch trials that implicitly drew contemporary parallels.

The first chair of HUAC, the Texas Democratic congressman Martin Dies, wrote and spoke vividly about a conflict between the teachings of Christ and Marx. He concluded that the only way to turn back the surge of communist activities in the US was with "the restoration of Christian influence in America."[32] Leaders of the Left, in turn, wondered if Dies and HUAC's other inquisitors had ever really read the words of Christ or Marx. "There have been a number of people recently who have been accused of Communist tendencies," Eleanor Roosevelt observed in a 1949 speech. "Yet, what they said was no more Communistic than some of the teachings of Jesus Christ."[33]

By exaggerating the threat of communism, the corporate-funded organizations that led the Christian Right could acquire interfaith and bipartisan support. In 1948, HUAC published a series of pamphlets called *100 Things You Should Know about Communism and Religion* to warn that communists in America would usher in an age of locked churches, imprisoned clergy, and burnt Bibles. "These are the same communists who crucified Jesus," one congressman stated on the House floor without a hint of irony.[34]

Figure 8. Rev. James Fifield (center) escorting Sen. and Mrs. Joseph McCarthy from his L.A. church in 1954. Credit: Los Angeles Herald Examiner Photo Collection/Los Angeles Public Library.

The man who would become the spokesperson for the congressional hunt for communist Judas Iscariots, Republican senator Joseph McCarthy of Wisconsin, echoed Fifield, Vereide, and Dies in portraying the conflict between Christianity and communism as nothing less than "that final Armageddon foretold in the Bible" (figure 8).[35] McCarthy, a devout Catholic, was allied with leading Catholic anticommunists like JFK's father, Joseph P. Kennedy Sr., a conservative who was one of the wealthiest investors in the world, and New York City's Cardinal Francis Spellman.[36] Revered as "the American Pope," Spellman has since taken a hit to his reputation from, among other things, multiple reports that the anti-LGBTQ+ moralist was having sex with men.[37]

Anticommunism was the foundation on which Fifield, Vereide, and their corporate allies attempted to build a Christian nation. The new Christian evangelism, Vereide averred, should "express itself in governmental affairs, in the legislative assemblies and in the political arena. Rebels against the Divine order must be firmly eliminated from positions of responsibility and leadership."[38] With a Christian Republican as president, this dream would start to become a reality in the 1950s.

BUYING A CHRISTIAN NATION

When Dwight Eisenhower, a fundamentalist Christian, became president, the emergent Christian Right wasted no time in seizing the opportunity to take over the government. With Eisenhower's help, the corporate-sponsored Christian Right purchased a Christian nation in the 1950s. This new product came shrink-wrapped in a mythic veneer of historical continuity, neatly packaged along with the batteries of Cold War mobilization. The rise of conservatism in the run-up to Eisenhower's election signaled the success of Spiritual Mobilization and the efforts of anti–New Deal Christians during World War II and its aftermath.

"We who are free must proclaim anew our faith," Dwight Eisenhower, the son of Mennonite parents, pronounced in 1953 during a presidential inaugural speech unlike FDR's in everything other than its mandatory deference to Christianity. "This faith is the abiding creed of our fathers," he said, recasting America's founders as wholesome Christians. "This faith rules our whole way of life. It decrees that we, the people, elect leaders not to rule but to serve. It asserts that we have the right to choice of our own work and to the reward of our own toil. It inspires the initiative that makes our productivity the wonder of the world. And it warns that any man who seeks to deny equality among all his brothers betrays the spirit of the free."[39] The "free," of course, refers to those who aren't pagan communists.

Eisenhower called for a "great crusade for freedom," using militaristic rhetoric that diverged sharply from the pacifism of the Mennonite tradition in which he had been raised.[40] The crusades, lest we forget, were a series of bloody wars waged by Catholics in the Middle Ages against Muslims, as well as Jews and Orthodox Christians. The president's appropriation of this medieval rhetoric was hardly cleansed of violence. "The enemies of this faith know no god but force," the celebrated World War II general alleged, implying that the godless communists who opposed free capital were those who instigated aggression. As the leader of the free world, the United States had to hold war "to be the first task of statesmanship to develop the strength that will deter the forces of aggression and promote the conditions of peace."

The historian Jonathan Herzog has described the Eisenhower era aptly as a "significant period of legislative sacralization."[41] With some bipartisan support, the Christian Right led a wide-ranging campaign to Christianize America through legislation. In 1953, Eisenhower attended the first National Prayer Breakfast (figure 9), an annual event spearheaded by Vereide and organized by "the Fellowship" for America's most prominent politicians and corporate leaders. A presidential version of the meetings Vereide had started for businessmen in Seattle, the first

Figure 9. The first annual National Prayer Breakfast on February 5, 1953. From left to right: Rev. Abraham Vereide, Rep. Katharine St. George (R–NY), President Eisenhower, Sen. Frank Carlson (R–KS), Conrad Hilton, and Rev. Dr. Edward Pruden. The poster in the background is Hilton's "America on Its Knees." Credit: Getty Images.

meeting was hosted by the hotel magnate Conrad Hilton. Hilton commissioned the event's iconic image of "America on Its Knees"—Uncle Sam confidently kneeling in prayer—and Eisenhower gladly hung a copy of the painting in the Oval Office.[42]

The first National Prayer Breakfast's purpose of promoting "government under God" came to fruition in several changes of the Eisenhower era. Pitting "Judaeo-Christian" principles—a formulation that covers all manner of sin[43]—against godless communism, the Christian Right and its obliging president resolved to add the words "under God" to the Pledge of Allegiance in 1954. Originally written in 1892 by Frank Bellamy, a socialist pastor who delivered sermons with titles like "Jesus the Socialist," the Pledge was now emended to suit the corporate agenda of the Christian Right.[44] Similarly, in the following year, Congress and Eisenhower passed a bill adding the words "In God We Trust" to all US currency (it hadn't previously been printed on paper money). The same words started appearing regularly on stamps in 1953, and in 1956 the phrase was officially adopted as the national motto.[45] Each day, this Christian slogan receives acclamation on the lips of unwitting schoolchildren across the country.

Eisenhower's government challenged the separation of church and state that Jefferson and the founding fathers had established, however nebulously. Suddenly, copies of the Ten Commandments began appearing in public spaces. This was much more than an expression of the nation's newfound piety: it was also a money-making scheme spearheaded by Fifield's wealthy Christian friend Cecil B. DeMille, director of *The Ten Commandments* (1956). This epic story of a man's struggle for religious freedom has raked in $2.4 billion, adjusting for inflation, and is the seventh-highest grossing film of all time.[46] To promote his blockbuster, DeMille joined ranks with the Fraternal Order of Eagles to have more than ten thousand framed posters and at least 194 granite monuments of the Ten Commandments put up from coast to coast.[47] DeMille and Moses himself, Charlton Heston—who would later become president of the National Rifle Association—personally endorsed the erection of the new monuments in public parks (figure 10). Could Hollywood ask for better billboards?

Corporate Christianity's crusade against the secular state in these years ravaged American civil law. We see the repercussions of Eisenhower-era precedents in legal debates today over (Judaeo-)Christian monuments in civic spaces. The Satanic

Figure 10. Dedication of the Ten Commandments monument at the International Peace Garden adjacent to the American-Canadian border crossing in North Dakota. From left to right: Charlton Heston, Minnesotan judge E.J. Ruegemer of the Fraternal Order of Eagles, Fargo mayor Herschel Lashkowitz, and Lt. Gov. Clarence Dahl. Credit: Institute for Regional Studies, NDSU Fargo.

Temple, most recently, has led the charge against the Christian monuments. When the Satanists—Far Left humanists and free-speech advocates whose appropriation of the imagery of Christianity's great villain is entirely tongue-in-cheek—announced that they would erect a statue of the hermaphroditic winged-goat deity Baphomet in Oklahoma, the state's Supreme Court decided to remove the Ten Commandments from the capitol. In 2017, thanks to the lobbying of Jason Rapert, a state senator and conservative Christian minister, a new Ten Commandments monument was set up on the grounds of the Arkansas state capitol. It was quickly destroyed by a rogue opponent who was not associated with the Satanic Temple and then was set up again in 2018. As part of a protest at the capitol building, the Satanists displayed their one-ton bronze statue of Baphomet, where it briefly stood tall as a sign that the debate over church and state rages on in America.[48]

But the Christian Right's encroachment into politics didn't go unchecked. Several key Supreme Court rulings in the early 1960s signaled the limits of the emergent Christian Right's political influence: *Engel v. Vitale* (1962) decided that New York public school teachers could not begin the school day with a prayer, and *Abingdon School District v. Schempp* (1963) outlawed devotional Bible reading in public schools. In the heyday of the civil rights movement, rulings like *Green v. County School Board of New Kent County* (1968) and *Swann v. Charlotte-Mecklenburg Board of Education* (1971) called for the desegregation of schools receiving public funding. This fired up many among the predominantly white Christian Right and instigated the formation of Christian academies and the Christian home-schooling movement.[49]

Certain corporate-backed Christianizing initiatives received bipartisan support during the Eisenhower era, a Republican takeover after two decades of Democrats in the White House. But with JFK as president and civil rights, sexual liberation, and antiwar movements on the rise, conservatives retreated into the Far Right of the Republican Party. The Christian Right resisted these progressive movements by adopting the language of traditional "family values," which opposed abortion, gay rights, and feminism and supported Christian schools, home schooling, and military service. With the help of some charismatic preachers, the Republican Jesus would soon become the official sponsor of those values.

REPUBLICAN JESUS GOES MAINSTREAM

Eisenhower's presidency enabled conservative Christianity and its Small Government politics to go mainstream. Charismatic preachers like Fifield and Vereide paved the way for the presence of "Court Evangelicals" among the president's advisers, to borrow the moniker applied to them by the progressive Evangelical scholar John Fea.[50] None of these Court Evangelicals did more to keep the flame of conservative Christianity alive in the government than Rev. Billy Graham, who advised every president from Eisenhower to Trump before his death in 2018.

Billy Graham was without a doubt the most influential Christian preacher of the last century. His "crusades," which started out in Ringling Brothers circus tents but soon filled stadiums, brought a watered-down conservative Christianity to many millions across the world.[51] Just about any country song you've heard about Jesus might as well have been a Graham sermon.

A slight against Graham, affectionately known as "America's pastor," is more likely to offend an American than an irreverent crack about Jesus. Graham's promoters valorize him as an honest farm boy who found Jesus and wanted nothing more than to bring Christ's redemption to the world. That's all well and good, but Graham was also a shrewd political influencer. He united a massive coalition of Christians around the simple message of a loving God who redeemed sinful humanity through the sacrifice of his son. But his gospel was also thoroughly individualistic and anti–Big Government, trading fears of communism and social progress for moral conservatism.[52]

Graham's economic liberalism shines through his sermon to the American Association of Bankers in 1974: "Unless we take moral and spiritual action and do it quickly, we may find ourselves in a totalitarian state, with all freedoms suppressed in a relatively short time. The Bible teaches you cannot serve the true God and another god called materialism, but you can serve God *with* materialism, if your heart is right toward God."[53]

This same Anti-Federalist stress on individuals' spiritual duties underlies Graham's mixed record on civil rights. It's true that Graham personally pulled down the ropes of segregation at some of his crusades as early as 1953, and he also said lots of nice things about racial equality *in Christ*.[54] But the reality is that his social consciousness receded whenever government intervention, which entailed the regulation of big businesses, was on the table. "The only possible solution" to the race problem, Graham pronounced, was "a vital, personal experience with Jesus Christ on the part of both races."[55] Graham opposed the Civil Rights Act of 1964 and was vocal in his disdain for Rev. Dr. Martin Luther King Jr.'s March on America in 1963. America's pastor besmirched MLK's famous dream, envisaging that "only when Christ comes again will the little white children of Alabama walk hand in hand with little black children."[56]

The #2 Court Evangelical, Baptist minister Jerry Falwell, was no better. His 1965 sermon "Ministers and Marches" insisted that civil rights activism was incompatible with the gospel.[57] And the civil rights laws, he quipped, "should be considered civil wrongs."[58]

Nobody did more to sabotage the civil rights and sexual liberation movements than conservative Evangelicals like Graham and Falwell.[59] Their segregationist performances served the Republican Party's "southern strategy" for turning racist white Democrats in southern states into Republicans.[60] At the same time, their aversion to cultural changes helped to galvanize the Christian Right around a subcultural identity characterized by what historians have called a "paranoid style" of politics and an "embattled mentality."[61]

For all of his disclaimers about not getting involved in politics, America's favorite crusader was a vocal supporter of war for decades—from Korea to Iraq. Graham soothed any presidential or popular Christian anxieties about the injustice of war by depicting military intervention abroad as a strategy for spreading Christian democracy in an increasingly communist world.[62] Graham envisioned the Third World as the site of an apocalyptic struggle between American Christianity and the Soviet Union's pagan communism. "God may be using Communism as a judgment upon the West," he warned about North Vietnam.[63]

Graham was more influential than ever during the Nixon presidency. For the first time in history, Graham led a full-blown worship service as part of President Nixon's inauguration in 1969. He also introduced the first of what would become regular Sunday worship services in the East Room of the White House.[64] The ministers who presided over these services, which were attended by conservative Christian politicians and corporate leaders alike, were hand-picked by Graham to ensure that their politics aligned with his and Nixon's—that is, that they preached a Jesus who favored Small Government, traditional family values, and whatever other Republican causes came to the fore.[65]

When Nixon, a paradoxically prowar Quaker who served as Eisenhower's vice president, faced criticism over his expansion of the Vietnam War into Cambodia in 1970, Graham invited him to speak at a massive crusade at the University of Tennessee (figure 11). Graham, Nixon, and all involved knew that this was an overtly political act, with Nixon calling on the mostly Republican crusaders to support bringing about "peace in the world" by resisting materialism and turning "to the great spiritual forces

Figure 11. First lady Pat Nixon, Rev. Billy Graham, and President Richard Nixon (left to right) examine the crowd of more than sixty-five thousand at Graham's Crusade for Christ at the University of Tennessee in 1970. Credit: Associated Press (photographer: Lou Krasky).

that have made America the great country that it is." The film of the crusade made by Graham's lucrative organization was conveniently edited to remove the protesters' booming chants of "Bullshit!"[66]

Just days later, Graham continued Nixon's prowar cause by announcing a pro-America rally. The Princeton historian Kevin Kruse has shown that Graham's Honor America Day relied on the corporate funding of many of the same business lobbies that had for decades relied on Christianity to resist the New Deal.[67] This celebrity-studded Fourth of July celebration in the capital put an innocent Christian face on a corporate, Republican cause. Its backers relished the profits of war as much as they loathed regulations.

Graham's mainstream appeal to Christians with a Republican gospel of limited government, individual freedom, and anticommunism set the stage for the Christian Right's startling choice of Republicanism over Christianity in 1980.[68] The Christian Right backed the divorced Hollywood actor Ronald Reagan, who went to church as often as a poor man goes to a tailor, over Jimmy Carter, the born-again Baptist and passionately pious Democratic incumbent. Reagan catered to the Christian Right by calling for "old fashioned values" and casting his bid as a renewal of Eisenhower's Christian crusade, constantly performing his contempt for those who wanted to get rid of "In God We Trust," school prayer, and unborn babies.

Falwell, the most outspoken of the Court Evangelicals on social issues, founded the Moral Majority organization in 1979 to mobilize Christian conservatives to vote for Reagan. The Reagan years were Falwell's heyday. With a Christian conservatism that was more blatantly political than Graham's, Falwell was primed to help Reagan achieve Christian support for his neoliberal program of Reaganomics. "The free-enterprise system is clearly outlined in the Book of Proverbs in the Bible," Falwell claimed in his influential 1980 book *Listen America!* "Jesus Christ made it clear that the work ethic was a part of His plan for man. Ownership of property is biblical. Competition in business is biblical."[69]

Like the Christian Right, the Republican Jesus had become more political than religious by the Reagan era. Graham, Falwell, and their corporate-sponsored media empires weren't alone in driving this transformation. Best-selling books like Hal Lindsey's *Late Great Planet Earth* (1970), and later Tim LaHaye and Jerry Jenkins's Left Behind series (1995–2007), helped to expand the mainstream sway of Republican Christianity, especially among white, middle-class Americans. They identified the signs of the end-times in the actions of communists at home and abroad, including university professors.[70] With an apocalyptic urgency, in the late twentieth century, such conservative prophets came out of the woodwork to scare the bejesus out of voters—or rather, to scare the Republican Jesus into them.

. . .

FDR's New Deal Jesus tried to chase away corrupt bankers and businessmen. But instead of running away, or reforming their practices, America's corporate leaders fought back by investing in a Jesus of their own. Between the inaugurations of FDR and Eisenhower, powerful corporations funded the emergence of a Christian conservatism that cut across denominations and even, to some degree, parties. By the time of Eisenhower's presidency, however, the Christian Right was proudly Republican, forcing America to be born again as a Christian nation.

In reaction to FDR's Big Government, the corporate-sponsored Christian Right sold a Republican brand of Jesus by appealing to Americans' patriotic love of freedom and fear of communism. This Republican Jesus didn't look the same to every consumer, but he was always a promoter of free enterprise, limited government, traditional family values, and individual freedoms. And his worst enemies were the communists, whether crypto-communists among the labor organizers, socialists, and left-wing Democrats in America or the fascist communists abroad. As the heir of Protestantism and classical liberalism, Republican Jesus didn't suffer Pharisaic legalists like FDR's people and the rulers of totalitarian states. He called individuals to faith in free enterprise, by the grace of God and government, letting the poor and marginalized fade into the background.

When the Christian Right backed a scarcely religious Hollywood Republican for president over a deeply religious Evangelical Democrat in 1980, they proved that their faith in the fearmongering politics of Small Government outweighed their solidarity with those washed in the blood of Christ. This prioritization of a leader's politics over his piety set the stage for the Christian Right's shocking sacrifice of Christianity on the altar of free enterprise in 2016. It set the stage for corporate interests to trump everything else.

CHAPTER FOUR

Tea and Prosperity in the Age of Trump

trump

//trəmp//

Etymology: from the Old French word *tromper,* to deceive

verb (transitive)

1. to get the better of
2. to override

noun

1. in card games, a playing card of the suit chosen to rank above the others, which can win a trick where a card of a different suit has been led
2. an older, thrice-married, stocky, yellow-haired corporate businessman who gets the better of the American people during a US presidential election, who tricks workers to construct buildings for him for less than half the union wage, who overrides usual rental practices when tenants are black, who calls women "fat pigs, dogs, and slobs," who mocks a woman for "blood coming out of her ... wherever," who brags about grabbing women by the pussy, who pays off porn stars with whom he has had extramarital affairs, who ridicules people with disabilities, who refuses to denounce white supremacists, who hires white supremacists, who relays anti-Semitic

conspiracy theories, who defends free speech when it is hateful toward anyone other than himself, who runs illicit campaigns that depend on Russian hacking, who bans Muslim immigrants, who declares a national emergency to build a giant border wall to keep out Mexicans he calls "drug dealers, criminals, and rapists" but not those Mexicans who work on his resorts for infinitesimal wages, who bans openly transgender troops from serving their country, who offers to pay the legal fees of white supporters who punch out black protesters at his rallies, who overrides the balance of powers by stacking the Supreme Court with judges who favor executive power, who takes pride in firing anyone who disagrees with him, who attempts to dismantle Social Security and affordable health care programs, who denies responsibility for climate change, who considers most of the press his enemy but Fox News his friend, whose net worth is allegedly in the billions but not fully clear because he won't reveal his tax returns, who plays the right cards to receive the support of the Christian Right.

Donald Trump would not have won the 2016 presidential election if he had not won the support of the Christian Right. The statistics are revealing: 58 percent of Protestants (including members of the Church of Jesus Christ of Latter-day Saints) and 52 percent of Catholics voted for Trump. Even more notably, Trump's support included 81 percent of white Christians who identify as born again or Evangelical, regardless of denominational affiliation.[1]

Like Reagan's first election, Trump's success in 2016 signaled how much more a candidate's Small Government, conservative politics matter to the Christian Right than any semblance of sincere commitment to Christ. Sure, Trump identifies with Christianity. "I'm a Protestant. I'm a Presbyterian," he said to Fox News in 2011. "I'm also busy and probably busier than I should be. But I am a Christian. I'm a Protestant. I'm a Presbyterian."[2] That was almost right on script.

When Trump goes off script we catch glimpses of his Christianity, and it combines an ethno-populist faith in freedom from government authority with a probusiness faith in individuals' freedom to prosper. When asked whether God helped him to achieve his business success, Trump responded that "God helped me by giving me a certain brain, whether that's a good or a bad thing." Whenever Trump speaks about free will in this way, Augustine and Calvin must roll over in their graves. But he goes further. In an interview, he divulged that he has never asked God for forgiveness. He allowed that "when we go in church and when I drink my little wine ... and have my little cracker, I guess that is a form of asking for forgiveness." Still, he strives "not to bring God into that picture."[3]

Trump's election represents the success of the conjoined forces of corporate leaders and the Christian Right to control the government. Wealth and Christianity are indivisible for Trump. "I think people are shocked when they find out that I am a Christian," he acknowledges in his 2015 book with a fittingly ableist title, *Crippled America: How to Make America Great Again.* "They see me with all the surroundings of wealth so they sometimes don't associate that with being religious. That's not accurate. I go to church. I love God, and I love having a relationship with Him."[4]

Trump rarely speaks about Jesus (unless the "little cracker" counts), but Republican Jesus has experienced a spirited rebirth in his America. Regardless of his personal convictions about

Christ and morality, there can be little doubt that Trump embraces Republicans' doctrines of neoliberal capitalism and Anti-Federalism. As we have seen, the Republican Jesus has been tailored by corporate-backed Christian leaders to promote these doctrines since FDR's day.

Trump is the heir to this legacy of probusiness Christianity and especially its Tea Party and Prosperity Gospel currents. By combining an allegiance to many of the traditional "family values" positions of the "old Religious Right" with the Tea Party's resentment politics and the Prosperity Gospel's glorification of wealth, Trump and his supporters have reinvented Republican Jesus as a wealth-loving, positive-thinking nationalist.

TEAVANGELICALS FOR JESUS

The Tea Party movement agitated the Christian Right with a wave of resentment that Trump rode to victory. This movement started in libertarian circles during the presidency of George W. Bush but became organized and influential only following the Great Recession and in the run-up to Obama's second election in 2012. It tied Christian conservatism together with fiscal conservatism and ethnic/racial conservatism.[5] For Christians who vote on the issues of abortion or same-sex marriage, supporting Tea Party candidates also entailed voting for Small Government restrictions on collective bargaining and xenophobic immigration policies.

The Tea Party, which we have already encountered as an influence on O'Reilly and Dugard's version of Jesus, is best known for protesting taxation. Its name refers to the Boston Tea Party of 1773, in which a group of colonists resisted British tariffs on the sale of tea by rushing onto ships and dumping their tea chests into the Boston Harbor. With a rallying cry of "No taxation without representation!" the dissenters rebuked the British for collecting revenue from commerce in the colonies without extending the colonists a reciprocal say in the affairs of state. While part of their resentment was directed at the British government's taxation of colonial citizens, their grievances were more especially directed at the crown's reluctance to tax the corporate British East India Company. Ironically, the modern Tea Party's hostility toward taxation is directed primarily at the government and fails to acknowledge, as the 1773 protesters did, that corporations swell with capital thanks to limitations on taxation.[6]

Aside from appropriating the heritage of the 1773 Tea Party, the more recent movement applies the backronym Taxed Enough Already to its name.

According to Tea Party activists, the core values of the movement are fiscal responsibility, constitutionally limited government, and free markets.[7] This movement blamed Obama's Big Government for the recession. The Tea Partiers reacted against what they viewed as a nonwhite president taking money from hardworking white people and giving it to freeloading nonwhites and especially "illegals." White nationalism found a platform in this movement and a leading voice in Steve Bannon, who became Trump's White House chief strategist.[8]

Though sometimes viewed as a Far Right fringe phenomenon, the Tea Party was multidimensional and widely influential, even among "establishment" Republicans. Its sprawling grassroots network and expansive funding sources enticed many Republican politicians to support the movement, or at the very least to be careful not to reject it. Tea Party causes and candidates received substantial funding from billionaires like the Coors beer family, the Walmart Waltons, and the Koch oil dynasty.[9] Since the mid-twentieth century, the libertarian Kochs have bankrolled conservative Christian and anticommunist organizations that even leading conservative intellectuals like William Buckley Jr. and Ayn Rand have considered radical.[10] As recent investigative studies have shown, corporate-run political lobbies like the American Legislative Exchange Council (ALEC) have played an increasingly big part in drafting and promoting the probusiness legislation that many Republican lawmakers propose. The political positions of the corporate lobbies often, but not always, cohere with Christian conservatism, since the Religious Right was itself shaped by probusiness corporate interests.[11]

Although the movement lacked an official leadership, it was organized as the Tea Party House Caucus in 2010 by Minnesota congresswoman Michele Bachmann. At its height in 2010–11, this House Caucus had more than sixty members.[12] According to Gallup poll data from early 2011, 30 percent of Americans supported the Tea Party.[13] With the help of the newly trendy Twitter platform and key media proponents like O'Reilly, Sean Hannity, and especially Glenn Beck (all at Fox News at the time), this movement spread at an astonishing pace.[14]

David Brody, a self-described "Teavangelical," has shown that the Tea Party and white, Evangelical Christianity overlapped considerably.[15] A Pew Research Center poll based on data from 2010 and early 2011 revealed that white Evangelicals were five times more likely than other Americans to agree with the Tea Party. Even more strikingly, of Americans who agreed with the Religious Right, 69 percent agreed with the Tea Party and only 4 percent disagreed.[16] The Tea Party unified the Religious Right with libertarians and white nationalists, much to the dismay of politically moderate and progressive Evangelicals.

After Mitt Romney won the Republican ticket over several more ideal Tea Party candidates, and then lost to Obama, the Tea Party appeared to have tapered out. The official caucuses disbanded and public interest in Tea Party causes waned.

Yet as Bryan Gervais and Irwin Morris have demonstrated, the Tea Party's "reactionary Republicanism" never faded. Instead, it became the base for Trump's campaign—a campaign that embraced not only the Tea Party's desire for limited government but even more importantly its affection for brash ethnonationalist rhetoric that is, quite deliberately, both grammatically and politically incorrect.[17] Without explicitly branding himself as a Tea Party candidate, Trump fit the mold perfectly.

To legitimize their politics of resentment, the Tea Partiers and their successors have relied on fake histories about race and religion in America. And these are not just fake histories but disturbingly problematic histories. Deciphering some of the ways that the Teavangelicals understand American history is important because it is what they think of when they hear Trump's slogan "Make America Great Again." For the Christian Right, the slogan calls for a return to when America was a Christian nation—that is, at its founding. This was precisely the historical connection Ronald Reagan broached when he used the same campaign slogan.[18] John Fea adds, however, that Trump and Christian nationalists also idealize the antebellum South and the Eisenhower era as times when America was great.[19]

Michele Bachmann, whose interminable meme trail has nearly broken the internet, has served as one of the gatekeepers of the Tea Party's fake history. The 2012 presidential hopeful memorably claimed that the founding fathers "worked tirelessly until slavery was no more in the United States."[20] Bachmann's notion that the founding fathers were antislavery whitewashes a century of harsh, institutionalized slavery.

At the same time, Bachmann has suggested that slavery was a good thing for African Americans. In 2011, she proudly signed a conservative Christian organization's pledge, "The Marriage Vow." The pledge laments that "a child born into slavery in 1860 was more likely to be raised by his mother and father in a two-parent household than was an African-American baby after the election of the USA's first African-American President."[21] In other words, slavery had a civilizing, Christianizing effect on African Americans that is now wanting among them, thanks to Obama (not coincidentally, this was around the same time that Trump, the "Birther-in-Chief," started suggesting that Obama wasn't born in the US and was a Muslim).[22] Entirely ignoring the facts that marriage between slaves was illegal, and that enslaved families were routinely separated at auctions, this deeply racist view of history asserts that African Americans were better off as slaves because they were exposed to the good Christian morals of white families.

Bachmann's comments and pledge fit with a broader under-standing of American history that equates Christianity, white-ness, and goodness. Her views invoke a fake history of the first century of the United States that became popular among some circles of Evangelicals in the mid-twentieth century.[23] According to this narrative, Africa was barbaric because of its pagan-ism, and American slavery was thus a prerequisite process in which lucky Africans could achieve what the Confederate general Robert E. Lee called "the sanctifying effects of Christian-ity." Therefore, the founding fathers supported slavery in prac-tice but not in theory. The Civil War, so it goes, was about religion rather than slavery: the godless North attacked the Christian South.[24]

Bachmann endorsed these views not only by making remarks about slavery but also by assisting her extremist Christian law professor John Eidsmoe with writing his book *Christianity and the Constitution: The Faith of Our Founding Fathers* (1987) and by listing fake histories of this sort as personal recommendations on her official website. Bachmann received a world-class training in using the Bible to falsify history while working with Eidsmoe at the Evangelical Oral Roberts University. Its Coburn School of Law sets out "to restore law to its historic roots in the Bible."[25] This type of revisionist history, flawed in both details and interpretation, has been quite common among Teavangelicals.

The historical primer of the Tea Party is a book by W. Cleon Skousen called *The Five Thousand Year Leap*. Published in 1981, the book smacks of the Cold War anxieties of conservative Christians. Its author is a Far Right member of the Church of Jesus Christ of Latter-day Saints (who taught the Book of Mormon as a historical source at Brigham Young University), a former FBI agent, and an ardent supporter of anticommunist organizations like the Koch-funded John Birch Society (which Eidsmoe also supported).

For Skousen, the founding fathers brilliantly combined biblical and classical Greco-Roman principles in the new nation's constitution for limited government. On the basis of cherry-picked sources lacking historical contextualization, Skousen claims that the founding fathers established a Christian nation: "The Founders were not indulging in any idle gesture when they adopted the motto 'In God We Trust.'"[26] As we've seen, this phrase first appeared on coins in 1864 and was not an official motto until the Eisenhower era.

Skousen's *Five Thousand Year Leap* touts a hard-right Republican Jesus. He places much emphasis on the founding fathers' commitment to Jesus's "second great commandment"—love thy neighbor.[27] Notably, though, he spends far more time appealing to the Roman orator Cicero than the gospels when trying to work out what this commandment means. He ultimately concludes that Jesus promoted the prosperity of the commonwealth, which implied the freedom (and responsibility) of individuals to improve themselves.

In his *Days of the Living Christ* (1992), Skousen more explicitly insists that Jesus's teachings oppose the welfare system.[28] And in his *The Making of America* (1985), he expounds on the racial implications of these biblical and American principles through discussions of slavery that characterize white slave owners as "the worst victims" of slavery.[29] For Skousen, like Bachmann, slavery was a stage in American history in which whites helped to Christianize African Americans so that they would no longer need handouts; as a result, they should no longer need handouts today.

Skousen's works would have had little appeal outside of the Far Right within the Church of Jesus Christ of Latter-day Saints if it weren't for repeated endorsements by Fox News's token Far Right Latter-day Saint, Glenn Beck, during the rise of the Tea Party. Beck wrote the foreword to the thirtieth edition of *The Five Thousand Year Leap* in 2009 and publicized the book whenever he had the chance.[30]

The centrality of Skousen to the foundational ideas of the Tea Party is celebrated in a painting called *One Nation under God* by the pro–Tea Party, pro-Trump artist Jon McNaughton, who fancies himself a political, Church of Jesus Christ of Latter-day Saints version of Norman Rockwell. A handsome, white Republican Jesus stands at the center of the painting, where he displays the US Constitution to past and present onlookers.[31] One of the few people of color in the painting—and the only one in the foreground, representing the present—is a black "college student" holding a copy of *The Five Thousand Year Leap.* McNaughton assumed, no doubt, that a black man would need this wisdom to improve himself. The only other books in the painting are the Bible, held by a white "Christian minister," and Darwin's *On the Origin of Species,* held by a "professor" who is stooping next to Satan among the heretics looking away from Jesus.

Inspired by Skousen, Teavangelicals provoked the Christian Right's post-9/11 fears of immigrants, postrecession fears of government spending, Obama-era fears of nonwhite leaders, and nostalgia for a time when America was great—when it was a truly Christian nation. Their efforts created a political vacuum in which a scarcely religious white man could easily attract the interest of Evangelicals through strident intonations of economic and racial nationalism and bombastic affirmations of fake history.

IS PELAGIUS LATIN FOR PEALE?

Trump validated the Teavangelicals' anger and anxiety by doubling down on the Tea Party's ethno-nationalist rhetoric, but he also needed to instill hope that a Trump presidency was more than a pipe dream. To do so, he appealed to the Prosperity Gospel, a theological movement that delivered strategies for spiritual, physical, and financial mastery.

The Prosperity Gospel refers to a multifaceted movement that gained traction in the healing revivals of the World War II years and the postwar age of anxiety. The Duke University professor Kate Bowler has shown that the Prosperity Gospel movement overlaps with fundamentalism, Evangelicalism, Pentecostalism, and Far Right conservatism (including the Teavangelicals), without corresponding strictly to any of them. What unites adherents to the Prosperity Gospel is a conceptualization of individuals' faith as an active power whose ability to turn thoughts and words into reality is demonstrated by wealth, health, and victory.[32]

Most of Trump's limited personal engagement with faith has been through the Prosperity Gospel. In 1975, his family started attending Norman Vincent Peale's historic Marble Collegiate Reformed Church in New York City. Peale soon became Trump's "spiritual father" and called Trump his "greatest student of all time." As Stephen Mansfield reports in his book *Choosing Donald Trump*, the Methodist minister officiated at Trump's first wedding, buried both of his parents, and was the distinguished clergyman at the Trump family's birthdays, anniversaries, births, and building dedications.[33]

Peale was very much a part of the mid-twentieth-century making of American probusiness Christianity that we explored in the last chapter. He was friends with Fifield and was a New York representative of his Spiritual Mobilization organization. In 1950, Peale became the first director of a New York offshoot of Spiritual Mobilization called the Christian Freedom Foundation, which published a periodical called *Christian Economics*. He resigned after a month but continued to support the organization and eventually returned as its treasurer.[34]

Like his Spiritual Mobilization peers, Peale was a bitter opponent of the New Deal. He bemoaned that, instead of praying to God to improve their lives, New Deal Christians "pray to the government to write another code."[35] A 1942 *New York Sun* article recognized him as "a vigorous assailant of the New Deal, preaching eloquent sermons against bureaucracy, official bungling, mudding and meddling, invasion of individual rights, wrecking of American traditions, coddling of the unemployed, providing relief for the undeserving, knuckling to union labor, the menace of a third term, in fact, the entire category of New Deal sins as he sees them."[36]

Peale's eclectic self-help theology combined New Thought and Christian Science philosophies with Baptist, Methodist, and Calvinist beliefs.[37] Peale's Prosperity Gospel became widely influential through his regular preaching, radio shows, and books. His best seller, *The Power of Positive Thinking* (1952), catapulted him to fame. The book, as Bowler puts it, "articulated middle class aspirations" with its simple positive thinking formula: "Picturize, prayerize, and actualize."[38]

Stressing a biblical portrait of Jesus as healer, *The Power of Positive Thinking* asserts that all it takes to transcend poverty is faith and positive thinking. "For a man to have lived in poverty when all the time right on his doorstep is gold indicates an unintelligent approach to life," Peale explains. "If you mentally visualize and affirm and reaffirm your assets and keep your thoughts on them, emphasizing them to the fullest extent, you will rise out of any difficulty regardless of what it may be. Your inner powers will reassert themselves and, with the help of God, lift you from defeat to victory."[39]

In many ways, Peale's gospel complemented those of his mainstream peers like Graham. Peale, too, was a Court Evangelical, especially under Nixon.[40] However, Peale's theological emphases formed a sharp contrast with Graham's. The latter addressed the anxieties of his listeners with a Calvinistic message in which everyone was a sinner but might be redeemed through faith in Christ and counted among the elect when he returned. Peale addressed the same postwar anxieties, but with an amped-up Arminian-Methodist theology of free will.[41] By controlling their thoughts and actions, individuals could improve themselves and reap the benefits of wealth and health in this world, not just the next.

Peale emphasized the individual's will to prosper and downplayed the human plight of sin so much that he was compared to Pelagius, the infamous ancient defender of free will. One critic even quipped, "Is Pelagius the Latin spelling for Peale?"[42]

The influence of Peale's gospel on Trump is unmistakable. Not only does Trump view wealth as commensurate with Christianity and believe that any individual can use positive thinking to prosper, but he also learned about "facts" from Peale. Trump's fake history and "alternative facts" are rooted in Peale's "name it and claim it" model of individual success. Much as Trump exaggerates crowd sizes, Peale was prone to hyperbole in his own self-promotion efforts—for example, he claimed responsibility for the "Largest Vested Children's Choir in the State" and "the Greatest University Audience in America."[43] Even more, Peale's books are littered with one-liners like "What you 'image' (imagine) may ultimately become a fact if held mentally with sufficient faith" and "Attitudes are more important than facts."[44]

Peale's gospel informed Trump's Arminian theology of free will and prosperity, but he died in 1993, long before Trump's irruption into politics. Paula White-Cain, a celebrity Prosperity Gospel preacher, succeeded Peale as Trump's spiritual mentor after the two became friends in 2002. A Mississippi native with what she has described as a "messed-up" childhood, White-Cain converted to Christianity as a teenager and found her way into ministry after marrying a megachurch Pentecostal pastor.[45] By the time Trump met her, she was preaching to thousands with her husband each week and also starring in her own television show.[46] Soon, the multimillionaire was also writing self-help books like *Deal with It!* (2004), which was aimed at women, and *Move On, Move Up* (2008).

Like Peale, White-Cain likes the portrait of Jesus as healer. She cites, for example, the story of Jesus healing the woman with an irregular genital discharge who pushed her way through the crowd to touch the hem of his prayer shawl.[47] This story has all the right components for White-Cain's interpretation of the gospel: a woman faced with obstacles who takes it upon herself to get the help she needs through faith in Christ. Seeing as the woman might have had "blood coming out of her … wherever," one wonders if Trump would view her as a faithful self-improver or just another pushy woman.

Though less philosophical than Peale, White-Cain is just as cheery and just as self-assured of the human will to prosper on earth. "Don't let anybody tell you," she demands, "that you can't find the money you need to pursue your dream."[48]

White-Cain is similar to Peale when it comes to theology, but she also has two additional qualities that no doubt ingratiated her to Trump: she embodies the same kind of physical and material prosperity that Trump likes to surround himself with (one of her homes is a $3.5 million condo in Trump Tower in New York City), and she has more appeal among people of color than many other televangelists (her weekly show was broadcast on BET).[49]

In 2015, Trump enlisted White-Cain to help him reach out to the Christian Right. Before taking to the campaign trail, however, she set aside her Pentecostalism and publicly announced that she was a free agent.[50] Becoming nondenominational was a strategic move aimed at widening Trump's appeal across Christian denominations. And she did just that by arranging for Trump to meet, and in some cases pray, with Christian leaders from different denominations.

Figure 12. Advisory meeting on the nomination of the conservative lawyer Neil Gorsuch to the Supreme Court. From left to right: Rev. Paula White-Cain, President Trump, and Wayne LaPierre (chief executive officer and executive vice president of the NRA) in the Roosevelt Room on February 1, 2017. Credit: Associated Press (photographer: Pablo Martinez Monsivais).

White-Cain did so much to make Trump palatable to Christians that Mansfield credits her with helping to "deliver the Oval Office into Donald Trump's hands." It didn't hurt that in 2015 she married the drummer from Journey, proving to voters that anyone can marry a rock star if they Don't Stop Believin'. And anyone can become president by the same tactic. White-Cain is now the chairwoman of Trump's Evangelical Advisory Board and a regular presence at White House events (figure 12).[51]

Peale and White-Cain provided Trump with a theological foundation for his campaign. By combining the Prosperity Gospel's doctrine of prosperity through faith with the Teavangelicals' racializing of Christian nationalism, and by appropriating both movements' flagrant disregard for facts, Trump managed to convince Christian conservatives that globalization and regulation were the biggest obstacles to their prosperity.

THE CHRISTIAN RIGHT'S NEW COURT JESTERS

Even with support from adherents to the Prosperity Gospel and Teavangelicals, there was still one sector that Trump needed to secure the Christian Right's vote. He needed endorsements from the "new old Christian Right," the families of the revered Court Evangelicals Billy Graham and Jerry Falwell.

The Graham and Falwell dynasties remain a force to be reckoned with in global Evangelicalism and American politics. Both families have many fans among the Tea Party and Prosperity Gospel movements but have not restricted their mainstream appeal through concrete affiliations with either.

Franklin Graham, Billy's son and the most influential member of the Graham clan, has inherited very little of his father's reluctance to make overt political endorsements. Despite thinly veiled displays of political allegiance, Billy Graham did not explicitly endorse presidential candidates and later in his life regretted aligning himself with political candidates in ways that he described as "non-Christian." Franklin, however, has been outspoken in this regard. During the Obama era, he joined Trump in questioning Obama's birth certificate. Like Trump, he went so far as to suggest that Obama was not a Christian and might even be a Muslim. According to Franklin, Islam is a "very wicked and evil religion."[52]

Franklin Graham arranged rallies for Evangelicals in all fifty states as part of his "Decision America Tours" during the 2016 campaign. He avoided an official endorsement, but his allegiance to Trump was obvious. After the first GOP debate, in which Trump used Megyn Kelly's question about him calling women "fat pigs, dogs, and slobs" as a platform to denounce political correctness, Franklin praised Trump for "shaking up the Republican party and the political process." A month after Trump won the election, Franklin accompanied Trump on his "Thank You" tour, where Trump said clearly that "having Franklin Graham, who was so instrumental," was the reason he "won so big with Evangelical Christians."[53] Franklin, for his part, chalked Trump's victory up to God answering the people's prayers.

Franklin has remained instrumental to Trump. He spoke at the inauguration and is one of Trump and Pence's most trusted religious advisers. He has defended Trump on even the most controversial of his comments and decisions, such as his victim-blaming response to the 2017 white supremacist riots in Charlottesville, the Stormy Daniels affair, and his immigration policies.[54]

Franklin has not escaped criticism from Evangelicals, though. Even his niece, Jerushah Armfield, has condemned his comments about Trump. Armfield contends that her grandfather "understood the love of Jesus that fought for the outliers while the president-elect [Trump] ostracized them."[55]

Jerry Falwell's son, Jerry Falwell Jr., has been an even more ruthless defender of Trump. Falwell Junior officially endorsed Trump in 2016, assuring his Evangelical contingent that he had "no doubts, no hesitations." The son of the Moral Majority's founder has gone to great lengths to allay Evangelicals' concerns about the values of a candidate who was a notorious playboy. He has stressed that Trump's personal values matter little; what matters is his commitment to key political issues for Evangelicals: "support for the state of Israel; strong national defense; traditional family values; and pro-life."[56]

Falwell Junior is deeply xenophobic—particularly when it comes to Muslims—and thus also agrees with Trump's ethno-nationalist immigration policies. After the 2015 San Bernardino attack by radical Islamic terrorists, he said, "I've always thought that if more good people had concealed-carry permits, then we could end those Muslims before they walked in."[57] He didn't seem troubled by the question of just how these brave white heroes would have been able to distinguish a radical Islamic terrorist from a normal, peaceful Muslim before shots were fired, because for him there is surely no difference.

None of the Court Evangelicals today can quite match the sway that Falwell Junior has over Evangelicals as the president of Liberty University, the world's largest Christian university. Trump first spoke at the university in Lynchburg, Virginia, at Falwell Junior's invitation, in 2012 and has returned to speak a couple times since (figure 13). This private university's total enrollment, including residential and online students, is over one hundred thousand, and its endowment is in the billions.[58] Its students receive over $445 million each year in federal student loans, the eighth highest in the country (no wonder the Prosperity Gospel is so popular among Evangelicals).

John Fea has pointed out that a major reason that Falwell Junior so fervently promoted Trump is that he believed Trump would protect Christian colleges and universities like Liberty from regulations that seemed to pose a threat under Obama.[59] In particular, he wanted to ensure that religious exemptions would still be available under Title IX of the federal Education Amendments of 1972.[60] Title IX states that students cannot be discriminated against "on the basis of sex" through programs or institutions receiving federal funding: that is, unless they file for an extension on the basis of religious liberty.

Figure 13. President Trump with Rev. Jerry Falwell Jr. at a Liberty University commencement ceremony on May 13, 2017. Trump received an honorary doctorate in business and delivered remarks. Credit: Wikimedia Commons (photographer: Shealah Craighead).

With its clear stance against homosexuality and its tendency to take the success of its football program more seriously than the reporting of sexual assaults, it should come as no surprise that Liberty University—like many other US institutions of higher learning—regularly files for and receives Title IX exemptions.[61] If such exemptions were barred on the basis that they unlawfully discriminate against LGBTQ+ students, Liberty could lose nearly half a billion dollars in federal student aid per year.

Since Trump became president, his administration has been eagerly trying to rework Title IX to limit protections for transgender students. At the same time, the administration has recently proposed that religious exemptions do not need to be declared in advance; they can be declared after a discrimination complaint has been filed.[62]

Trump also gained the trust of Falwell Junior and other Evangelical elites by promising to repeal the so-called Johnson Amendment to the IRS tax code. This 1954 addition to the code bars tax-exempt organizations like churches from endorsing political candidates. It certainly hasn't stopped such endorsements, though, and the law has been enforced only in a single instance.[63] Trump also can't repeal it on his own, as this requires an act of Congress. But this didn't stop him from holding an outdoor ceremony at the White House in May 2017 in which he signed an executive order on religious liberty with his Court Evangelicals around him. The order's vaguely worded statement that the Department of the Treasury would not take action against individuals or organizations for speaking from a religious perspective about political issues was an entirely symbolic gesture—but a symbolic gesture that made all the wealthy Evangelical Trump supporters who run tax-exempt religious organizations very happy.

In addition to protecting the Christian Right from paying its taxes and from having to reject discrimination, Trump repaid his Evangelical allies for their support by moving the US embassy in Israel from Tel Aviv to Jerusalem—a nod to the Religious Right's Christian Zionism.[64]

To be sure, Trump didn't just offer promises to safeguard the wealth of Christian corporations like Liberty University in exchange for the votes of Evangelicals. His campaign also gave tens of thousands of dollars to Liberty University's chief information officer as payment for falsifying online polls to enhance Trump's profile. The Trump campaign's corrupt dealings with a Liberty administrator began as early as 2012, but the limits and details of the scandal remain—like so many of Trump's dealings—obscure.[65]

With Court Evangelicals having greater wealth and political influence than ever before, it is vital to recognize that they are motivated consistently, if not exclusively, by profits and self-interest. This hasn't stopped them, to be sure, from turning to the Bible to justify their moneymaking political schemes.

THE WHITE HOUSE BIBLE STUDY

Each week in the Trump White House, some of the world's most powerful leaders meet for a sixty- to ninety-minute Bible study session run by a fundamentalist Evangelical organization. All of the attendees have been chosen by Trump and Pence to partake in these sessions, whose explicit aim is "to evangelize elected officials." Seeing as the officials involved are already evangelized, it'd be more accurate to infer—if these sessions are anything more than a publicity stunt catering to Trump's Evangelical base—that their aim is to instruct elected officials in strategies for using the GOP (garble-omit-patch) method to make the Bible support their right-wing politics.[66]

The White House Bible study is overseen, and usually led, by Ralph Drollinger. A former pro basketball player, Drollinger is an Evangelical preacher and the president of the "nonprofit" organization Capitol Ministries. He received a master of divinity degree from a fundamentalist Evangelical institution in California known as the Master's Seminary. It's worth noting that the accreditation of this seminary (and its related university) is currently under official review because of its "pervasive climate of fear, intimidation, bullying, and uncertainty," along with other alleged ethical violations.[67] But maybe it was different when Drollinger attended.

Drollinger founded Capitol Ministries with his second wife, Danielle, in 1996, to evangelize the American government. Prior to starting Capitol Ministries, Danielle was active behind the scenes in California politics and founded and served as the first executive director of the Independent Business PAC, whose goal was "to help Christians win election to office."[68] Ralph had previously worked in conservative sports-related ministries.

With its explicit mission of making biblical faith the basis of American government policies, Capitol Ministries runs Bible studies for elected officials. It is active in forty-three state capitals and more than twenty international locations but is best known for its influence in Washington, D.C. The organization holds weekly Bible classes in the House, the Senate, and—since Trump's election—the White House. The congressional Bible studies have been celebrated by Evangelical politicians. Bachmann, for instance, praised Capitol Ministries for its intent of "making disciples amongst the members of both Houses."[69]

The White House Bible study has a number of official sponsors who are regular participants: Vice President Mike Pence, Secretary of State (and former CIA director) Mike Pompeo, Health and Human Services Secretary Alex Azar, NASA administrator Jim Bridenstine, Housing and Urban Development Secretary Ben Carson, Education Secretary (and billionaire lobbyist) Betsy DeVos, Agriculture Secretary Sonny Perdue, and Energy Secretary Rick Perry.[70] Attorney General Jeff Sessions and Labor Secretary Alexander Acosta were also involved before Trump gave them the boot.

Even though he calls the Bible his favorite book, Trump does not personally attend the classes, but he receives printouts of the Bible studies.[71] According to Drollinger, sometimes he writes back notes on the printouts with commendations like "Way to go Ralph, really like this study, keep it up!"[72]

To be clear, then, the people who currently decide US policy on issues ranging from international relations and climate change to urban development and education are attending weekly classes in which they learn how to apply biblical values from a politically conservative fundamentalist with questionable ministerial credentials. Or, at the very least, they are choosing to publicly endorse the exclusionary conservative biblical interpretations of a leading Republican Christian political influencer.

In response to a *New York Times* op-ed describing Drollinger as a Christian nationalist, the pastor issued a lengthy rebuttal on his website that labeled the article "fake news."[73] His main points were that he does not believe Christians should have dominion over government and that he upholds the separation of church and state. But if he didn't believe Christians should have dominion over government, why would he head an organization whose strategy is to "evangelize elected officials"? His argument is special pleading. On the basis of Jesus's "Render unto Caesar" statement, he affirms an institutional separation of church and state. But he believes that Christianity should "influence" the state, and his organization's activities show that he aggressively pursues this influence over government.[74] He even published a book in 2012 called *Rebuilding America: The Biblical Blueprint.* I'm no Webster, but that doesn't sound like any definition of "separation" I'm familiar with.

Drollinger believes and teaches that women should not serve as ministers or even teach adult men (does he make an exception for Paula White-Cain?), that abortion is infanticide rather than a woman's choice, that homosexuality is a sinful abomination, and that Catholicism "is one of the primary false religions of the world."[75] Liberal Protestants and Jews are also shunned by his exclusionary theology because, like Catholics, they "reject the Jesus of Scripture" whereas "Scripture is clear; those who are at enmity with Him—who passively or actively reject the Son of God—their prayers are worthless and go unheard. And the State suffers for want of His blessing."[76]

Irony barely scratches the surface of describing Drollinger's view of Islam, which he considers another false religion and a warrior faith. "Any serious and objective student of the Koran understands this," declares the biblical fundamentalist, "The book instructs its adherents to advance Islam by the sword. This is not in question."[77] One wonders if Drollinger has ever read the book of Joshua, in which the Israelites wipe out the Canaanites at God's command.

In addition to his conservative views on women, sexuality, and non-Protestant religions, Drollinger asserts that the Bible unequivocally promotes Small Government, the free market, and the development of business and commerce for personal gain. One of his Bible studies advances this claim in clear language: "Free Market Capitalism is God's blueprint for growing a nation's economy."[78]

All of Drollinger's Bible studies, which are posted on his organization's website, suffer from the same flawed methodology. He assumes that the Bible can be interpreted literally without modern assumptions framing how it is understood. For example, he takes it for granted that the Bible affirms capitalism without even considering whether "free-market capitalism" existed in biblical times. Most professional historians agree that it didn't. To support his argument, he patches together a number of disparate biblical quotations without supplying any literary or historical context, without appealing to the original languages of the texts, and without addressing the differing views represented by each of the biblical texts.

The Drollingers' support of the conservative Museum of the Bible in D.C. betrays their understanding of the Bible as part of the fake history of America as a Christian nation—or, more specifically, a "Bible nation." As the Bible scholars Candida Moss and Joel Baden have shown, the museum, which was founded by the conservative, Evangelical Green family and opened its doors in 2017, has relied on an unethical trade in ancient Bible-related artifacts, some of which have been exposed as modern forgeries.[79] This illicit trade has helped to fuel extremist organizations like ISIS, with the ironic result that the museum's founders and supporters are funding the very people they most despise. At the same time, the Museum of the Bible has maintained close ties with the right-wing Israeli government, funding Israeli archaeological excavations in the West Bank and promoting its own Christian Zionist tours of the Holy Land.[80]

Before opening the museum, the billionaire Green family had already made the news for a conservative cause. In 2014, they won a case against the federal government on the basis of religious freedom. They fought against having to provide employees in their Hobby Lobby craft stores with health care coverage for birth control under the Affordable Care Act.[81] This political stunt helped to publicize the Green family as a new conservative powerhouse in American politics.

And then they established the Museum of the Bible, supposedly to engage *all* people with the Bible. Much in the same way that fundamentalists treat biblical texts, however, the Green family has plucked artifacts from their ancient contexts and assembled them in this museum so that they form a coherent picture of the Bible as history. The artifacts are presented as tangible proof of the self-interpreting truth of the Bible.[82]

By positioning their gigantic museum near the National Mall in D.C., in sight of the Capitol, the Greens went a step further. They strategically portrayed this biblical history as central to America and its history.

The Drollingers are part of the story of the founding of this conservative biblical museum in the nation's capital. To show his support for the museum, Ralph Drollinger deliberately held a meeting there for eighty international associates on the topic of ministering to political officials. His wife, Danielle, has represented the museum as an ambassador abroad.[83] Meanwhile, Betsy DeVos, a regular participant in the White House Bible study sessions, has made substantial donations to the museum through her family's foundations. Biblical history is, after all, the type of history the education secretary would like taught in public schools, and creationism is her preference for science education.[84]

It is crucial that we understand the Drollingers' fundamentalist approach to the Bible as part of the Christian Right's project of falsifying history for its own benefit. Whether its focus is the ancient worlds of the Bible, the founding fathers, or the antebellum South, this project pries snippets of texts from their original literary and historical contexts and patches them into a preconceived narrative without any regard for nuance, uncertainties, or potential counterarguments. If we follow the money trail, we find that it is big businesses that stand to benefit the most from the narratives the Christian Right spins as "history."

.   .   .

Many of the Christians who voted for Trump in 2016 believe the brash outsider is an unwitting agent of God. Some have likened him to the Persian king Cyrus, who is described as the Messiah who would save Israel from the Babylonian exile in the book of Isaiah.[85] They imagine that God chose Trump, like Cyrus, to save his people even though he is an idolatrous despot.

For his part, Trump hit many of the right notes with Christian Republicans. His status as a political outsider and his ethno-nationalist language and ideas appealed to the Teavangelicals. His personal success and neoliberal glorification of wealth attracted those indoctrinated by the Prosperity Gospel. His promises to protect the lucrative "religious freedoms" of Christian colleges and businesses charmed the elites of the new old Religious Right. And his hatred of Big Government appealed to all of the above.

In the age of Trump, the Republican Jesus has hit his stride. The Trump administration's fanning of an anti-intellectual fire among Republicans has created a post-truth haze in which fake histories gain traction more easily than ever. Christian nationalist interpretations of the Bible are interspersed within these fake histories in multiple ways—whether by casting the Bible itself as a clear and uniform historical source or coloring the foundations of America as biblical. There have been attempts to resist this Christian nationalism from both left and right, but they have not yet made much of an impact.[86]

Trump's "Make America Great Again" is a dangerous slogan that, for much of the Christian Right, means returning America to its imagined foundation in a particular self-serving understanding of biblical values. Organizations like Capitol Ministries are working hard to make conservative interpretations of the Bible influence politics at every level—to inject their warped interpretations of Jesus's teachings into the story of what America once was and what it should be again.

The remainder of this book demystifies, one issue at a time, the claims Republican influencers have made about Jesus since the Roosevelt era and continue to make today. It calls out the teachings these Republicans attribute to Jesus for what they are—fake history.

PART THREE

What Does Republican Jesus Stand For? Is He Right or Wrong?

CHAPTER FIVE

Family Values

"Instead of being liberal," Billy Graham announced in 1953, the first year of Eisenhower's presidency, "*Christianity Today* will be conservative, evangelical, and anti-Communist."[1] Graham decided to create a new magazine that would outflank the *Christian Century,* a widely respected Christian magazine that leaned left. Along with his father-in-law, Dr. L. Nelson Bell, Graham secured enthusiastic financial support for *Christianity Today* from J. Howard Pew, a wealthy oil executive who was indignant that the crude money he invested in conservative efforts like James Fifield's Spiritual Mobilization organization had not yet scorched away the New Deal social consciousness of much of mainline Protestantism. With Pew's patronage, Graham and Bell launched the periodical that would do more than any other media to shape Christian conservatism in the coming decades—to promote "biblical" ideals of "family values" as a defense against any form of government investment in the liberal project of sexual liberation.[2]

Christianity Today provided a platform for leaders of the emergent Christian Right to attract support for their faith in free enterprise and limited government. By the late 1960s, its authors began to target abortion and homosexuality under this pro–limited government rubric because they feared that "a government which controls the economic life of its citizens today will control their thoughts and souls tomorrow."[3] Protecting the conservative ideal of a traditional nuclear family consisting of a working father, homemaking mother, and their children meant safeguarding a key principle of modern capitalism: men control politics and economics while women are restricted to the domestic sphere.[4]

Prior to the proliferation of conservative Christian propaganda about "family values" during Eisenhower's presidency, Evangelicals showed little sustained interest in the morality of homosexuality and abortion. Graham's magazine, Falwell's Moral Majority movement, and other conservative efforts like the Evangelical psychologist James Dobson's Focus on the Family organization eventually succeeded in the 1970s and 1980s at persuading Evangelicals that opposition to abortion and homosexuality were part of the biblical foundations of Christian faith and were therefore integral to Evangelicals' subcultural identity.[5] Even more, Republican influencers cast these as fundamental "family values" that the embattled defenders of biblical Christianity must strive to protect in their cosmic struggle against the pagan culture of liberals and communists.

Republican politicians have persistently abused the Bible to support their positions on abortion and homosexuality. According to Drollinger, who runs the White House Bible Study, the Bible is clear and unswerving in its presentation of God's views that "life begins at conception" and that "homosexuality and same-sex ceremonies are illegitimate."[6] Jesus, conservative influencers insist, was an antichoice heterosexual man who exemplified the family values of modern American conservatives.

But would Jesus and his earliest followers really have recognized fetal personhood from conception and rejected homosexuality and same-sex marriages? Or were their family values, in fact, totally different from those of modern American conservatives?

FAMILIES IN THE NEW TESTAMENT WORLD

Most American marriages involve a traditional Christian exchange of vows—something like "to have and to hold from this day forward, for better, for worse, for richer, for poorer, in sickness and in health, to love and cherish [brides are also expected to say "obey"], till death do us part"—and the completion of a legal marriage license signed by the couple, the officiant, and two witnesses. US marriages endow each partner with rights to the other's property and employment benefits, among other things, but spouses usually take note of these economic details only when one partner requests a prenuptial agreement. The focus of most modern American weddings, whether Christian or implicitly Christianized by the American wedding-industrial complex is the couple's mutual love and desire to start a family together.[7]

Marriages in the New Testament world—an agrarian society characterized by harsh conditions of life that resemble those in modern low-income countries—were also about family, but family meant something different then. In the words of the Roman jurist Ulpian, "We call family [*familia*] a number of people who are by birth or by law subjected to the power of one man, i.e., the *pater familias* [father of a *familia*].... *Pater familias* is the title given to the person who holds sway in the house."[8]

Roman authorities and their subject peoples around the Mediterranean conceptualized the ideal family in patriarchal terms as a social and economic unit much broader than the modern "nuclear family." In this unit, the *pater familias* held full legal authority over his wife, children, slaves, and certain other dependents, and he also controlled their estate (which could also be called a *familia*).[9] As land was the foremost commodity in the Roman Empire, it was, in some sense, part of the family.

This Roman family structure determined how someone's inheritance (or *patrimonium*, from *pater*, "father") was distributed among offspring deemed legitimate through the institution of marriage (or *matrimonium*, from *mater*, "mother").[10] Like father and mother, patrimony and matrimony went hand in hand.

A few surviving marriage contracts from Jews who lived on the Arabian side of the Roman provincial border between Judaea and Arabia in the early second century CE show that this ancient Corleone-esque understanding of family was not just an Italian fashion. Though recorded nearly a century later than Jesus's life, these documents provide us with precious traces of the actual lives of ordinary Jews in a Roman provincial setting quite similar to Jesus's—lives that are often ignored, mocked, or romanticized in the ancient literature written by elites.

One important set of documents belonged to a Jewish woman named Babatha, who lived in a village on the south side of the Dead Sea and owned some property there. When Babatha married her first husband, incidentally named Jesus, her father gave her four productive date orchards and gave her husband a dowry. Jesus died a few years after their marriage, not long after the birth of their son. Soon after Jesus's death, Babatha married Judah, a Jewish man from Judaea, and entered into a polygynous arrangement with him and his other wife, Miriam.[11]

The marriage contract between Babatha and Judah sheds light on the purpose of marriage at this time. In this Aramaic contract, Judah declares Babatha his wife "according to the law of Moses and the [customs of] Judaeans."[12] He vows to Babatha to "bring you [into my house] by means of your dowry." Babatha paid Judah a cash dowry (or *ketubba*) of about a year's income, which probably originated with her father and was returned to her from her first husband's estate after his death. Judah did not take responsibility for Babatha's orphan son because he was maintained by a trust out of Jesus's estate. Judah did, however, formally vow to provide Babatha with food, clothing, and conjugal rights and to pay from his own estate to redeem her should she be taken into captivity. He also agreed to provisions from his estate for any children that they would have together in the case of his death.[13]

From Babatha's documents and similar archives from Roman Egypt, we can see that marriage and family in the general setting of the gospels revolved around the transmission of property from a father to his dependents. Even the conventional marriage ages reflect this purpose. Most men married in their late twenties or thirties, whereas most women married in their early teens and sometimes as young as twelve. To be clear, the marriage of a thirteen-year-old girl to a thirty-year-old man was not only socially acceptable but typical. Because the average life expectancy of a man who was fortunate enough to survive his first decade of life was only forty-five to fifty years, if women married young it was more likely that their fathers would still be alive at the time of their marriage to authorize their unions and pay their dowries.[14]

Compared to modern American marriages, marriages in the New Testament world were more contractual than religious or romantic. These weren't primarily sacraments or celebrations of love; they were legal agreements in which a bride's family paid about a year's worth of income as a dowry in exchange for her husband taking responsibility for basic protections for his bride and their children together.[15] Since marriages were not construed as sacred bonds, they could be terminated within the parameters of the original contract. Divorce was commonplace.[16]

The close link between Roman marriage and inheritance law, which also applied in Judaea, assumed that married couples would have children. Average households in the Roman Empire were nearly double the size of modern American households: having three or more children was both normal and encouraged.[17] Primitive contraceptive methods were used, but fertility rates were still high.[18]

Infant mortality rates were also high. Whereas about 0.6 percent of American babies die in their first year after birth today, upwards of 25 percent did in the Roman Empire.[19] Since infant death was so likely, Romans didn't name their children or ceremonially welcome them into the family until their eighth or ninth day.[20]

Families that didn't want a child would usually "expose" it after birth—a practice of setting a newborn by the roadside that was not necessarily infanticide since rejected babies were sometimes rescued—only to be enslaved. A disconcerting ancient letter from an errant Egyptian husband to his wife suggests that exposure was a more likely fate for girls than boys: "If you bear a child and it is male, let it be; if it is female, cast it out."[21]

Exposure was more common than abortion in the case of unwanted children, but abortion was also practiced. Influential Roman physicians cautioned against abortion for the specific reason that the methods used endangered the life of the mother. "It is safer to prevent conception from taking place," Soranus asserted, "than to destroy the fetus."[22]

The question of when a fetus becomes human was mainly entertained by philosophers staking speculative positions as to how and when a fetus acquires a rational human soul. The most widely held position followed the "gradualist" approach of the Greek philosopher Aristotle, who argued that a fetus gradually becomes human in form and soul over the course of gestation: at first it's like a plant and has a vegetative soul; then it becomes like an animal with a sentient soul; finally, when it becomes human in shape, the fetus has a rational soul.[23]

Some, however—especially Stoic philosophers—asserted that the fetus was not even a living being until birth, at the first breath. Only a small minority of Platonists and Pythagoreans advanced the view that a human soul is present in the embryo from conception.[24] Each of these different philosophical positions, it's worth noting, is known only from the writings of elite men who attributed little or no agency to the mother in generating the child.

Tara Mulder, a historian of Greek and Roman medicine, has observed that the philosophers who believed that life began before birth understood this only as "potential" life, or what we might call fetal vitality. Roman philosophers and jurists did not recognize the fetus as a legal person until its birth, at which point it came under its father's legal power. Before that, it was legally a part of the mother with increasing potential to become its own person.[25]

Jesus and his peers weren't privy to these technical Greco-Roman philosophical debates and probably had much more pressing concerns. Most likely, they assumed a general Aristotelian perspective in which fetuses gradually became human. Not only was this the prevailing view in the Greco-Roman world, but it was also the position of the Septuagint, the Greek translation of the Hebrew Bible that was read and quoted by the Greek-writing authors of the New Testament. Where the Hebrew version of Exodus 21:22–25 stipulates that the life of a mother is worth more than the preservation of her fetus, the Septuagint translation of this passage alters its meaning so that a fetus is worth the full value of a human life if and only if it is "formed"— that is, if it has reached that uncertain point at which it takes the form of a human.[26] Unlike Greco-Roman philosophers, the Septuagint ordained that a fetus had the legal rights of a person once it was "formed" in the womb.

It is difficult to imagine any ordinary ancient Jews thinking that a fetus constituted a human person with full legal rights at conception. They would, instead, have agreed either with the Septuagint that legal personhood begins at an imprecise point during gestation or with Roman law and the Hebrew version of the Bible that it begins at the first breath, which Genesis repeatedly describes as the "breath of life."[27]

In the only world Jesus and his earliest followers knew, abortion was a legal way to end the gestation of a fetus.[28] Critics of the practice were typically concerned that abortion methods imperiled the life of the mother and therefore recommended abortion only when the mother's life was already at risk. Whereas several sources reported that Jews in Jesus's time shunned the Roman practice of exposure, equating it with murder, abortion was not a hot-button issue; it was only occasionally discussed by ancient Jewish authors.[29]

Homosexuality and same-sex marriage were similarly not hot-button moral issues in the New Testament world. But unlike abortion, they were totally unthinkable prior to modernity.

Because marriages in the New Testament world were used to establish property relations between a man and his children through his wife, same-sex marriages weren't even a question. Roman literature furnishes a few references to same-sex marriages between men, but these tend to re-gender one of the men as the bride: one partner needed to be deemed socially subordinate for marriage to make sense.

People in the Roman Empire thought of sex in terms of active and passive power. Penetration was considered masculine—even virtuous (a word derived from the Latin *vir,* "man")—while being penetrated marked a person as effeminate and socially inferior. "Surely no one," the first-century CE Stoic philosopher Musonius Rufus declared, "considers men inferior to women."[30]

Gay sex was pervasive in the Greco-Roman world, but Romans would understand the categories of "homosexuality" and "heterosexuality" about as well as they would understand "capitalism," which is to say not at all. They would recognize that a man could have sexual relations with a man, or a woman with a woman, but they wouldn't infer biological or psychological motivations for these acts that amount to the modern notion of a "sexual orientation."

The word *homosexual* didn't even appear in an English dictionary until 1892.[31] As the French philosopher Michel Foucault famously argued, prior to the twentieth century, religious conservatives often deemed same-sex acts ("sodomy") as sins for which one could repent. It was nineteenth- and twentieth-century psychologists who first portrayed "homosexuality" as a mental disorder or disease that required ongoing treatment. And they defined "homosexuals" as an aberrant species that deviated from their natural "heterosexuality." By and large, the medical community has renounced the equation of homosexuality with a disorder since the 1970s and now recognizes sexual orientation as innate and sexual identity as more complex than sexual orientation and more fluid than the homosexual/heterosexual binary allows.[32]

Men from Pompeii who painted graffiti like "I want to fuck a boy" and "Here I fuck Rufus ... Eat your heart out, girls!" would balk at the idea that their sexual acts with men defined their sexuality or identity.[33] Ancient literature, inscriptions, and art demonstrate that it was acceptable, even admirable, for a man to have sex with both women and men. The idealized Roman man could penetrate, and even brutally rape, a woman or lower-status man as he wished. Meanwhile, a man who was penetrated by a man would be derided as an effeminate pervert whose moral and physical integrity was seized by the man who raped him.[34]

When Roman moralists condemned a man for orally or anally penetrating another man, it was for one of two reasons: the sexual act expressed a lack of masculine self-control, or the sexual act exploited a vulnerable person of lower status—usually a slave.[35] Unlike homophobic preachers and politicians today, the ancient moral philosophers who reproved same-sex sexual acts tended to treat them under the rubric of adultery, an act of excessive passion that compromised a man's self-control. "Of other types of embraces," Musonius Rufus observed, "those involving adultery are the most unlawful, and those involving two males are no more tolerable."[36] This clarification about two males was needed, to be sure, because many Romans would have considered it more offensive for a married man to have an extramarital affair with a woman than for him to regularly rape his male slaves. The apostle Paul, a contemporary of Musonius Rufus who was also fond of Stoic moral philosophy, similarly implied that same-sex sexual acts were immoral while touting celibacy as the best state in which to await Christ's return and marriage as a "plan B" for those with less self-control.[37]

Modern conservatives, like O'Reilly and Dugard, have been quick to characterize ancient Romans as insatiable homosexuals in order to draw a contrast with the supposedly conservative sexual morality of ancient Jews and Christians. The usual foundation for this assumption is those favorite verses of every homophobic picket sign, "You shall not lie with a male as with a woman; it is an abomination" (Lev. 18:22) and "If a man lies with a male as with a woman, both of them have committed an abomination; they shall be put to death; their blood is upon them" (Lev. 20:13). These verses, which are even more perplexing in the original Hebrew, do seem to denounce sexual contact between two men, but they take no position against "homosexuality" or gay marriage as such.[38] If this were the point, we should expect this legal literature to say something about sex between women, but Leviticus stipulates only that two women *who are related* cannot have sex with a man at the same time.[39]

These ancient Israelite laws about sex between men were likely motivated by a concern to protect socially inferior men from sexual exploitation. This is, after all, how other ancient Near Eastern societies presented their laws about sex between men. A Middle Assyrian (mid-second millennium BCE) law, for instance, even specifies that a man who is prosecuted and convicted for lying with "his neighbor" (a man of equal social status) will be raped by a man as his punishment.[40] The fact that the punishment is forced anal intercourse shows that "homosexual" sex was not the problem. At issue, instead, was the reduction of a social equal's status, because anal penetration was understood as feminizing the receptive male partner. The laws in Leviticus (or, at least the version in 20:13) diverge from neighboring societies' laws on sex between men of equal status only by requiring the punishment of both partners instead of just the penetrative male. To some degree, this is unsurprising because this section of the law code doesn't differentiate special laws for people of different social classes to the extent that other ancient law codes did. The Leviticus laws therefore represent a more comprehensive attempt to prohibit a form of sex that—in an ancient context so unlike our own—often expressed and maintained unequal social statuses among men.

Despite the presence of these laws in Leviticus, Jewish and Christian complaints against gay sex are not especially common in ancient literature and usually occur within ethical discussions that prohibit a wide range of sexual acts within marriage and outside of it. We don't have sufficient evidence to conclude that Jewish and Christian scruples about gay intercourse were much more common than the minority views of Stoic moralists like Musonius Rufus were among Romans.[41] What is clear, in any case, is that none of our ancient sources reject gay people or gay marriage, and those that take issue with gay sex are mainly concerned with barring adultery or the sexual exploitation of slaves and other low-status men.[42]

Daily life in the New Testament world was harsh in ways that most Americans can scarcely imagine. With low rates of life expectancy, high rates of infant mortality, no modern medicine, no modern waste removal, regular food shortages, widespread disease, and the constant threat of being reduced to slavery, the ordinary Jewish family had much more to worry about than the modern Republican fixations on fetal personhood and homosexuality.

LEAPS OF LOGIC IN ELIZABETH'S WOMB

The question of when a fetus becomes a human life that is protected by all laws that protect personhood has not always been a Christian interest. It was made into one by right-wing influencers who advanced a "family values" agenda. While asserting traditional gender roles in response to the sexual revolution of the 1960s, these influencers also turned the fetus into the symbol of a private citizen deprived of its individual rights through government regulation.[43]

Many conservative Protestants had viewed opposition to abortion as a pesky "Catholic issue" before liberal state governments started to regulate access to abortion in the late 1960s. Graham and Bell's *Christianity Today* declared the beginning of the "War on the Womb" only following New York's momentous statewide legalization of abortion in 1970, three years before *Roe v. Wade* made abortion legal nationwide.[44] But during the 1960s, the magazine rarely covered abortion, and, when it did, its Evangelical authors openly admitted that the Bible was "strangely silent" on abortion and fetal personhood.[45]

Staunch Evangelical "prolife" advocates were, prior to *Roe,* willing to allow abortion in certain cases: Graham made exceptions for rape and incest, and Bell, a surgeon, admitted that he had performed "therapeutic abortions" in order to protect mothers' lives in extreme cases.[46] Even after *Roe,* many Evangelicals were reluctant to jump onto *Christianity Today*'s antiabortion bandwagon, given that it meant linking arms with Catholics and Latter-day Saints.

After an official publication of the US Presbyterian Church printed a minister's article in favor of legalizing abortion in 1972, Bell retorted in *Christianity Today* that doctors like himself—the overwhelming majority of whom were male at that time—should control decisions about abortion. He expressed outrage at "this Presbyterian minister's cavalier statement that a fetus is not a person." There is irrefutable biblical proof of fetal personhood, he stated, in the story of the meeting of Elizabeth and Mary in Luke 1:39–45, in which Elizabeth's "child," John the Baptist, "leaped in her womb."[47] Since the passage refers to a "child" in the womb and describes him as leaping for joy, antichoice Christians have regularly cited it as God's word that life begins before birth and, therefore, that abortion is murder.

The garbling of this verse by Bell and countless other anti-choice Christians as biblical evidence of fetal personhood before birth has influenced the heated debates over abortion as Republicans have sought to turn back *Roe* under Trump's administration. Conservative interpreters of this verse spin it as a blanket rejection of abortion by conflating the "life" of a fetus with its legal personhood and disregarding the stages of fetal development between conception and birth. No prochoice advocate would deny that life begins at conception inasmuch as cells are living organisms. The difficult question is, instead, at what point the fetus constitutes an independent person from the mother and therefore warrants its own legal rights.

The language used in these debates often misrepresents embryological science. Republicans, for instance, have identified the "fetal heartbeat" as a palpable characteristic of human life that warrants personhood. Their "heartbeat" rhetoric is a political tactic that tugs at our heartstrings, making us think of a tiny person capable of kindheartedness and heartache, but it is misleading at best. At about six weeks, an ultrasound can detect electrical activity in what's known as the "fetal pole" of a two- to four-millimeter fetus, but this electrical activity does not evince a cardiovascular system or any type of emotional capacity.[48]

Trump's equation of abortion with a baby being "ripped from the mother's womb moments before birth" similarly misrepresents the practice of abortion.[49] Statistics are important here: a 2015 report by the Centers for Disease Control and Prevention found that more than two-thirds of abortions occurred before eight weeks; 91 percent occurred in the first trimester; 7.6 percent occurred between fourteen and twenty weeks; and only 1.3

percent occurred at or after twenty-one weeks (these are misleadingly known as "late-term abortions"). This 1.3 percent of
abortions that were performed in the third trimester occurred
under extreme conditions in which either the fetus was not via-
ble or the mother's life was at risk.[50] The types of abortions
Republican influencers vividly describe in order to influence
legislation don't actually happen.

When Republican Christians interpret Luke's story of Elizabeth and Mary, they make these exact assumptions that all abortions are the same and that life before birth entails prenatal via-
bility and legal personhood. Modern conservatives weren't,
however, the first to mine this story for a biblical theory of when
life begins. One of the most prolific early Christian writers, Tertullian of Carthage (ca. 160–220 CE), is often credited with being
the first to articulate a *comprehensive* Christian platform against
abortion.[51] This is because in works like *On the Soul,* Tertullian
rooted his position that abortion is a form of homicide in his
theory that a human receives a soul at conception rather than at
the first breath, as his "Gnostic" Christian opponents believed.
He cited the child leaping in Elizabeth's womb as proof.[52]

But in other books such as *Against Marcion* and *On the Flesh of
Christ,* Tertullian agreed with Aristotle that fetuses only gradually became human. He waged this argument in these works
because he wanted to show that Jesus became human during
gestation and was not actually God in a human costume, as his
opponent Marcion claimed. Like modern politicians, Tertullian—who was not a physician and who wrote misogynistic
books like *On the Apparel of Women,* a set of prescriptions for
female behavior that refers to women as "the devil's gateway"—
wavered between different views on fetal ensoulment as it suited
his ends in a given theological debate.[53]

Since antiquity, then, some Christians have identified the story of the meeting of Elizabeth and Mary as a significant testimonial on life before birth. But the text deserves more careful attention than it usually receives.

The story of Elizabeth encountering Mary while both women are pregnant occurs only in Luke, a gospel written by the same author who wrote Acts of the Apostles. This gospel was likely written in the last decades of the first century or the first decades of the second century CE by an anonymous Christ follower in a city of Asia Minor (modern Turkey), although scholars call the author "Luke" for the sake of convenience. This author drew heavily on the Septuagint and Greco-Roman philosophical and mythological traditions to tell his version of the story of the beginnings of Jesus's movement.

In the crucial scene, Mary has traveled to visit her relative Elizabeth, whom God helped to become pregnant in her old age. An angel has just announced to Mary that God will make her pregnant even though she remains a virgin. Mary is portrayed as young and, considering the marital norms at the time, should be envisioned as twelve to sixteen years old.[54] Joseph, her legal husband, should be imagined as being about thirty years old (an age discrepancy to which some misguided conservatives appealed in 2017 in defense of US Senate candidate Roy Moore's statutory rape of a fourteen-year-old while thirty-two).[55]

The scene begins with Mary entering the house and greeting Elizabeth. It then recounts that "when Elizabeth heard Mary's greeting, the child leaped in her womb" (1:41); later the text clarifies that the child has "leaped for joy" (1:44). To be clear, this passage—and the rest of the New Testament, for that matter—is silent about the practice of abortion itself, but this text may still be relevant to discussions of fetal vitality and personhood.

The Greek word translated "child" here, *brephos,* was used for both fetuses and infants in antiquity and does not divulge anything concrete about the author's view on fetal personhood. Luke's word for "leaped," *skirtaō,* may allude to the Septuagint version of Genesis 25:22, where the same word is used for the twins Jacob and Esau cavorting in Rebekah's womb.[56] God explains to Rebekah that these two twins represent two nations in her womb (Israel and Edom) and that "two peoples out of your womb will be distinguished" (25:23). It might be noteworthy that Genesis refers to Jacob and Esau as "nations" (*ethnē*) while in the womb but as "peoples" (*laoi*)—indicating groups of humans—after birth, although Luke doesn't take up these metaphors.

To determine whether this text conveys an early Christian view on fetal personhood, we need to take stock of details from the text's literary context. One phrase of interest emerges in the blessing Elizabeth imparts on Mary: "Blessed is the fruit of your womb" (1:42). Plant metaphors are abundant in ancient embryological discussions. These usually begin with agreement that the father implants a seed in the mother and then proceed to debate whether the mother contributes very little or nothing at all to the seed during its growth.

Stoics, in particular, used to employ the language of "fruit" as a metaphor for gestation and birth. Fetuses, they argued, were part of the maternal viscera and did not become their own beings until birth. They compared birth to a fruit falling when it is ripe: only when it separates from the tree does it become its own entity.[57]

Does "fruit of the womb" in Luke imply that a fetus does not become a person until birth, as it did for Stoics? Perhaps, but it is more likely that Luke borrowed the phrase from the Septuagint, where "fruit of the womb" occurs several times, since he makes regular use of these scriptures in his gospel.[58]

If "fruit of the womb" were to be understood in the Stoic way, this would mean that a fetus becomes human when it takes its first breath. Stoics had a single concept, *pneuma,* for the divine life-giving spirit in the universe and for its presence within humans as the breath of life. But Luke explicitly counters the idea that human life begins with the first breath when he describes an angel telling Elizabeth's husband, Zechariah, that their son John the Baptist "will be filled with the Holy Spirit even from his mother's womb" (1:15). The word *even* signifies that this prenatal infusion of the spirit (*pneuma*) of God was remarkable and perhaps contrary to expectation.

This verse strongly suggests that Luke thought human life begins before birth, but it doesn't specify when exactly. If the author assumed that human life began at conception, we should expect him to have had the angel tell Zechariah that his own seed—his sperm—was infused with the Holy Spirit. Instead, the text implies a gradualist theory of when life begins.

The moment at which Luke thought that a fetus became human and took on the spirit of God is unclear. By focusing on John the Baptist's movements in the womb, Luke insinuates that he considered the fetus a living being at that point. Interestingly, the gospel is explicit about the age of the fetus during Mary's visit: it was six months old (1:26, 36). Antichoice interpreters tend to read past this detail.

While this influential text probably does reflect its author's view that a fetus is endowed with the Holy Spirit and becomes a living being and potential person during gestation, it requires only that this potential personhood begin by six months. Luke is not clearer about the point at which a fetus becomes a potential person because the author's purpose here was not to comment on fetal personhood but to show that John the Baptist was a precursor to Jesus and not the Savior himself. Historians have long recognized that Luke goes to great lengths to show that John the Baptist, whose own following likely competed with Jesus's in its earliest stages, was only the opening act for something much greater.[59]

Luke invokes the prophet Malachi to explain this relationship between John and Jesus: John is the one who "will go before the Lord to prepare his ways" (1:76, referring to Mal. 3:1). According to the Septuagint version of Malachi, on the day the Lord comes, the righteous "will go out and *leap* like calves let loose from tethers" (4:2).[60] When Luke used this same verb, *leap*, to describe John the Baptist's prenatal joy at Mary's pregnancy, his purpose was not to explain when a fetus becomes its own person but to relegate John the Baptist to a harbinger of the true Messiah coming in fulfillment of the scriptures.

By releasing this text from the tethers of Republican politics, then, we are inclined to discover much richer insights into its literary and theological significance.

GOD MADE THEM MALE AND FEMALE . . . AND EUNUCH

Another text that Republican Christians have tethered to their "family values" agenda is Matthew 19:3–6. In this passage, Jesus quotes from Genesis in the course of his teachings on marriage and divorce: "[God] made them male and female." For many conservative Christians, this verse shows that Jesus deemed gender biological and binary and that he sanctioned only heterosexual marriages as legitimate. Republican influencers' interpretations of this verse undergird Christian transphobia and homophobia ranging from Jerry Falwell's berating of the "effeminate" purple

Teletubby, Tinky Winky, to extremist pastors' public praise of the actions of the radical Islamic fundamentalist who slaughtered forty-nine people at a gay nightclub in Orlando in 2016.[61]

Many conservative Christians have believed that liberals' campaigns for sexual rights would bring about God's wrath. AIDS "may be a judgment of God on the nation," Billy Graham proclaimed as gay men and other marginalized persons fought for their lives during the AIDS epidemic in the late 1980s.[62] Falwell concurred and added that homosexuality was "Satan's diabolical attack against the family."[63] For Tim LaHaye, the coauthor of the best-selling Left Behind series and author of a similarly apocalyptic book called *The Unhappy Gays,* homosexuality had been the cause of the Flood and the Babylonian captivity and remained "part of the buildup of the 'perilously evil times' that are prophesied for the last days."[64]

Since homosexuality was a sign of the end times, Dobson urged Christians to think of the struggle to fight homosexuality as "our D-Day, or Gettysburg or Stalingrad."[65] Love Won Out, the now-defunct gay outreach program of Dobson's Focus on the Family, put a happy face on this extreme homophobia: it taught Evangelicals to love the sinner but hate the sin.

The apocalyptic urgency of conservatives' political agenda against equal rights for LGBTQ+ people has experienced a resurgence in the benighted epoch of Trump. Vice President Pence has echoed the Evangelical influencers by prophesying that same-sex couples will be the cause of "societal collapse."[66] And while Trump claims to be good for the gay community, his administration has sought to diminish nondiscrimination protections for LGBTQ+—and especially for transgender—people in employment, health care, and military service.[67]

At the same time, there has been more support for LGBTQ+ people than ever in traditionally conservative Christian churches in recent years. From the emergence of organizations like DignityUSA (Catholic) to pro-LGBTQ+ protests at Liberty University and the schism over LGBTQ+ rights within the United Methodist Church, it is clear that LGBTQ+ equality is an issue that increasingly causes rifts among politically moderate and conservative churches.

Hard-nosed conservative leaders persist, nonetheless, in reciting verses from Leviticus and Matthew as God's Word—and the final word—on the issue. Matthew 19:3–6, for instance, remains the biblical foundation of Franklin Graham's strident defense of binary gender against the extension of Title IX to protect transgender people from discrimination, against the recognition of "X" as a sex classification on birth certificates, and even against Target's gender-neutral makeover of its stores. Inciting Evangelical boycotts of the retail giant, Graham minced no words: "I have news for [Target] and for everyone else—God created two different genders. Jesus said, 'Have you not read that He who created them from the beginning made them male and female' (Matthew 19:4)." Presenting this verse as a self-evident argument, Graham rested his case, saying, "You can't get any clearer than that."[68]

In fact, we can get much clearer by reconsidering this verse within the literary and historical contexts Graham persistently omits. Matthew's version is more popular, but this teaching also appears in Mark (10:2–12) and in short form in Luke (16:18). Historians have long recognized that Matthew and Luke independently used Mark as a source, so Mark should be considered the earliest form of the passage. The anonymous author we call "Mark" wrote his gospel shortly after the First Jewish Revolt against Rome (66–70 CE) somewhere in the Eastern Empire, whereas the unknown author we call "Matthew" wrote during the 80s or 90s in the Galilee or just north of the region in Syria.

Matthew's gospel is both the most traditionally Jewish gospel and the gospel that most fervently vilifies the Pharisees, the predecessors of the rabbis whose teachings are recorded in the Mishnah and Talmud. It seems that a main reason Matthew wrote his gospel was to distinguish Jesus's movement from the rabbinic movement that emerged in the Galilee in the decades following the revolt.[69]

Matthew's social context of "sibling rivalry" with the rabbis is important because the impetus for Jesus's teaching on divorce in his gospel is a legal challenge raised by the Pharisees, who stand in for the rabbis of Matthew's day. The Pharisees provoke Jesus by testing him with the question "Is it lawful for a man to divorce his wife *for any cause?*" (Matt. 19:3). *Lawful* here means acceptable according to the Jewish Law of Moses, or Torah—the instructions contained in the first five books of the Bible.

Mark's version of this story begins in the same way, but without the phrase "for any cause." This divergence reveals one of Matthew's motives in rewriting Mark's version. In Mark, Jesus rejects the stipulation of the law in Deuteronomy 24:1 that allows a man to divorce his wife in cases of "something objectionable." Jesus, in Mark, is opposed to divorce and remarriage under any circumstances.

Matthew's Jesus, however, engages in an androcentric rabbinic-style debate over what constitutes a lawful exception instead of rejecting the exception clause in Deuteronomy as Mark's Jesus did. He concludes that a man getting divorced and remarried constitutes adultery *except* in cases in which a wife has herself committed adultery (Matt. 19:9).[70] This was, in fact, the same view held by Rabbi Shammai and his followers in the first century CE, although other rabbis allowed for additional exceptions.[71]

In both Mark and Matthew, Jesus quotes Genesis 1:27 ("[God] made them male and female") in tandem with Genesis 2:24 ("For this reason a man shall leave his father and mother and be joined to his wife, and the two shall become one flesh") to prove to the Pharisees that these Genesis verses necessitate a stricter view of marriage than what appears in Deuteronomy. But the gospels disagree about how much stricter Jesus's interpretation was than Deuteronomy's.

As the Duke University professor and progressive Baptist pastor Jennifer Wright Knust has shown in her book on sex in the Bible, Jesus takes a different position on divorce in each gospel. Mark's Jesus rejects divorce under any circumstances, while Matthew's Jesus makes an exception if a wife has been adulterous. Meanwhile, Luke's Jesus does not prohibit divorce at all but still considers marrying a divorced wife to be adultery (16:18).[72]

Which of the gospels correctly conveys Jesus's teaching on divorce? We can't know for certain, but there are reasons to suspect that Mark, the earliest source, is right that the historical Jesus discouraged divorce and made no exceptions. This is the same general view found in Paul's letters.[73] Matthew rewrote Mark's version of this teaching so as to engage in a more complicated legal debate with rabbis who were rising to prominence when he wrote. In both Mark and Matthew, though, Jesus's teaching on divorce is more restrictive than was typical among Jews or Romans.

Most likely, this restrictive teaching on divorce was intended to protect wives. As we've seen in the case of Babatha, marriages mandated that husbands provide wives with certain securities that they might otherwise lack. One wonders, if this were the case, what Jesus and the gospel writers thought about polygyny as a strategy for protecting women. Intriguingly, Jesus's teachings prohibit a man from marrying a second wife only *if* he has divorced the first.

Republican influencers focus on "made them male and female" as a prooftext for binary gender and for marriage as exclusively heterosexual, but in the process they pluck the line from Jesus's strict teaching on divorce, adultery, and remarriage. Polling data might shed some light on this selection bias. According to wide-ranging quantitative data compiled by sociologists in 2014, white Evangelicals have higher divorce rates than most Americans and most other types of Christians.[74] And according to a survey by Ashley Madison, the scandalous dating service for people already in relationships, Evangelical is the most common religious affiliation of users (25.1 percent) and Catholic is the second most common (22.75 percent), indicating that these groups are by no means less likely to pursue adultery online because of their religious affiliation.[75] Since Christian conservatives consider the gospels such authoritative texts for modern sexual ethics, perhaps they should spend some more time studying the parts of Matthew surrounding 19:4.

Conservatives, in any case, are right that the passage in Matthew depicts marriage as being between a man and a woman. This is not surprising, for the Pharisees specifically asked Jesus about a law pertaining to marriage between a man and a woman, and, besides, there were no same-sex marriages in the New Testament world. Mark and Matthew present Jesus's teaching as a narrowly defined discussion pertaining to the interpretation of a law in Deuteronomy. The texts don't reject gay marriage; they don't even address it.

Matthew's Jesus does, however, recognize nonbinary gender in the grand finale of his teaching on divorce in another verse that conservatives routinely omit. After learning of his position on divorce, Jesus's disciples ask him, "Is it better not to marry?" (Matt. 19:10). Jesus answers, "For there are eunuchs who were born that way from their mother's womb, and there are eunuchs who have been made eunuchs by others, and there are eunuchs who have made themselves eunuchs for the sake of the kingdom of heaven. Let anyone accept this who can" (19:12).

In the course of his teaching about marriage, Matthew's Jesus thus recognizes the existence of three types of sexual minorities— those born eunuchs, those who were castrated, and those who voluntarily became eunuchs for the Kingdom of Heaven.[76] The first group—eunuchs who were born that way—is particularly interesting, for Jesus uses the same phrase "from their mother's womb" to describe them that Luke uses to recount the moment at which John the Baptist received the Holy Spirit. Eunuchs from the womb could refer to men born with one or two undescended testicles (cryptorchidism) or with some other genital-related physical or sexual condition that the ancients perceived as a defect.[77] Like slaves who were castrated so that they could serve in political administration without the ability to pass their office on to their progeny, eunuchs from birth were widely derided as incomplete and unmanly men.[78]

Eunuchs, in Pliny the Elder's censorious words, belonged to a "third class of half-males."[79] The satirist Lucian from Syria concurred, classifying eunuchs as "something composite, hybrid and monstrous, outside of human nature."[80] Some Jewish authors like Philo and Josephus were also quick to degrade eunuchs as a detested class of gender-ambiguous people who were able neither "to disseminate seed nor to receive it."[81] Since eunuchs were unable to procreate (and thereby pass on their patrimony), they were not regarded as true men in the Roman world and were not always assigned all the legal rights of adult men.[82]

Matthew's Jesus, however, recognizes—shortly after speaking of those "made male and female"—that some people are born as neither women nor fully men. According to the Mishnah, Jewish rabbis in the first century CE also recognized the existence of natural eunuchs ("eunuchs of the sun") as distinct from eunuchs castrated by humans ("eunuchs of man") (figure 14). The rabbis specifically debated the legal capabilities of eunuchs in relation to marriage and procreation, just like Matthew's Jesus. Rabbi Akiva, for instance, reasoned that eunuchs could not perform the rite of levirate marriage—a brother's duty to marry the wife of a brother who dies (Deut. 25:5–10)—because they could not procreate, but Rabbi Eliezer retorted that natural eunuchs might be able to procreate and therefore fulfill this commandment.[83] Both of these rabbis upheld the significance of marriage and did so because they viewed the purpose of marriage as procreation.

Matthew's Jesus was not as quick to encourage marriage and thus used the example of the eunuch to stake a different position in the rabbinic debate about marriage and procreation. Unlike the rabbis, he forecast the imminent end of the world and therefore idealized eunuchs precisely because they often did not marry. As a response to his disciples' question about whether to marry, Jesus's proclamation about eunuchs implies that celibacy is the ideal state in which humans should await the Kingdom of Heaven.[84] Jesus's enjoinder to "let anyone accept this who can" mirrors Paul's preference for celibacy with a special allowance for those who don't have enough self-control to be celibate: "To the unmarried and the widows I say that it is well for them to remain unmarried as I am. But if they are not practicing self-

Figure 14. Statuary relief of a *gallus,* a priest of the Great Mother goddess, from second-century CE Italy. To show their devotion to this Anatolian goddess, priests castrated themselves and dressed as women, as seen in this relief. Photograph courtesy of Brent Nongbri.

control, they should marry. For it is better to marry than to be aflame with passion" (1 Cor. 7:8–9).

Jesus in Matthew calls on his followers not to self-castrate but instead to be celibate. Eunuchs here function as an example of the unmarried. Like Paul's letters, Matthew's gospel presents celibacy as an ideal in part because it requires renouncing conventional gender roles. For the earliest Christians, celibacy anticipated the androgynous, or at least sexually ambivalent, state that their resurrected bodies would take in the Kingdom of Heaven. Resurrected bodies will be neither male nor female: "For in the resurrection they neither marry [male] nor are given in marriage [female], but are like angels in heaven" (Matt. 22:30).[85] Apparently, there are no men's and women's restrooms in heaven.

The earliest Christians believed that androgyny—a mixture of male and female characteristics—was the perfect, primal form of humans to which they would return in the afterlife. Through the ritual of baptism, they symbolically assumed non-binary gender by clothing themselves with Christ so that "there is no longer male and female" (Gal. 3:28).[86]

Ancient understandings of androgyny assumed an interdependence of the sexes but by no means an equality of the sexes.[87] Christians sought out the unification of male and female during their earthly lives, but this unification almost always favored male characteristics because female bodies were thought to be imperfect. As Jesus says in the Gospel of Thomas, a very early gospel that many ancient Christians deemed authoritative, "Look, I shall lead her so that I will make her male in order that she also may become a living spirit, resembling you males. For every woman who makes herself male will enter the kingdom of heaven."[88] The incorrigible misogynist Tertullian directly instructed women to this same end: "You too (women as you are) have the self-same angelic nature promised as your reward, the self-same sex as man."[89]

Celibacy, according to New Testament texts, was a way for the baptized to experience during their remaining time on earth the relinquishment of conventional gender roles that would be their reward in heaven. In this sense, celibacy was construed as androgyny with regard to gender identity and expression (being clothed with Christ means expressing as neither male nor female). But through the example of the eunuch, Matthew's Jesus also relates celibacy to androgyny in terms of biological sex: eunuchs' bodies are physically different from those of men, as defined in this ancient context.[90]

Franklin Graham and other conservative leaders preach that "you can't get any clearer" about traditional marriage and binary gender than their narrow-sighted interpretation of Matthew 19:4. It turns out that their interpretation of the verse is about as self-evident as the gender of resurrected bodies.

. . .

Jesus was no family man. According to the gospels, he was an itinerant ascetic who rejected his family. When his mother and brothers came to visit him while he was delivering a sermon, he gave them the cold shoulder: "Who is my mother, and who are my brothers?"[91] He then turned to his disciples and proclaimed them and anyone else who does the will of God to be his mother and brothers.

Jesus called on his disciples to abandon their families, take up their belongings, and follow him. "Let the dead bury their own dead," he admonished a disciple who wanted to bury his father before joining the movement.[92] To follow Christ, a man was supposed to become a eunuch for the Kingdom of Heaven. If he could, he should renounce traditional gender and marriage as he soon would in the afterlife.

The earliest Christians lived in a very different world than modern Americans, and they also had very different priorities. To create an antichoice heteronormative Jesus who was a model family man, Republican influencers have had to recite the same verses automatically, without paying any attention to their literary and historical contexts—to what these verses would have meant in the world of Jesus and the authors of the gospels.[93]

A close reading of the gospels shows that Republican influencers have been too quick to put Jesus in a box. The gospel writers' Jesus was not a proponent of heterosexual marriage and binary gender but a critic of divorce and adultery who advocated for celibacy as a form of nonbinary gender expression. Likewise, Jesus did not comment on abortion, and the Gospel of Luke suggests only that a fetus becomes a potential person by the sixth month.

According to the gospels, Jesus and his earliest followers did not preoccupy themselves with policing reproductive rights and marginalizing sexual minorities like modern Republican leaders because they had much bigger fish to fry—or rather, to fry and then distribute to the poor.

CHAPTER SIX

Charity

Stripped naked, beaten, robbed, and left for dead on the roadside, what is a man to do? According to one of Jesus's most celebrated teachings, the "Parable of the Good Samaritan," the injured man can expect a neighborly passerby to show mercy on him by bandaging his wounds and paying for him to receive hospitality at a local inn. To modern American readers, this story poses a quandary: Does it mean that Jesus would support universal health care and social welfare or that he would insist that charity should come from individuals instead of the government?

A president's interpretation of this parable serves as a reliable litmus test for his approach to welfare. To Hoover, it meant that individuals should be their brother's keeper, but FDR insisted that it entailed that the government should be "on the same side of the street with the Good Samaritan."[1] To Reagan, who vigorously attacked the social programs established by FDR's New Deal, the moral of Jesus's story was that the Samaritan "didn't go running into town and look for a caseworker to tell him that there was a fellow out there that needed help. He took it upon himself."[2] Reagan's self-motivated Samaritan fit nicely with his neoliberal rhetoric about welfare turning people into freeloaders and breaking up families. He also popularized the "welfare queen" as a symbol for poor people as lazy criminals and parasites leeching the earnings of hardworking Americans. Even though the majority of welfare recipients were white, Republican influencers typically portrayed the "welfare queen" as a hefty black woman flaunting extravagant furs and driving a Cadillac to pick up her welfare check.[3]

Despite persistent efforts, Reagan and his administration didn't manage to repeal FDR's welfare programs. To many liberals' dismay, it was Clinton who signed off on the 1996 welfare reform that replaced FDR's Aid to Families with Dependent Children (AFDC) with Temporary Assistance for Needy Families (TANF). The reform bill was crafted by the Republican-majority Congress under the leadership of House Speaker Newt Gingrich and then approved by Clinton, whose main stipulation was that it wouldn't restructure Medicare and Medicaid. Clinton, for his part, had campaigned on the promise to "end welfare as we know it" by imposing time limits on cash benefits—"Two years and you're out!"—and turning welfare into temporary aid to get people back to work. The Republican-drafted bill made good on Clinton's own promises but went even further than Clinton intended by imposing work requirements as a prerequisite for aid and transferring power over the distribution of welfare from the federal government to states.[4]

Jesus's Samaritan was a central figure among supporters of the bipartisan 1996 welfare reform. The Samaritan, for Gingrich, reminded Americans that they should "reach out to humans and forget the bureaucracies."[5] For Clinton, the parable taught that "when people do want to behave, they're entitled to a little help from their friends, from their Samaritans."[6] Clinton's interpretation of the parable disclosed his interest in making welfare conditional on individuals' behavior rather than maintaining it as a legal entitlement. By raising the minimum wage and expanding the Earned Income Tax Credit, Clinton acknowledged that poverty was not simply a result of whether people "want to behave," yet he still approved time limits and work requirements that overlooked the manifold ways that low wages, inadequate benefits, harsh working conditions, inflated prices and interest rates, and an inequitable labor market prolonged and compounded poverty for people who wanted nothing more than "to behave."[7]

Democratic heads of charitable organizations invoked Jesus to criticize the reform bill. Marian Wright Edelman, founder of the Children's Defense Fund, wrote an open letter to Clinton urging him not to sign the bill, since "the New Testament Messiah made plain God's mandate to protect the poor and the weak and the young." Fr. Fred Kammer, a Jesuit priest and president of Catholic Charities USA, similarly resisted the reform by quoting Jesus: "Whatever you do to the least of my sisters and brothers, you do to me."[8]

Liberals and conservatives agree that Jesus called on his followers to show compassion to the poor, but they radically disagree about how Jesus expected believers to meet this goal. Today, with the negative effects of the 1996 reform clearer than ever as one-third of Americans live in or near poverty, Jesus's teachings on social justice have once again become a battlefield.[9] Christian conservatives and liberals remain deadlocked over the question of whether Jesus advocated government assistance for the poor and outcast, and they remain trapped in solipsistic readings of the relevant texts. A closer look at these texts in light of Jesus's historical context will reveal that both sides have ignored some significant obstacles to interpretation—namely, that each gospel presents a somewhat different approach to poverty and that none of the gospels comments on the government as a provider of welfare because this wasn't even seen as a possibility in the world of Jesus and the gospel writers.

WELFARE IN THE NEW TESTAMENT WORLD

Homeless beggars on the streets of Rome were "the poverty-stricken scum of the city" who should "be drained off to the colonies," ranted the ever-snobbish senator Cicero.[10] Elite authors like Cicero slandered the poor, but they also posited a distinction between the poor and beggars. Like modern Republican politicians, ancient writers were more willing to tolerate the working poor than the destitute.

There was no consistent and uniform safety net for the poor in the Roman Empire. Citizens of the city of Rome enjoyed access to free monthly provisions of grain, which ancient authors described as a strategy to keep the poor from rioting since "the harmony of the masses depended on their well-being in this respect."[11] But noncitizens in Rome and inhabitants of the rest of the empire had no access to the imperial capital's grain dole.

There were no imperial or civic welfare programs in the Roman Empire. Instead, public benefaction was widely practiced in the Greek-speaking cities of the eastern provinces of the empire. Wealthy benefactors made personal donations to citizens in the form of public buildings, festivals, one-time food distributions, and occasional monetary handouts. In return, they were publicly honored with statues and inscriptions praising them for their largesse. Philosophers from Aristotle to Seneca the Younger warned that the motivation for this civic munificence should not be what it invariably was—the "love of honor" (Greek: *philotimia*).[12] Benefactors, on the whole, were not as interested in helping the poor as they were with boosting their own status in the city.[13] Their gifts went a long way toward monumentalizing cities, but they did little to relieve poverty.

A character in a play by Plautus conveyed a widespread elite bias about giving alms to beggars: "You do no service to a beggar by giving him food or drink, for you both lose what you give him and prolong his life for misery."[14] Some philosophers believed that a rich man should give a coin to beggars in need, so long as they weren't on the brink of death (since they considered that a waste of a coin). For the most part, though, giving to beggars was a topic that ancient writers were as uncomfortable discussing as the average American driver waiting at a red light with a panhandler outsider the car window.

Jews in Jesus's time also did not yet have formal institutions of charity like a soup kitchen or a collection cup.[15] They did, however, assign a great deal of theological value to different types of almsgiving. "Atone for your sins with alms and for your iniquities with compassion for the needy," Daniel counsels King Nebuchadnezzar in one of the ancient Greek versions of Daniel. Several ancient Jewish authors identified giving to the poor as a way to atone for sin but not strictly as a way to help the poor.[16] Similarly, observant Jewish farmers in the land of Israel were supposed to set aside a tithe in the form of one-tenth of their agricultural produce for the poor once every three years, but these tithes were handed over to priests and were viewed as a form of divine benefaction rather than charity.[17]

Ancient texts, on the whole, are not very useful guides to the reality of poverty in the New Testament world. Not only were their elite authors prejudiced against the poor, but also each ancient author construed poverty in his own way. There were no attempts to measure and define poverty in antiquity—no Gini coefficients or poverty lines. All literary depictions of the "poor" were relative. Depending on the author, time, and place, people might be considered poor because they didn't own slaves, because they had to perform manual labor, because they couldn't afford a proper dowry, or because they were homeless and starving. Meanwhile, certain philosophers extolled voluntary poverty because they believed it elicited the virtues of self-sufficiency and indifference. "Poverty does not consist in not having money," boasted one Cynic philosopher, "but poverty consists in desiring everything."[18] Surely those who didn't choose to be poor would have begged to differ.

Loath to settle for these broad and self-serving ancient characterizations of poverty, modern scholars have endeavored to define poverty in the Roman Empire more precisely in terms of income distribution. Drawing on information from ancient legal and financial documents and comparative data from other preindustrial agrarian societies, historians have determined that 80 to 90 percent of the empire's population lived in poverty. More specifically, they lived just above, at, or below subsistence level (the minimum amount of income required for survival). Only about 2 percent of the population were superwealthy elites, but they controlled 25 percent of total income. The remaining 8 to 18 percent of "middlers" caught between the poor and the elites had moderate surplus resources and therefore enjoyed some economic stability.[19]

There are important differences between poverty in the Roman Empire and modern America. In the US, 12 to 13 percent of the population lives below the unrealistically low official poverty threshold, but one-third overall lives in or near poverty.[20]

Poverty, then, was much more widespread in the Roman Empire: almost three times as many people were poor, and there wasn't a substantial middle class. Whereas in the US a main cause of poverty is restricted access to education and professional training, the main cause of poverty in antiquity was restricted access to land. A person who owned or rented a productive plot of land could eke out a subsistence through farming.[21] Then as now, however, inflation, debt, and low wages were major hurdles to economic stability.

Another main difference involves variables of discrimination that predispose certain groups to economic disadvantages. In the US, black and Latino persons are more than twice as likely to be poor as non-Hispanic whites because of structural discrimination in education, employment, housing, and criminal justice.[22] Racial difference was not similarly correlated with poverty in the Roman Empire, and it also was not the basis for slavery.[23] On the other hand, mental and physical disabilities were even more likely to result in poverty in antiquity than today.

Much as the Roman Empire didn't provide its subjects with regular financial relief, it also didn't provide any sort of public health care. Compared to the standards of modern developed nations, public health in the Roman Empire was appalling. Forms of medical care were scarce, dangerous, and often ineffective.[24] By investigating ancient skeletons, researchers have found that Romans were severely malnourished and often suffered from weakened immune systems and intestinal worms.[25]

Roman medical texts corroborate this evidence with their descriptions of "plagues" of malaria causing people to "flee … [and] raise their fists at the gods."[26] Even though aqueducts, running water, and sewage were hallmarks of Roman innovation, stone and brick cities pocked with sitting pools made the Roman

Empire into what one historian has described as "an unintended experiment in mosquito breeding."[27] Malaria predisposed people to other diseases and caused widespread suffering and death across the empire. This was only exacerbated by the accumulation of waste—both human excrement and refuse. Jews and followers of Christ were not immune.[28]

People in the New Testament world didn't have a concept of "hygiene" that was backed up by modern medical science as we do today. On the contrary, ancient notions of "purity" and "cleanliness" had more to do with things being in their proper place and moral rectitude than preventing the spread of infections and disease.[29] Jewish ritual baths, for instance, were used for religious purification from "impurities" like menstruation and seminal emissions, but their water was neither frequently replaced nor treated with chemicals in a way that would satisfy modern standards.[30] Reflecting pools and cisterns in cities and villas were no better.

Poor people had fewer protections from these insalubrious conditions than anyone else. Ancient authors speak about the same stray dogs who rummaged through urban dung heaps and dragged human bones around the streets tormenting beggars who couldn't defend themselves.[31] Elite prejudices and authorial embellishments aside, there can be little doubt that, as in any unequal society, the poor were especially susceptible to malnutrition and disease.[32]

Jesus and the gospel writers would have gotten a kick out of the idea that the Roman imperial government should provide financial assistance to the poor and affordable health care to all of its residents. This perspective depends on a democratic view of society that asserts health care as a human right and recognizes poverty as a consequence of systemic inequalities. Living in a world ravaged by poverty, malnutrition, and disease—a world dominated by indifferent elites—many within the first generations of Jesus's followers found it easier to envision justice for people who were poor and disabled in the Kingdom of God than on earth.

BLESSED ARE THE POOR (IN SPIRIT?)

As common as it is to hear the Bible quoted in congressional sessions, it's a rare day in which a debate zeroes in on the meaning of a Greek word in the New Testament. During a hearing held by the House Budget Committee in June 2019 on "Poverty in America," ten white male Republicans challenged a progressive budget for poverty relief designed by the Rev. Dr. William Barber II and the Rev. Dr. Liz Theoharis. Sparks flew.

In response to Barber and Theoharis's argument that extending the nation's deficient safety net was a moral imperative, Rep. Bill Johnson of Ohio—who was neither a minister nor a scholar—claimed to know the Bible better than the witnesses. "I been a Christian since I was ten years old," he stated as his credentials in this matter. "I don't find anywhere in the scripture," he proceeded, "where Jesus said that it was Caesar's job to feed the poor, and to clothe the widows, and take care of the orphans. It's the church's responsibility, the community's responsibility, your neighbor's responsibility, it's your responsibility to do those things."

Barber, a respected activist-theologian and NAACP leader, countered with "First of all, it's interesting that you would define yourself as Caesar." Then he flexed his biblical muscles. "Next, you haven't read the 2,000 scriptures in the Bible that talk about how societies are supposed to treat the poor, the immigrant, the least of these. And you don't know that Jesus started his first sermon with the Good News to the *ptōchos*—a Greek word that means 'those who have been made poor by economic systems.' … It is bothersome that in the 21st century we still have these weak, tired old mythologies. See the people [in poverty]! Stop just talking about how you know poverty and hear what these folks are saying, and put together a full plan to deal with this issue."

Instead of listening to the testimonies of the people on the ground working with the poor, the Republican congressmen persisted, with no dearth of narcissism, to cite their own lives as examples. "The only way out [of poverty]," one professed, "was to work my tail off."[33]

The congressmen's uniform assumptions about poverty being caused by laziness, which Barber bemoaned as "weak, tired old mythologies," derive from the long-standing entanglement of Protestantism and economic liberalism that I earlier described as economic Arminianism. According to this prevalent class theology, whether one is poor or rich is as much a result of free will as whether one will be eternally damned or saved.

A 2017 poll by the *Washington Post* has exposed the far reach of economic Arminianism among Americans. When asked whether lack of effort or difficult circumstances are to blame for poverty, Christians were 2.2 times more likely than non-Christians to cite lack of effort. White evangelicals were the most likely to attribute poverty to laziness—3.2 times more likely than a person who is not affiliated with any religion. While the trend toward citing lack of effort does not fully adhere to party lines, the poll found that a person who leans Republican is 4.3 times more likely to blame laziness than one who leans Democrat.[34] All of this amounts to a high probability that a Christian Republican will blame poverty on its victims' indolence.[35]

Proponents of the Prosperity Gospel are among the most influential Christians who interpret Jesus's ministry as calling on the poor to improve themselves—to shake off their "poverty mentality" because it doesn't glorify God. Joel Osteen, the coiffed and preened celebrity televangelist who preaches in the former Houston Rockets arena, for example, proclaims that Jesus helped the poor by announcing God's favor to them. In his 2010 book *It's Your Time: Activate Your Faith, Achieve Your Dreams, and Increase in God's Favor,* Osteen focuses—like Barber—on the beginning of Jesus's ministry in Luke. Osteen latches onto Jesus's words in Luke 4:18: "The Spirit of the Lord is upon me, because he has anointed me to bring good news to the poor. He has sent me to proclaim release to the captives and recovery of sight to the blind, to let the oppressed go free, to proclaim the acceptable year of the Lord."

Except Osteen misleadingly crops this verse so that Jesus only says, "The Spirit of the Lord is on me to help the poor, to comfort the hurting, and to announce the acceptable year of the Lord," cutting out the proclamations for captives, the blind, and the oppressed. He adds that "one translation"—the one that best fits his agenda—"says 'to declare the year of God's favor.'"

What matters for Osteen here is that Jesus declared to the poor that it is their time to accept God's favor by acting to earn prosperity. Osteen goes on to chide those who have "missed their season of favor" by refusing to pull themselves out of debt and poverty.[36] In this light, Osteen's reluctance to open up his megachurch as a shelter for Houston's evacuees after Hurricane Harvey was not hypocritical at all: he preaches that God gives people the opportunity to help themselves, so why should he interfere?[37]

Ironically, the passage from Luke that Osteen clipped to advance his own gospel of wealth not only recognizes disadvantages that cannot be overcome (captivity, blindness, and oppression) in concert with poverty but also casts Jesus as providing structural relief to the poor. Jesus, according to Luke's narrative, is reading these words from a scroll of the prophet Isaiah in front of the congregation of his local synagogue in Nazareth. After his reading, Jesus declares to his townspeople that "today this scripture has been fulfilled in your hearing." Jesus, in other words, is the Messiah who will do all the good things Isaiah prophesied.[38]

By proclaiming a "year" that is "acceptable" to the Lord, Luke's Jesus is not explaining to the poor that God has made it an opportune time for them to bootstrap their way out of poverty. Instead, he uses Isaiah to declare the inauguration of his ministry as a jubilee. According to the law code in Leviticus, the jubilee is a "year of release" every fiftieth year in which fields are not sown, confiscated properties are returned, debts are forgiven, and slaves and prisoners are freed. Historians debate whether the jubilee was ever actually practiced in ancient Israel, but, regardless, it is presented in our sources as a plausible institution designed to relieve social and economic disadvantages caused by difficult circumstances, not lack of effort.[39]

In the scriptural verses that Luke's Jesus reads, Isaiah's prophecy expands the jubilee into a vision of the felicitous state that the righteous will enjoy in a coming age.[40] The phrase "God's favor" that Osteen dwells on is better translated (from both the Hebrew and the Greek) as "acceptable to the Lord." It is the language used in the Bible for a ritual practice, such as a proper animal sacrifice, that God considers acceptable.[41] Neither Leviticus nor Isaiah nor Luke refers to favor that God offers to the people as an opportunity for them to improve themselves. Quite the reverse, Luke's depiction of Jesus as invoking the Jewish jubilee traditions implies that Jesus viewed poverty as a structural problem.

When Barber stressed that Jesus began his ministry by bringing good news to the *ptōchos,* he was commenting on the characterization of poverty as systemic in this same passage from Luke. There were two common words for a "poor person" in ancient Greek, *penēs* and *ptōchos,* and they have different connotations. *Penēs* was usually used for a person struggling for subsistence but still able to find work. *Ptōchos* (plural: *ptōchoi*), on the other hand, was the term that the gospel writers used. Ancient writers typically applied this label to destitute persons who were reduced to begging to survive.[42]

Those identified as *ptōchoi* are often portrayed as sickly. In a parable in Luke, for instance, dogs lick the *ptōchos* Lazarus's sores as he begs outside the gate of a rich man's mansion. When Lazarus dies, he goes straight to heaven. The parable states no conditions for Lazarus's prosperous afterlife, not even faith in Christ. The rich man who didn't help Lazarus, on the other hand, met his fate in the torments of hell.[43]

The gospels consistently portray *ptōchoi* as unable to help themselves. In some cases, *ptōchoi* have severe physical disadvantages such as blindness, like Bartimaeus, whom Jesus heals in Mark, or the man with disabled legs "from his mother's womb," whom Peter heals outside the Jerusalem Temple in Acts of the Apostles.[44]

Luke often lists *ptōchoi* alongside the blind, deaf, disabled, and diseased as people deserving of justice.[45] This juxtaposition is important because every other one of these scorned social groups pertains to individuals who are unable to do much, if anything, to alleviate their circumstances. A blind man cannot heal himself. A deaf woman cannot heal herself. And, presumably, Luke believed that *ptōchoi* are unable to escape their position of economic disadvantage on their own.

Luke is many social progressives' favorite gospel. It contains teachings about social justice that appear in none of the other gospels—for example, the parable of Lazarus and the rich man, the Samaritan parable, and the story of the tax collector Zacchaeus who gave his possessions to the poor and received salvation in return.[46] Luke's Jesus calls on believers to give at least some of their surplus wealth to the poor if they wish to be saved. This implies that at least some people in Luke's own community had surplus wealth and were therefore part of the top 10 to 20 percent of society in terms of income.[47] This is also why Luke assumes that some believers receiving Jesus's teaching can give loans and why only his gospel has Jesus direct certain teachings to slave owners.[48]

Luke's social ethics were developed for a specific community and cannot be taken as representative of the historical Jesus or other early believers. Whereas Luke shaped the traditions he inherited about Jesus to suit a community that included a cross section of urban society, Jesus and his earliest followers would have been among the rural working poor. Luke was careful to omit Mark's detail that Jesus was a *tektōn*—the Greek term used for a skilled profession such as a carpenter or stonemason—because it would have signaled to readers that Jesus was a member of the working masses, better off than most farmers or fishermen but still poor compared to Luke's wealthier readers (figure 15).[49]

Mark calls Jesus a *tektōn,* while Matthew refers to him as the son of a *tektōn* and the other gospels fail to describe Jesus or his stepfather's occupation.[50] The historical Jesus probably was a *tektōn* because it's the sort of potentially embarrassing detail that an early believer wouldn't have made up. It also fits with the social profile of Jesus's disciples in all of the gospels: they were fishermen, tenant farmers, day laborers, and toll collectors from

Figure 15. Statuary relief from Rome showing carpenters working in a busy urban workshop. The historical Jesus would have served as Joseph's apprentice in this skilled, yet low-paying profession or one much like it. Credit: Wikimedia Commons (photographer: Carole Raddato).

the small Jewish villages around the northwestern rim of the Sea of Galilee.

The closest that historians can get to the original words and deeds of the historical Jesus is a substantial block of material that both Matthew and Luke relate in such a similar way that they must have taken it from the same source—a source other than Mark. Scholars have reconstructed this common material, known as the "double tradition," and refer to it as Q (from *Quelle,* the German word for "source," because the German scholars who first proposed this theory couldn't come up with a cleverer name). This lost Greek gospel contains some of our earliest and most reliable traditions about Jesus and was likely written in the Galilee in the three decades following Jesus's death. Even still, this material doesn't contain the actual words of Jesus, and it reflects the evolving memories and changing concerns of the communities Jesus left behind.[51]

What is remarkable about Q is that almost all of its teachings are about social ethics in an agrarian milieu. Some of the most memorable sayings of Jesus that Matthew and Luke inherited from this source include "Blessed are you poor [*ptōchoi*], for yours is the Kingdom of God"; "Give us our daily bread today"; "Cancel our debts for us"; "The day laborer is worthy of his wages"; and "You cannot be a slave to God and mammon [Aramaic for "wealth"]."[52] These sayings show that concern for the indigent and hostility toward wealth were fundamental convictions at an early stage in the development of Jesus's movement.

In their early form in Q, these ideas were rooted in the expectation that Jesus's life and death signaled the emergence of the Kingdom of God, in which the poor would be exalted. Q's maxims didn't provide much of a rubric for how the poor should live their this-worldly lives because its authors believed that an other-worldly age was rapidly dawning. This source also wouldn't have advised the rich to do things like give alms or divest themselves of their possessions because it wasn't written for people with wealth.[53]

Whereas the gospels of Mark and John focus relatively little on Jesus's social ethics, both Matthew and Luke adopted Q's social teachings but reworked them in different directions.[54]

Luke, as we've seen, took Jesus's beatitude about the poor and admonishment against being a slave to mammon and developed them into a radical vision of social justice based in practices of almsgiving and divestiture. Luke's social consciousness is a function of his conviction that the end-times were not as imminent as earlier generations of Christ's followers believed.

This author didn't give up hope that Christ would return to establish God's Kingdom, even though it had been decades since Jesus's resurrection. He endeavored to show, instead, that the salvation of the world had been gradually unfolding since the birth of Christ.[55] The radical social practices of believers, some of whom he romanticized as owning all things as "common property" (Acts 2:44; 4:32), contributed to this unfolding history of salvation.[56]

Matthew took a quite different tack by theologizing Q's sayings about poverty. He turned "Blessed are the poor" into "Blessed are the poor *in spirit*" and he interpreted "cancel our debts" in the Lord's Prayer as a metaphor for the forgiveness of sins.[57] Matthew's Jesus, like Luke's, promotes almsgiving but emphasizes that the motivation for almsgiving should be storing up treasures in heaven: "Jesus said to him, 'If you wish to be perfect, go, sell your possessions, and give money to the poor, and you will have treasure in heaven" (Matt. 19:21). In Matthew's theological economy, alms are loans paid to God in exchange for eternal riches in the afterlife.[58] This theological framework directs attention to the rich man's opportunity to earn salvation instead of the plight of the poor. The poor are living altars on which people can make a sacrifice to God with the expectation that it will be repaid in the afterlife.[59]

Matthew's social vision is summed up in Jesus's justification for a woman anointing him with expensive oils instead of giving that money to the poor, as his disciples suggested: "For you always have the poor with you, but you will not always have Me" (Matt. 26:11). Matthew appropriated these words from Mark's gospel but took away Mark's important reasoning that "you can show kindness to [the poor] whenever you wish" (Mark 14:7). Luke, meanwhile, was quick to omit Mark's saying entirely.[60] According to Matthew, poverty is a problem that cannot be resolved on earth, so there's little sense in trying.

Matthew and Luke agreed that Jesus brought good news to *ptōchoi*, but they disagreed about how and why they should be helped. Like most ancient authors, Matthew portrayed beggars as a natural feature of society and only urged believers to engage with them to achieve their own ends.[61] Luke's Jesus promoted a more radical plan to help poor, oppressed, and disabled persons that drew from Jewish traditions of social justice like the jubilee and emphasized the predicament of persons who were poor and disabled.

Barber was right that the *ptōchoi* in Jesus's world were impoverished by economic systems and had to rely on begging to survive, but it's important to recognize that the gospels—like modern Christian communities—do not all respond to the situation of *ptōchoi* in the same way.

THE SAMARITAN'S PURSE STRINGS

When Representative Johnson asserted that nothing about poverty relief in the gospels requires Caesar to provide welfare to the poor and marginalized, he aligned himself with the usual Republican position in the long-standing debate over the interpretation of Jesus's famous Samaritan parable. While liberal politicians have often turned to this parable in Luke as proof that Jesus supported welfare and public health care, Republican influencers have appealed to it as biblical evidence that individuals and private organizations, not the government, are responsible for helping the sick and poor.

"A hundred years ago," Franklin Graham pontificated in a 2012 interview, "the safety net, the social safety net in the country was provided by the church…. But the government took that. And took it away from the church."[62] Graham's strategic church-versus-state rhetoric obscures several basic facts: American public welfare funds outweighed private funds long before the New Deal, there was considerable Christian support for the

New Deal's standardization of welfare, and today's leading Christian charities rely on federal funding.[63]

Franklin Graham is the president of an international humanitarian aid organization known as Samaritan's Purse. Founded in 1970, it states its mission as the fulfillment of its namesake parable: "Samaritan's Purse travels the world's highways looking for victims along the way. We are quick to bandage the wounds we see, but like the Samaritan, we don't stop there. In addition to meeting immediate, emergency needs, we help these victims recover and get back on their feet."[64] Samaritan's Purse's evangelical missionary work is aimed at proselytizing, but they also insert themselves, and their eager corporate friends like Monsanto, into economic development in disaster-torn countries.[65] As the renowned Yale professor Inderpal Grewal elucidates, "Rescue, proselytizing, missionary saving, and development collaborate as the group preaches American Protestant evangelical ideas that combine neoliberal capitalism with individual responsibility, Bible study, and an antiabortion, antigay agenda."[66]

Samaritan's Purse presents itself as a private Christian international nongovernmental organization, but it has received millions of dollars in US government funds, which it has considerable discretion in distributing. The *New York Times* reported that Graham's missionaries distributed resources to victims of the 2001 earthquake in El Salvador only after subjecting them to a prayer service and asking them to accept Christ as their savior.[67] Similarly, after the 2010 earthquake in Haiti, Graham's organization was at the forefront of the effort to save Haiti not from a natural disaster but from sin and the Vodou religion: "Will voodoo continue or will this be a time for Christ?" According to the Billy Graham Evangelistic Association, Samaritan's Purse helped nearly two thousand Haitians "come to Christ."[68] More recently,

Franklin Graham, who has denounced Islam as an "evil religion," has taken a special interest in focusing his organization's development and proselytizing activities in Muslim-majority countries.[69] In this light, Franklin Graham's concern about the government wresting control of the social safety net from churches appears to be motivated not by a moral objection to government funding but instead by a desire to put private, Christian interests in charge of how, and to whom, government aid is given.

The 1996 welfare reform bill paved the way for old and new conservative Christian charitable organizations to privatize government spending for domestic and international relief. It included a "Charitable Choice" provision that enabled states to disburse public funds to faith-based social service programs, blurring the already arbitrary line between church and state and allowing for faith-based discrimination in the use of public funds. George W. Bush then expanded the role of faith-based social services through the introduction of an Office of Faith-Based and Community Initiatives (OFBCI). This office made it easier for faith-based organizations to compete for federal grants to provide social services, and it has existed under different names ever since its formation.[70]

Bush's speech about the founding of OFBCI is revealing. Entitled "Rallying the Armies of Compassion," his remarks praised the work of charities because they use "care and compassion" to offer assistance in "ways that government cannot." Much like Franklin Graham, Bush implied that the welfare state had co-opted the church's mandate. The government does not have "a monopoly on compassion," he declared. Christian charities have been "neglected or excluded," but thanks to the Bush administration's efforts they could now hope for a "level playing field" and a "seat at the table."[71]

Bush and the OFBCI deployed "compassion" as a red herring to distract Americans from their political aims. According to one conservative activist who pursued Bush's reforms, Christian conservatives wanted "religious groups receiving federal funds [to have] an unfettered right to hire and fire people based not only on their professed religion but also on whether they lived according to the 'rules' of their religion."[72] Charitable Choice and the OFBCI protected discrimination in how these organizations hired and how they disbursed funds. The OFBCI, for its part, discriminated in its decisions as to which religious organizations obtained funding: Christian organizations, and especially white-majority, Christian conservative organizations, received the majority of federal grants.[73]

Bush applauded charities' "compassion" because this is the word used in Luke's parable: the Samaritan "had compassion on" the injured man. Whether with respect to international aid or local charity, Republican Christians exalt the Samaritan as a biblical symbol of the superiority of individual and communal forms of charity over and against what they consider dependency-creating, sin-validating government welfare programs.

The Samaritan stands for having your cake and eating it too: under the flag of "religious freedom," Christian "armies of compassion" can shirk responsibility for anyone they consider morally unfit, yet they can still take advantage of government funding and tax exemptions. A notorious example is the Salvation Army, which uses federal funding to lobby for conservative causes such as legislation that discriminates against the LGBTQ+ community.[74]

Compassion is a key word in Republican influencers' interpretation of the parable in Luke (10:25–37) because they understand it to mean that the Samaritan was motivated by apolitical Christian altruism instead of compliance with the government. They are right that Luke's Jesus presents the Samaritan's compassion as apolitical. The Greek verb usually translated as "show compassion" or "have pity," *splangchnizomai,* means to be moved from one's bowels and indicates that the Samaritan was motivated by a visceral, personal feeling of concern for the man dying on the road. But it is misleading for Republicans to contrast the Samaritan's compassion with state welfare, which didn't even exist as a potential point of comparison in the time of Jesus and Luke.

Luke's parable, instead, distinguishes the Samaritan's actions from the benefaction practices of Greco-Roman cities like that of Luke's community.[75] The parable twice uses forms of the Greek word *epimeleomai* to describe how the Samaritan "took care" of the victim.[76] This is a very rare word in the New Testament, where it is used only by the author of Luke and Acts of the Apostles and the author of 1 Timothy, both of whom wrote for communities in Greco-Roman cities in Greece or Asia Minor (modern Turkey).[77] This word calls to mind the concept of *epimeleia,* which is often used in Greek political writings and inscriptions for a public commission that facilitated the civic dynamics of benefaction. *Epimeleia* and *epimeleomai* often referred to a benefactor "taking care" of the city or to the duty of civic administrators or voluntary associations to "take care" to erect a public monument to honor a benefactor. Cities like Ephesus were peppered with honorary statues standing on bases whose inscriptions praised these exceptional citizens for their care (*epimeleia*) for the city.[78]

Luke's parable cleverly undermines this widespread Greco-Roman practice of politics- and honor-motivated giving by using the same vocabulary to describe the actions of a man motivated by compassion. The parable doesn't endorse aid managed by private religious associations over and against state welfare (government welfare didn't even exist yet). Instead, it endorses compassion-motivated giving over and against giving motivated by political legitimation. The moral of the story of the Samaritan is that humanitarian aid should have no strings attached—no religious, economic, or political enticements.

Whereas Republican Christians lobby on behalf of charitable organizations that promote Christianity, neoliberal economics, and conservative politics, the Samaritan parable encourages inclusive giving. Because modern readers are keen to interpret the Samaritan as a model for charity, we often miss the ways that this parable revolves around ethnic interaction.

In the first century, Jews and Samaritans were two separate ethnic and religious groups that occupied neighboring territories. They shared the same God and some of the same scriptures and both considered themselves "Israel," but they worshipped at different cultic sites—the Jews at the Temple in Jerusalem and the Samaritans at Mount Gerizim near Shechem, where their own temple had stood before it was destroyed by the Jewish ruler John Hyrcanus in the 120s BCE. Jews and Samaritans were often in conflict over their divergent histories and places of worship. Some ancient Jewish authors refused to recognize them as "Israel," opting instead to call them Sidonians, Shechemites, or Chuthaeans and lambasting them as "not even a nation."[79]

The Samaritan parable engages this ethnic conflict by setting the scene on a road in a Jewish territory that connected Jerusalem, the city of the Jewish Temple, to Jericho, where many Jewish priests lived. After the victim was beset by thieves, two functionaries of the Jerusalem Temple—a priest and a Levite—passed by. Stereotypically, both of these figures would have been seen as prone to neglect the near-dead victim for fear of contracting impurities that would render them unfit to serve in the Temple for a time.[80]

Ancient audiences of the parable who were familiar with the Hebrew Bible would have expected the next person to come onto the scene to be a lay Israelite. Instead, it was an outsider, a Samaritan whose human compassion moved him to cross the symbolic ethnic border between Samaritans and Jews to help a neighbor in need.

According to Luke, Jesus preached this parable in a debate with a Jewish legal scholar over how to interpret the law. "What must I do to inherit eternal life?" the Jewish scholar asked Jesus, whom he addressed as "Teacher." Jesus replied by asking him what it said in the law, the Torah. The scholar answered by reciting the famous prayer from Deuteronomy known as the Shema: "You must love the Lord your God with all your heart, and with all your soul, and with all your strength, and with all your mind." The scholar also added, "and [love] your neighbor as yourself" (Luke 10:25–28).[81]

Jesus affirmed his answer, but then the scholar asked, "And who is my neighbor?" This question provoked Jesus to use his famous parable to show that the Samaritan acted as a neighbor.

Whenever I teach the Samaritan parable, I begin by asking my students who invented the "Golden Rule"—the law to love your neighbor as you love yourself. They know I'm up to no good, but the overwhelming majority still humors me by answering "Jesus." I then point out that this ethic long predated Jesus and is found in ancient cultures ranging from China to Greece. They are most surprised, however, to learn that Jesus picked up his "Greatest Commandment" from the law code of Leviticus.

To understand this parable in its ancient context, we need to resist two problematic assumptions: that Jesus's Christian "law of love" superseded the Jewish "law of ritual" and that the Samaritan should be described as "good" (a word never used in the passage). The potential of contracting impurity from a corpse was a legitimate legal concern among ancient Jews. Rabbinic literature shows, though, that some Jews prioritized the law of neighbor-love above the law about avoiding corpse impurity much as Jesus's parable advocates.[82] The modern branding of this story as the "Parable of the Good Samaritan" makes the prejudicial assumption that Samaritans were not normally "good" while also turning the parable itself, rather than its framing narrative as a legal debate, into the central focus.[83]

Jesus's inter-Jewish debate with the legal scholar frames the Samaritan parable as a technical discussion as to who constitutes a "neighbor" according to God's law laid out in the Torah. In Luke's Greek, the word for "neighbor" is *plēsion*. The Septuagint version of Leviticus uses this word in its command that "you shall love your neighbor as yourself" (19:18), but it issues this command in a speech directed at "the whole community of the sons of Israel" (19:2). It extends the commandment to the "resident aliens" living among Israel in 19:34, but it never explicitly extends the commandment to a foreigner.

It was debatable, then, whether the law should be extended to a Samaritan. Luke's Jesus gave his parable to demonstrate that he considered a Samaritan a neighbor, just as the Samaritan considered the injured man a neighbor. Elsewhere, Luke's Jesus clarifies that the Samaritan is a "foreigner," or, more literally, "a person of another race" (*allogenēs*).[84] Luke's parable thus relies on the ancient Jewish stereotype that Samaritans were not actually Israelites (as they claimed to be)—that they were "of another race"—but does so to show a Samaritan exemplifying the law of Israel as Jesus interpreted it.[85]

The Samaritan parable has nothing to do with sources of funding but everything to do with showing compassion across religious, political, racial, and ethnic boundaries. Luke's Jesus advocates for an expansive legal definition of the neighbor who should give and receive compassion. Franklin Graham's Samaritan's Purse organization should take special note that the Samaritan in Jesus's parable does not attempt to convert the incapacitated man into a Samaritan.

.   .   .

Jesus, according to all of the gospels, personally distributed free fish and bread to the poor and free healings to persons who were sick and disabled. Because he possessed the power to perform miracles, he was able to provide aid without the help of the government or religious organizations, but he's a tough act to follow. Since Jesus's death, his followers have debated how best to carry forward his ministry to people who are poor, sick, disabled, and oppressed.

The gospels don't address government welfare and universal health care because nobody in Jesus's time could envision an empire-wide social safety net while living in a brutal empire that relished the profits of slavery and conquest. Our best method for deciphering what Jesus would think about government aid is to examine his understanding of poverty and charity. But the sources are inconsistent.

Our earliest retrievable form of the teachings of Jesus, the Q material, characterizes Jesus as an apocalyptic prophet who preached good news to people who were poor and disabled. His good news, though, was only that their suffering would cease in the Kingdom of God.

Matthew theologized Q's social teachings. His gospel portrays Jesus as addressing the "poor in spirit" instead of the poor and construes almsgiving as a strategy through which the donor may obtain treasures in heaven.

Luke is the only gospel that focuses on poverty as a structural problem. Its author scripts Jesus as calling on people of means to give alms to the poor and urging the rich to divest themselves of their wealth. In his narrative of Jesus's encounter with the Jewish legal scholar, Luke also has Jesus interpret the Jewish law on neighbor-love as transcending religious, racial, and ethnic boundaries.

According to Luke's gospel, the most developed social vision in the New Testament, the ideal form of humanitarian aid is motivated by compassion and is not political or discriminatory. Republican Christian leaders flout this message when they seek to control the social safety net in order to discriminate against non-Christians, people they consider immoral, and so-called welfare queens. Like the caricatured priest and Levite in the parable, modern right-wing religious leaders use their positions of influence to preserve their status at the expense of those in need.

Whether modern Americans determine that the Samaritan should represent the government, religious organizations, or individuals, they're left with one glaring problem: the parable's Samaritan bandages the victim but doesn't change the conditions that predisposed him to become a victim in the first place. The Rev. Dr. Martin Luther King Jr.'s lucid criticism of the Samaritan parable still resonates today: "True compassion is more than flinging a coin to a beggar. It comes to see that a system that produces beggars needs to be repaved. We are called to be the Good Samaritan, but after you lift so many people out of the ditch you start to ask, 'Maybe the whole road to Jericho needs to be repaved?'"[86]

CHAPTER SEVEN

Church and State

"A man may be down but he is never out." Bruce Barton, the same ad man who coined this famous neoliberal slogan for the Salvation Army, wrote a best-selling biography of Jesus in 1925 that was as popular among Hooverist proponents of the free market as O'Reilly and Dugard's novel has been among Teavangelicals. These promarket interpretations of Jesus's life and teachings share much in common but differ in one striking way: Barton's story, written prior to FDR's New Deal, doesn't portray Jesus as an opponent of excessive federal taxes.

Barton was a Don Draper–like advertising executive who had worked for the Coolidge and Hoover campaigns and thought of advertising as a way to manipulate viewers' "subconscious minds." He valorized "men's men" and put Betty Crocker in the kitchen, mocked Jews and marveled at Hitler's anti-Semitic propaganda, advocated for corporations and regarded poverty as a test of character. It's no wonder that his book *The Man Nobody Knows* portrayed Jesus as a "nobody" carpenter who used

Christian advertising tactics to become "the founder of modern business" and the greatest executive of all time.[1]

Barton's rags-to-riches story about a muscular, tanned, upwardly mobile Jesus is "perhaps the most influential forgotten book of the twentieth century."[2] Barton and his book have been praised by twentieth-century conservatives ranging from leading Klansmen to such familiar figures as DeMille, Peale, Eisenhower, and the former CEO of Chick-Fil-A. The book helped to propel Barton into the political spotlight as he went on to become a Republican congressman and a vocal opponent of FDR.[3]

Separated by nearly a century, the fan-fiction books by Barton and O'Reilly and Dugard agree that Jesus was a hypermasculine white man who applied his talents in pursuit of prosperity in a free market economy. Yet Barton's book doesn't depict Jesus as an opponent of oppressive taxes imposed by the Roman-Jewish establishment like O'Reilly and Dugard's. Instead, Barton emphasizes that Jesus was a fair-minded businessman whose "muscles were so strong" that when he drove out the "fat" and "flabby" money changers, "nobody dared to oppose him."[4] Written on the brink of the Great Depression, Barton's "portrait" of the life of Jesus envisions robust Christian business practices founded on hard work and diligent service as saving America from a scourge of greedy business practices motivated by the desire for comfort and wealth.

Prior to the New Deal, even a full-blown probusiness rewriting of the gospels like Barton's didn't interpret resistance against taxation and Big Government as Jesus's adze to grind. Since the emergence of the Christian Right, opposition to excessive taxation has become a common trait of Small Government interpretations of Jesus.

Republican influencers' Small Government interpretations of Jesus's economics depend on modern notions of "religious freedom" and the separation of church and state that don't align with the ancient sources. In the New Testament world, religion and economics were two sides of the same coin.

RELIGION AND ECONOMICS IN THE NEW TESTAMENT WORLD

One of the "seven wonders" of the ancient world, the Temple of Artemis at Ephesus was widely renowned, according to a first-century CE governor's decree engraved in stone, "because of the magnitude of its work, the ancientness of the reverence for the goddess, and the abundance of revenues having been paid by the emperor to the goddess."[5] Modern readers should have a knee-jerk reaction to that last clause. Could you imagine an American state governor boasting that a church in his or her domain was so great because Jesus Christ received lots of money from the president?

The pervasive US political rhetoric that idealizes religious freedom in concert with the separation of church and state (where "church" stands for religion and "state" comprises law, economics, and politics) would have made little sense to a person in the New Testament world. To be clear, tax exemptions for churches and religious organizations are one of many reminders that the US separation of church and state is more rhetorical than actual.[6] Nonetheless, the very idea of the isolation of religion and state into discrete spheres is distinctly modern.

The words in ancient texts often translated into English as "religion" are more precisely translated as "worship," "ritual," "rule," "custom," "piety," "law," or "scruples." Even Latin texts that use the noun *religio,* from which the English *religion* is derived, don't easily jibe with modern connotations of religion. Take, for instance, Cicero's indictment of an opponent's actions for being "against the law, contrary to the auspices, against all divine and human *religiones.*" Cicero is speaking specifically about Roman customs here. His use of *religiones* (the plural form of *religio*) thus can't refer to multiple different religions in the modern sense. Instead, he is referring to series of rules established by the gods and humans.[7]

Much of our understanding of religion developed only in the early modern period. Whereas many American Christians understand religion as an individual relationship with God, a cognitive system of beliefs, or an isolable sphere of social life, people in the New Testament world understood their worship as a more collective endeavor based in practices like rituals and fully integrated with a holistic social experience that also involved activities moderns classify as political or economic.[8]

This is why an ancient inscription could describe an emperor paying revenues to a goddess by contributing to a temple. Temples in the New Testament world evade simple description according to our modern categories of religion, politics, and economics. They were sacred spaces in which humans could secure the protection of a god or gods through various ritual transactions. They were also political sites at which individuals demonstrated their allegiance to their city, nation, empire, or all three simultaneously.

Subjects of the Roman Empire, including Jews, worshipped their gods by sacrificing animals to them, offering them agricultural products, or pouring out wine for them. In an ancient land-based economy, these were substantial economic transactions in which the god—not the temple or its priests—was viewed as the recipient.[9] These were not unilateral transactions, though.

People believed that the gods reciprocated with various forms of support and protection.[10]

The inseparability of religion, politics, and economics in the New Testament world made it easy for a political authority who was also a priest to abuse his control over funds designated for a god. In the Ephesian decree pertaining to the Temple of Artemis, the provincial governor, who was also a high priest, proceeded to complain about temple officials who, "using the scheme of the divine temple as their front, ... sell the priest-hoods ... at public auction."[11] Because of such politicians' attempts to profit from the economics of worship through their roles as temple functionaries, laws were often established to protect sacred funds by differentiating them from public funds.

Half a century before Jesus's ministry, the emperor Augustus issued a decree protecting "sacred monies" that diaspora Jews set aside to send to the Jerusalem Temple: "If anyone is caught stealing ... their sacred monies ... he shall be regarded as sacrilegious."[12] According to this decree, "sacrilegious" individuals could have their property confiscated. A later Roman jurist from the province of Syria specified that being found "sacrilegious" was a crime punishable by hanging—that is, crucifixion.[13] Stealing from sacred funds was a serious criminal offense that was enforced by the state.

Like the Temple of Artemis at Ephesus, the Jewish Temple in Jerusalem was, to use our modern terms, as much a political and economic institution as it was a religious center. From ancient literary and archaeological sources, we know that pilgrims who came there to make offerings to their deity created considerable economic demand for the plants and animals they sacrificed. They also stimulated a booming tourism industry in Jerusalem.[14]

The Jerusalem Temple had a number of additional economic functions besides facilitating sacrifices. Its priests collected annual half-shekel "Temple taxes" from Jews throughout the empire as well as agricultural tithes from Jews in the Land of Israel. According to the Torah, farmers were supposed to tithe 10 percent of their agricultural products to priests six out of seven years. It's not clear how many Jews actually observed the laws of tithing, but the ancient Jewish historian Josephus complained that his relentless fellow priests sometimes sent slaves to the threshing floors to exact tithes by force.[15]

The Jerusalem Temple also acted as a bank where Jews could deposit funds for safekeeping or take out loans, it collected fines from people who committed crimes like grave robbing, and it might even have leased out land.

Like temple officials in any major city in the Eastern Empire, Jewish priests also played some part in collecting imperial and municipal taxes. But they must have taken care to keep these streams of revenue separate, since stealing from the emperor was a recipe for disaster. From ancient tax receipts, we can tell that the Roman Empire collected land tributes from its provincial subjects at an average rate of about 14 percent of the harvested products of the taxpayer's land, but there were significant regional variations. They also collected "head taxes" from adult men at an average rate of five denarii per year, or about five days' wages for a subsistence-level laborer. High-status individuals often received tax discounts and exemptions.

Jerusalem's priests, like Ephesus's, encouraged and facilitated the collection of imperial taxes, but—barring any corruption—they transmitted these taxes to the emperor. When Rome introduced the census to exact tributes in Judaea, "the Judaeans were at first shocked to hear of the registration," according to Josephus. But "they gradually condescended, yielding to the arguments of the High Priest Joazar."[16] As Galileans, Jesus and his earliest followers did not pay any of these tributes to the emperor as Jews in the southern region of Judaea did beginning in 6 CE. Instead, Galileans paid taxes—probably at a relatively similar rate—to Herod Antipas, who had some autonomy in his appointment as the ruler of the Galilee on behalf of Rome. It is interesting, in this regard, that the gospels depict Jesus instructing people to "render unto Caesar" in Jerusalem, not Galilee.

Jewish priestly elites, as far as we can tell, did not increase their wealth through Caesar's taxes as they likely did from tithes and by capitalizing on the pilgrimage economy centered on the Temple in Jerusalem. They did, however, have considerable power over municipal taxes such as sales taxes, tolls, and customs duties, whose rates ranged from 2 to 25 percent. Archaeologists have discovered stone scale weights inscribed with the name of a family of high priests, which suggest that elite priests also played some official administrative role in calibrating the weights used to sell goods in Jerusalem's markets.[17]

There were separate streams of taxation that affected Jews in first-century CE Jerusalem—taxes destined for the Temple, which were collected and used by priests for the upkeep of the Temple; tributes destined for the emperor, which were facilitated by priests but transmitted to the emperor; and various occasional taxes that were exacted by municipal officials including priests and were supposed to be used for municipal services.

Taxes for Caesar and the city were kept separate from taxes for the Temple and tithes for God, but priests were involved to varying degrees in the collection of all taxes. In an economy where there were no major capital investments, industrial technologies were underdeveloped, and trade and labor markets were only partially integrated because of limited mobility and transport technologies, temples were among the most powerful economic institutions.[18] Temples were viewed as protected spaces because of the presence of gods within them, but also because written and unwritten laws recognized the violation of temples and theft of their monies as a punishable sacrilege.

Temples in the ancient world served many of the functions that moderns associate with banks. There were efforts to keep public taxes and sacred taxes and other offerings separate, but this was not a separation of economics and religion. The emperor and civic leaders were often religious officials, and temples were centers of economic activity. Jesus's teaching to "render unto Caesar" must, then, mean something other than to separate religion from government.

RENDER UNTO JUPITER'S TEMPLE

"The American Civil Liberties Union didn't invent the separation of church and state," rasped Russell Moore, the president of the Southern Baptist Convention's Ethics and Religious Liberty Commission, in the midst of the Supreme Court battle over whether Hobby Lobby should be required to provide medical coverage for contraceptives. "Jesus did," Moore explained, "when he said that we should render unto Caesar that which is Caesar's and render unto God that which is God's."[19]

In his 2014 *Time* op-ed, Moore goes on to distinguish his interpretation of Jesus's teaching on "church/state separation" from that of ACLU tote bag–carrying liberals, who he claims think the church should be dominated by the state. With the exception of Christian Dominionists, who go so far as to profess that America should be a theocracy, most conservatives would agree with Moore that Jesus's "Render unto Caesar" saying serves as a blueprint for the separation of church and state. But then, under the rubric of "freedom of religion," they assert that religion should "influence" the state. "The Bible," Drollinger quibbles, "clearly teaches that today, there is to be an *institutional* separation of Church and State.... What the Bible does not teach—and what the secularist would like to say the U.S. Constitution supports—is an *influential* separation of Church and State."[20] Or, as Rick Warren has put it, "I believe in the separation of church and state, but I do not believe in the separation of politics from religion."[21]

For Stephen McDowell, who runs a conservative Christian nonprofit that takes schoolchildren on "Christian history" tours of Washington, D.C., the separation of church and state, which is affirmed in the First Amendment, is "rooted in this historic political teaching of Christ."[22] Jesus, so it goes, established the separation of church and state.

Many liberals and conservatives would agree that Jesus's saying addresses the separation of church and state, but they disagree about how to apply this teaching. Both sides tend to assume that religion and the state were separate in antiquity and that Jesus's statement referred to all taxes. Neither of these assumptions is supported by the textual and historical evidence.

The earliest source of the "Render unto Caesar" passage is Mark (12:13–17), which Matthew (22:15–22) and Luke (20:20–26) used as a source for their versions. In each gospel, the teaching is framed by a debate in which either the Pharisees and Herodians (Mark), just the Pharisees (Matthew), or spies sent by the Jewish authorities in Jerusalem (Luke) attempt to trap Jesus by asking him whether it's lawful to pay taxes to the emperor or not. If he says "yes," he might risk losing followers who opposed Roman taxes. If he says "no," he could be indicted by the Romans and tried as a tax rebel.

Jesus's key phrase in Mark's version (and the other gospels' too) is garbled by most translations. The King James Version is particularly misleading, for it has Jesus respond to his opponents by asking them to bring him a "penny." In fact, he asks them to bring him a denarius: "Bring me a denarius and let me see it." A denarius (plural: denarii) is a silver Roman coin that is equal to about the daily income of the average day laborer. It's not a generic term like *coin* but names a specific coin like the English words *nickel* or *quarter.*

"Whose head is on this, and whose title?" Jesus queries after they show him the coin. When they answer that it is Caesar's, Jesus responds, "Return to Caesar the things that are Caesar's, and to God the things that are God's." In its literary context "the things" he speaks of must refer to the taxes his opponents quizzed him about. The word that they used for "taxes," *kēnsos,* is a Greek transliteration of the Latin *census,* whose meaning is the same as its English derivative. It stands in as a circumlocution for taxes that are collected by means of an official Roman census. The opponents' original question is, therefore, best translated as "Is it lawful to pay census (taxes) to Caesar, or not?" (Mark 12:14).

Of the two taxes typically collected by the Roman census, this must refer to the head tax, which was the only one paid in denarii, since the land tax was paid in crops.[23]

There are several problems with the idea that the historical Jesus would ever say these words. First, Jesus was from Galilee, where people did not pay taxes to Caesar at this time. The sources do depict him saying these words in Judaea, however, so we might allow that Jesus understood that Judaeans paid taxes in coin to Caesar. Second, it is unclear whether the census was used to collect head taxes in Judaea as it was in other provinces. Judaeans may have only paid land taxes to Rome.[24] Third, and most importantly, archaeological finds indicate that denarii were rarely used as currency in the Galilee and Judaea prior to 68 CE, during the First Revolt. They circulated more widely in this region only after 68 CE.[25] The historical Jesus would never have asked his opponents to bring him a denarius because he probably had never seen one before.

Mark puts a saying about an anachronistic tax into Jesus's mouth. There are good reasons to suspect that Mark wrote his gospel somewhere in Palestine or Syria shortly after the turbulent years of the First Jewish Revolt (66–70 CE), which culminated in the destruction of the Jerusalem Temple.[26] Mark's postwar context emerges in what is known as the "Little Apocalypse" (13:1–37). In this section, Jesus "predicts" the destruction of the Temple: "Not one stone will be left here upon another; all will be thrown down" (13:2). He explains that there will be famine, war, and false messiahs before the destruction, but he exhorts his disciples that "when you hear of wars and rumors of wars, do not be alarmed; this must take place, but the end is still to come.... This is but the beginning of the birth pangs" (13:7–8).

Mark scripted Jesus in direct response to anxiety among his community that the First Jewish Revolt was the apocalypse they anticipated but that Christ had failed to return. At one point in this narrative, Mark even makes the unusual move of interrupting Jesus's words with a cue to his audience that these words have special meaning for them. "Let the reader understand" (13:14), he says, alerting his postwar audience that the war and Temple destruction are only the "beginning of the birth pangs" of the end-times. They should take comfort in knowing that the Son of Man should still be anticipated (13:24).[27]

Mark addresses his audience's postwar concerns through Jesus's teaching on taxes just as he does through the Little Apocalypse. Although anachronistic in Jesus's context, a census used to collect taxes paid in denarii would have made perfect sense to Mark's postwar audience.

This is where things get interesting. After the First Jewish Revolt, Jews throughout the empire were required to pay a special "Jewish tax" (*Ioudaikon telesma*) as a punishment for the actions of the Jewish rebels in Judaea. The Jewish tax replaced the annual "Temple tax" once paid to the Jerusalem Temple, but it was exacted from all Jews regardless of age and gender. A special administrative office with its own personnel was even created to collect these prejudicial taxes. Numerous tax receipts that have survived from Egypt show that Jews paid this tax in the usual amount of two denarii.[28]

We cannot be sure whether Mark's community openly identified as "Jews," but they might have. Some members of Mark's audience, at least, would have identified as ethnically Jewish, and some would have come from—or still resided in—Judaea. Even Gentile followers of Christ among Mark's earliest audiences would have closely resembled Jews in practice and beliefs and could have been easily mistaken for Jews by outsiders. This is important because the Roman officials collecting the taxes were not always discerning in their racial profiling. The Latin author Suetonius describes an incident in which "an old man of ninety was inspected by a financial officer and a very crowded court to see whether he was circumcised."[29]

Suetonius's account might be embellished, but multiple ancient sources present the collection of this tax as an unrelenting persecution during the last three decades of the first century CE—the exact time in which the four gospels were written. The Flavian emperors minted coins during these decades that portrayed Jews as captives and proclaimed "Judaea captured"

Figure 16. The reverse of a coin minted by the Roman emperor Vespasian in 71 CE, declaring "Judaea captured" (*Iudaea capta*) after the First Jewish Revolt. The woman mourning is a personification of Judaea. The man standing with his hands bound is a Judaean captive, and behind him are captured weapons (which are clearer on other issues of this coin type). Nowhere does this image differentiate the rebels in the province of Judaea from other Jews throughout the empire. Credit: American Numismatic Society.

(figure 16). Nerva, the first to rule after the Flavian emperors, claimed to have rectified the harshness of these Jewish tax exactions to some degree. He issued coins with the inscription "To commemorate the suppression of wrongful accusations in regard to the collection of the Jewish tax."[30]

The late first century CE was a particularly hard time to be a Jew or part of a community that included Jews or resembled Jews.

Through Jesus's teaching on taxes, Mark urged his postwar community to pay the emperor the monetary taxes collected by the census—namely, the head tax and Jewish tax—as they lay low in anticipation of Christ's impending return. Both Matthew and Luke appropriated Mark's version of this teaching without any significant changes, but Matthew elsewhere doubled down on Mark's use of Jesus's teaching to address the Jewish tax.

Matthew, who crafted his gospel to differentiate his Jewish community from the emergent rabbinic movement, composed a story about taxes that is not found in the other gospels (17:24–27). Most translations begin this story with "collectors of the Temple tax" coming to Peter and asking, "Does your teacher not pay the Temple tax?" This translation misleads by translating the Greek word *didrachma* as "Temple tax." The didrachma, literally referring to two drachma coins, is the Greek monetary equivalent to both the half-shekel required for the Jerusalem Temple tax and the two-denarii Jewish tax that the Romans imposed in place of the Temple tax.

After Peter answers, "Yes, he does," Jesus poses the didactic question, "From whom do kings of the earth take toll or census taxes [*kēnsos*]? From their children or from others?" These questions reveal that Matthew's Jesus is addressing specific taxes collected by "kings of the earth" (the Roman emperors) and not by the Temple priests. When Peter correctly responds "From others," Jesus replies, "Then the children are free." Commentators debate to no end about what this cryptic saying might mean, but it might be as simple as it seems: Matthew's Jesus is saying that the Roman emperors do not tax their own children, but instead tax others—that is, foreign subjects like the Jews. In other words, the rulers are exempt from taxes but tax others.[31]

The story ends with a subversive twist. Despite his observation about this inequality in imperial tax collection, Jesus directs Peter as follows: "So that we do not give offense to them, go to the sea and cast a hook; take the first fish that comes up; and when you open its mouth, you will find a stater [a coin equal to two didrachmas]; take that and give it to them for you and me." Any reader or hearer who paid attention to the miraculous feedings that preceded this story in Matthew would know by now that fish are a symbol that God will provide for believers. In this case, he provides not only dinner but also the money to pay taxes. While Matthew's Jesus advocates paying taxes, then, he implies that God makes it possible to do so.

The "Render unto Caesar" passages similarly include an element of subversion in their depiction of Jesus endorsing the payment of Jewish taxes to the Romans. In this story in Mark, Matthew, and Luke, Jesus calls attention to the portrait and title on a denarius just before saying, "Return therefore to Caesar the things that are Caesar's, and to God the things that are God's."[32] Among the titles typically listed on Roman denarii, the emperor is often described as a "son of God" because his father was recognized as a god upon his death. During the first century, it was increasingly common for people living in the eastern provinces to worship the emperors as gods.[33]

By distinguishing Caesar from God, Mark, Matthew, and Luke depict Jesus denying the divinity of the emperor, but there is yet another level to this slight. According to ancient authors, the Jewish tax did not actually go to the emperor but to the Temple of Jupiter Capitolinus in Rome.[34] The gospels' Jesus, therefore, endorsed paying taxes to the temple of a Roman god at the command of an emperor who was revered by many as divine. His words reject the divinity of Jupiter and the emperor, but he nevertheless instructs believers to comply with taxes determined by an imperial census and credited to a temple. That's a far cry from an endorsement of the separation of church and state.

FLIPPING TABLES IN THE BANDITS' CAVE

"Stop making my Father's house a marketplace!" "My house shall be called a house of prayer; but you have made it a den of robbers!" These verses from the gospel accounts of Jesus's impassioned encounter with the money changers in Jerusalem are often cited by both liberals and conservatives alongside the

"Render unto Caesar" passages as proof that Jesus proclaimed the separation of religion from economics. Republican influencers, as we've seen, often interpret the money changers as representatives of Big Government, while liberals tend to understand them as representing the superwealthy. But both sides tend to agree, in any case, that Jesus sought to cleanse religion of economics.

The modern title for this passage, the "Cleansing of the Temple," misleadingly primes modern readers to expect that Jesus was trying to cleanse religion of economics—or worse still, that he was trying to cleanse the true Christian religion of faith from the economic trappings of Jewish ritual.[35] Yet, living in a world in which religion, economics, and politics were interdependent and indistinguishable, Jesus and the gospel writers could not have endorsed a separation of church and state. What, then, was Jesus so incensed about?

Each of the four gospels includes this episode, but they differ in their details.[36] Mark, Matthew, and John depict Jesus entering the precincts of the Jerusalem Temple during a Passover pilgrimage and interfering with the activities of the money changers and those selling doves. Luke's abbreviated version of the story is consistent but only depicts Jesus driving out "those who were selling things."

In John, this confrontation occurs at the beginning of Jesus's ministry. The other three gospels place it at the end of his ministry, in the week of his arrest and crucifixion. All of the gospels have Jesus cite scriptures in support of his actions. In Mark, Matthew, and Luke, Jesus combines verses from Isaiah and Jeremiah as "My house shall be called a house of prayer; but you have made it a den of robbers."[37] Meanwhile, John has Jesus cite Psalm 69 as "Zeal for your house will consume me" and allude to Zechariah with his command to "stop making my Father's house a marketplace!"[38] Only John includes the salacious detail that Jesus used a whip to drive out those selling sheep and cattle.

Because this event is mentioned in two independent sources, Mark (which Matthew and Luke use as a source) and John, and because it helps to explain why Jesus was crucified as a criminal, most scholars accept that this event should be considered historical in some form. At the very least, it is likely that the historical Jesus staged some sort of protest against the money changers and dove sellers at the Temple. But why would he do this?

If the historical Jesus did indeed target the money changers, this must have been at least in part an indictment of the Temple tax. The requirement for all Jews to pay an annual Temple tax was based on a loose interpretation of the law in Exodus 30:13 that lay male Israelites over the age of twenty should pay a half-shekel tax "as an offering to the Lord." In Exodus, this was a once-in-a-lifetime payment. Yet in the Persian period, Nehemiah recounts an annual payment of one-third of a shekel "for the service of the house of our God."[39]

By the time of Jesus, priestly elites had established the Temple tax as an annual half-shekel contribution to the maintenance of the Temple. Not all Jews acquiesced to this annual payment, however. The Qumran community associated with the Dead Sea Scrolls, for instance, seems instead to have followed the Torah by requiring initiates to pay a once-for-life Temple tax when they joined the community.[40]

Jesus may have rejected the annual exaction of this tax for the same reason as the Qumran community—namely, that it was not in the Torah. He might also have rejected it because the silver coins that were most often used to pay this tax featured graven images. The coins were minted in Tyre and featured

Figure 17. A Tyrian shekel (equal to two half-shekels) minted in 17/16 BCE. The obverse portrays the head of the god Melqart, and the reverse depicts an eagle. From other coins, we know that the inscription on the reverse of these coins, only partially visible on this coin, reads, "Of Tyre the holy and inviolable." Credit: American Numismatic Society.

images of the god Melqart and an eagle, as well as an inscription naming Tyre as a "holy" city (figure 17).[41]

Considering that Jesus also targeted those selling doves (and perhaps those selling cattle and sheep, as John adds), however, there must have been a greater purpose for his outburst. Our evidence allows only a provisional sketch of what might have gone down.

The historical Jesus's objective was likely to protest the high priests' abuse of their positions of power to gain wealth. From archaeological remains of their homes and tombs, it is clear that priestly elites were among the wealthiest people in Judaea. They earned their wealth through landownership and their control over commerce in Jerusalem, probably including control over the sale of animals for sacrifice. Even still, they collected tithes that the Torah required as a form of compensation for priests, who were not supposed to earn any other income. They also determined how the revenue from Temple taxes was spent, and they may have profited from the 4 to 8 percent surcharges collected by money changers, who were likely either priests or their agents. These men were, for all intents and purposes, the big bankers of Jesus's day.

When Jesus disrupted the activities of the money changers, the sales of sacrificial animals, and the transport of vessels that probably contained tithes (a detail only found in Mark 11:16, but arguably historical), he blocked the flow of revenue to priestly elites.[42] It is noteworthy that our sources do not recount Jesus blocking people from bringing *their own animals* to sacrifice at the Temple or from making deposits or seeking loans from the Temple.[43] The economics of worship was not his problem. The corruption of the economics of worship by priestly elites was.

I want to pause to emphasize how this historical interpretation differs from Republican interpretations like O'Reilly and Dugard's. Whereas O'Reilly and Dugard cast Jesus as a tax protester who opposed a Big Government represented by a coalition of high priests and Roman rulers ("The Temple priests and their Roman masters get most of the profit through taxation and money changing"), I contend that there is only evidence to suggest that Jesus protested the Temple tax and to observe that these Temple taxes were transmitted to the high priests, not Rome.[44] Whereas O'Reilly and Dugard perpetuate anti-Semitic stereotypes by casting Jesus as an opponent of *Jewish* ritualism and profiteering, I argue that Jesus was opposed to what he viewed as the exploitative practices of the high priests but was not at all opposed to the Temple, its sacrifices, or its role as an economic institution.

Jesus's protest, as I've reconstructed it, is entirely consistent with the critiques of the wealth of high priests that we find in a number of Jewish texts from the Roman period. A text known as the Psalms of Solomon, for instance, condemns priestly elites because "they would plunder the sanctuary of God."[45] Similarly, some of the Dead Sea Scrolls issue warnings about "wealth" and "defilement of the sanctuary" as nets in which Belial (a Satan-like personification of evil), working his evil through the high priests, traps Israel.[46] And a book called the Testament of Moses spares no words when castigating the priestly elites as "deceitful men, self-pleasers, hypocrites in all their dealings, ... who love to have banquets each hour of the day, devourers, gluttons ... who eat the possessions of the [poor] ... from sunrise to sunset saying: 'Let us have luxurious seats at the table, let us eat and drink. And let us act as if we are distinguished leaders.'"[47]

The authors of these Jewish texts despised the high priests for continuing to collect tithes and Temple taxes when they were already wealthy men. They didn't reject the Temple or priesthood as institutions but only the Temple's current management, which blurred the lines between sacred and public finances.

Like some of his Jewish peers, the historical Jesus seems to have charged the high priests with sacrilege—with violating sacred funds. Ironically, the Romans might have crucified Jesus on the basis of the same charge—sacrilege—for disrupting the flow of sacred funds to the Temple. If not sacrilege in particular, the Romans must have charged him with potential sedition for inciting riots like what would have ensued when Jesus confronted the money changers and sellers during a major urban festival. The Romans weren't fond of leaders of provincial social movements whom people hailed as kings, whether they were belligerent rebels or not. Crucifying potential rebels was, as the distinguished Hebrew University professor Paula Fredriksen explains, "a Roman form of public service announcement: Do not engage in sedition as this person has, or your fate will be similar."[48]

Only the Romans could legally execute someone in their empire. However, all of the gospels shift the blame from the Romans to the Jewish authorities. Why would the gospel writers blame the Jewish authorities for Jesus's death? And how does this motivation color their depiction of Jesus's quarrel with the money changers?

Each gospel presents a slightly different narrative to explain why Jesus was killed. John presents Jesus's raising of Lazarus as the reason that the Jewish authorities started plotting to kill him.[49] Matthew and Luke, on the other hand, imply that all of Jesus's actions since entering Jerusalem, but especially his teachings, set the Jewish leaders against him. Only Mark links his death directly to his outburst at the Temple: "When the chief priests and the scribes heard it"—that is, his "den of robbers" accusation—"they kept looking for a way to kill him; for they were afraid of him, because the whole crowd was spellbound by his teaching" (Mark 11:18).

The phrase "den of robbers," which comes from the prophet Jeremiah, would have been rife with meaning for the postwar audiences of Mark, Matthew, and Luke. A better translation of the Greek here is "cave of bandits." Josephus describes the Zealots, the sundry bands of lawless rebels who fomented the First Jewish Revolt, using this same word, *bandits* (*lēstai*). Some of these violent brigands, according to Josephus, hid out in caves before managing to occupy the Temple during the war.[50] Josephus, who himself had been a general fighting for the rebel government before defecting to the Romans, was very careful in his postwar writings to censure these rebels while clarifying that they didn't represent the position of all Jews.[51]

Much as Josephus sought to defend all Jews from responsibility for the revolt, all four gospels may be viewed as efforts to differentiate Christ followers in the sharpest terms from the rebels involved in the revolt. Christ followers found themselves in an awkward position after the war. They professed a Jewish messiah who was crucified by the Romans as a criminal at the exact time that all Jews throughout the empire were slandered as treasonous barbarians and punished for the revolt in Judaea through special taxes.

Regardless of what the historical Jesus's mission really was, the gospels leave their earliest audiences with little doubt that their savior was no rebel. The two men crucified beside Jesus were criminals but he was not.[52] He was, instead, killed for standing up to the corrupt authorities who supported the rebels. According to a historical-critical interpretation, the gospels portray Jesus as denouncing the corruption of the people who ran the Temple, not trying to cleanse religion of economics. This explains why the gospel writers shifted the blame for Jesus's crucifixion—a death sentence that only Roman authorities could declare—to the Jewish leaders.

.   .   .

It is difficult for us as modern Americans to read the passages in the gospels about taxation and Temple corruption without transposing our own assumptions about the separation of church and state onto them. It doesn't help that English translations often obscure details that were significant when the gospels were written. With better translations and a fuller sense of the historical context of the gospels, it's easier to recognize that Jesus and the gospel writers were totally unconcerned with our modern bipartisan ideal of the separation of church and state.

Our gospel accounts of Jesus's teachings on taxation and his conflict with the money changers and merchants were carefully crafted to address the concerns of Christ followers negotiating their relationship with Jews and the Roman Empire in the decades following the Judaean revolt against Rome. With Rome punishing all Jews for this provincial uprising in Judaea, followers of Christ found themselves in a difficult position because they proclaimed that a crucified Jewish criminal had risen from the dead and would soon return to bring an end to the world as they knew it.

The gospel writers were careful to defuse this tension. Mark, Matthew, and Luke present Jesus as exhorting his followers to pay their census-based taxes to Caesar, the head of the empire's official priesthoods. For Christ followers who identified, or were identified, as Jews, this also meant paying a tax to the Temple of Jupiter. These accounts imply that Jesus denied the divinity of the emperor and Jupiter, but they do not identify Jesus as a critic of the intermingling of practices that modern readers separate as religion, economics, and politics.

Even though these gospels encourage compliance with the Jewish tax, they also go to great lengths to redeem Christ followers from any culpability in the revolt. All four gospels are adamant that Jesus was a critic of the Temple authorities and a victim of their corruption. The accounts of the Temple incident are important because they show that Jesus tried to expose the corruption of the Temple authorities and prophesied the destruction of the Temple. For a postwar audience of Christ followers, these narratives protected the Jewish progenitor of their movement from being perceived as one of the Judaean rebels.

Conservative and liberal readers are equally prone to transforming the gospels' Jesus into a spokesperson for the separation of church and state, but they differ in their emphases. Barton and FDR agreed that Jesus lashed out against the greed and corruption of businessmen, but they disagreed about how to imitate Jesus in their own time. Like Hoover, Barton seemed to think that corporate greed would be resolved if businessmen traded practices motivated by greed for a business model based on Christian service: bankers and corporate executives should act more like Christ. FDR, on the other hand, thought that the government should act more like Christ by regulating the ways that banks treat their clients and businesses treat their employees.

As a reaction to progressives' interpretation of Jesus's outrage against the money changers and merchants as a model for government regulation and taxation in the wake of the Great Depression, conservatives cultivated interpretations of Jesus as a critic of Big Government. Whereas Barton's 1925 book doesn't present Jesus as a tax protester or view the money changers as representatives of the government, these interpretations became commonplace among conservatives during the era of the New Deal.

O'Reilly and Dugard's narrative is a full-blown expression of this anti–New Deal interpretation of Jesus with a twenty-first-century Christian nationalist edge. Whereas the gospels portray Jesus as a tax-compliant Jew who was no rebel, O'Reilly and Dugard have twisted him into a Christian rebel against taxes and Judaism.

CHAPTER EIGHT

Protection from Invaders

By mid-June 2019, the Republican governor of Texas, Greg Abbott, had signed all ten pro–Second Amendment bills backed by the NRA and passed in recent sessions of the Texas legislature. Abbott and progun Texan legislators defeated measures that would have banned bump stocks and placed restrictions on sales at gun shows. They also passed laws restricting schools, landlords, housing associations, and places of worship from being able to prohibit the carrying of firearms on or near their premises. Abbott even vetoed a bill that would have banned firearms from airports.[1]

Six weeks after a Texan NRA lobbyist gloated about this highly "successful" legislative defense of the Second Amendment in Texas, a white supremacist wielding a legally obtained semiautomatic rifle slaughtered twenty-two people and injured twenty-four more at a Walmart in El Paso. The white shooter confessed to police that he had traveled 650 miles from his home in Allen, Texas, to the border city of El Paso to target "Mexicans." Prior to the attack, he posted a manifesto online that explained his motive: "This attack is a response to the Hispanic invasion of Texas. They are the instigators, not me. I am simply defending my country from cultural and ethnic replacement brought on by an invasion."[2]

How did President Trump respond to this massacre? Did he consider regulating or banning weapons that automatically cycle a new round after each shot? Did he condemn white nationalism? No. He tweeted that we must "get strong background checks, perhaps marrying this legislation with desperately needed immigration reform."[3] Trump connects buying guns to protection from immigrants. Sadly, he's not the first to do so.

The connection between gun ownership and protection from outsiders dates back to the Second Amendment. In her new book, *Loaded*, the historian and activist Roxanne Dunbar-Ortiz reveals the concealed history behind the typical bipartisan claim that the Second Amendment was created to enshrine the rights of revolutionaries to form militias to defend themselves from the British Empire. The amendment states that "a well regulated Militia being necessary to the security of a free State, the right of the People to keep and bear Arms shall not be infringed."

This amendment may have been used to justify American colonists owning guns to shoot British soldiers. However, historical evidence shows that it was designed to give *settler*-militias the right to use firearms to drive Native Americans off of their lands and the right to control the African slaves whom they forced to create profits for them on their stolen land.[4] A century and a half before the Constitution was written, the governments of individual colonies had already established laws *requiring* colonists to own firearms and ammunition. Why? To shoot any Indigenous people who might resist having their land stolen. These colonial laws were the basis for the Second Amendment, a pillar of the Constitution of a new nation eager to send settler-militias westward to conquer Indigenous territories.[5]

The romanticizing narrative that the Second Amendment protects hungry turkey hunters and patriotic Johnny Tremains erases its persistent and historical connection to violent white supremacy throughout American history. This right has repeatedly been affirmed as a way to assert whites' control over people of color and other outsiders—whether Native Americans, African Americans, Muslims, Latinos, or Jews.

Opponents of gun control cite the Bible to legitimate their right to arms and their right to put refugees and other immigrants in cages like animals. The day after seven people were killed by a shooter in Odessa, Texas—less than a month after the El Paso shooting—the staunchly anti-immigration Texan politicians Ted Cruz and Matt Schaefer took to Twitter to defend Second Amendment rights as "God-given" and to argue that "the right to self-defense is recognized repeatedly in the Bible."[76] Republican influencers interpret the Bible as showing that the solution to gun violence is stricter immigration laws and looser gun laws.

When Republican Christians troll the New Testament for prooftexts that Jesus taught his followers to bear weapons to defend themselves from outsiders, they miss an important fact: if it weren't for the people of different ethnicities among Jesus's earliest followers and their ability to move across the provincial borders of the Roman Empire, Christianity would never have spread across the empire and probably wouldn't exist today.

PROTECTION FROM OUTSIDERS IN THE NEW TESTAMENT WORLD

The Roman Empire was a dangerous place to live. In no small part because of widespread poverty, banditry was a constant threat. Bandits were armed thieves who used violent force to rob people of their possessions. "Only the poor man is safe from bandit attacks," concluded Seneca the Younger.[7] A number of ancient gravestones even state that the deceased was "killed by bandits."[8]

Most bandits targeted merchants and travelers on rural roads, where they were less likely to have soldiers or guards to protect them. Bandits often attacked their victims with swords or knives, but they sometimes brandished clubs or improvised weapons like tools.[9] They didn't, of course, have guns because the gun is a modern invention. This simple point deserves special emphasis because, even in the hands of a skilled terrorist, a sword is nowhere near as lethal as an assault rifle. Unlike swords, the semiautomatic assault weapons that American gun control advocates are trying to ban enable shooters to slaughter large crowds of unsuspecting people in a matter of seconds.

Importantly, bandits in the New Testament world didn't come in disproportionate numbers from marginalized ethnic groups, nor was banditry motivated by ethnic prejudices.[10] Ancient authors described banditry as a countryside phenomenon, but they usually didn't blame it on ethnic groups they reviled the way modern right-wing politicians do.[11] The modern discourse that associates violent crime against whites with people of color is, in any case, a fiction. Though in 2015 Trump tweeted the false white nationalist fiction that "crime statistics show blacks kill 81 percent of white homicide victims," the FBI's data actually shows that 82 percent of white homicide victims were killed by other whites.[12] According to another study released in 2017 by the US Department of Justice, the majority of violent crimes in America are committed by people who are the same race as their victims.[13] The idea that people of color are more prone to violent crime than white people is a white nationalist myth.[14]

People in the New Testament world carried weapons while traveling to defend themselves from the very real and constant threat posed by bandits.[15] The physician Galen says that he once inspected the corpse of a bandit who had been killed by a traveler "repelling his attack."[16] Josephus even relates that the Jewish sect of Essenes associated with the Dead Sea Scrolls "carry nothing whatever with them on their journeys, except arms as a protection against bandits."[17]

Banditry was a major problem in first-century CE Judaea and Galilee, especially in the decades leading up to the First Jewish Revolt. The rebels who instigated this revolt, misleadingly conflated under the label "Zealots" by Josephus, included multiple rival gangs of bandits.[18] While some of these bandits may have been motivated in part by aspirations of social justice or political independence from the Roman Empire, they should not be valorized as ancient Robin Hoods.[19] They stole from the rich, but they didn't give to the poor. In most cases, they were violent outlaws.

The Roman government was not very effective at curtailing banditry. Roman officials sometimes tried to quell the violence of bandits, particularly if it resembled sedition. They posted guards on certain dangerous roads, and sometimes they raided houses to seize bandits' weapons.[20] Mainly, however, they relied on the army to suppress banditry.

Even though popular films about Jesus tend to represent the sword-wielding Roman army as Italian, the Roman auxiliary units stationed in Judaea were, in fact, ethnically mixed and would have consisted of a substantial percentage of people from Judaea and the greater province of Syria. In the provinces, these auxiliary soldiers acted as the empire's local police forces.[21] Locals and foreigners with swords were together tasked with protecting the empire's subjects in the provinces. They spent most of their time maintaining the "peace" by violently suppressing anything resembling a revolt by Roman subjects.

But many inhabitants of the Roman Empire weren't confident enough in the Roman Peace and its military enforcers to leave their swords at home when traveling. While laws would have varied in different times and places, it appears that Roman officials generally allowed people to carry weapons on roads while traveling but not in cities. This remains a matter of debate among scholars because there is little evidence one way or the other as to whether civilians were permitted to carry weapons in the cities of the Roman Empire.[22]

What seems clear, regardless, is that any unsheathing of a sword by a civilian in the context of a city could be viewed as a revolutionary action.[23] Josephus explains that during the run-up to the First Jewish Revolt, one group of anti-Roman Jewish rebels known as the Sicarii (Dagger-Wielders) carried daggers in Jerusalem during festivals and murdered their pro-Roman enemies, including certain Jewish leaders.[24] The "Judaea captured" coins minted by the Romans after the First Jewish Revolt even depict arms surrounding the captive Judaeans as a way to signify that Judaeans were violent rebels against Roman law and order (figure 16). It was rebels like these men from whom the gospel writers were so eager to differentiate Jesus, as we've seen.

Don't get me wrong: ancient Roman authors were no less xenophobic than American right-wing politicians. But they expressed their ethnic prejudices against outsiders differently. Whereas the modern American Far Right advances a nationalist agenda that seeks to separate white Christian America from racial, ethnic, and religious others, many ancient Roman authors embraced an imperialist agenda that sought to subject ethnic and religious others to Roman hegemony. Both discourses rely on problematic representations of ethnic outsiders as inferior people, but to different ends. The current American Far Right seeks to exclude certain foreign persons, but the Romans would have endeavored to dominate them.[25]

Another major difference between the ancient and modern contexts of ethnic prejudice and immigration involves citizenship. While modern immigration debates focus on immigrants' suitability for US citizenship, the majority of residents in the Roman provinces were not even enfranchised as Roman citizens during the New Testament period. In the eastern provinces where the Jesus movement took root, only a small percentage of inhabitants enjoyed the privileges of Roman citizenship. The overwhelming majority of the population of the provinces consisted of noncitizen residents and slaves.[26]

The only legal impediments to immigration in the Roman Empire were tolls for crossing district and provincial borders. There were no passports, visas, or other immigration documents.[27] Roman officials weren't concerned about noncitizens living in lands they claimed as their own, but they also didn't pass up any opportunity to collect revenue from them.

The beliefs and practices of Christ followers were able to spread rapidly around the Mediterranean because the Roman Empire didn't erect giant border walls between its different provinces and peoples.[28] As the Jesus movement expanded, it encompassed not only Jews but also a diverse group that the New Testament writings label *ta ethnē*—that is "the nations," also known as "Gentiles." Paul professed that in Christ "there is no longer Jew or Greek" (Gal. 3:28), and the author of Colossians expanded this inclusive ethic to the "barbarian" and "Scythian" (Col. 3:11). It also developed an increasingly international identity and began to embrace the positive roles of the noncitizen as defined in the Hebrew Bible. The Hebrew scriptures present diverse views on the treatment of foreigners that range from the legitimation of genocide (e.g., the conquest of Canaan in the book of Joshua) and the authorization to keep non-Israelites as slaves (Lev. 25:44) to commands to treat immigrants like Israelite citizens (Lev. 19:33–34).[29]

The early Christ followers found different ways to forge a common identity that connected believers across racial/ethnic and citizenship boundaries. They often used the "resident alien" and exile motifs in the Hebrew Bible as a way to include themselves among Israel without necessarily affirming the ethnic identity of Israelites. The author of 1 Peter, for instance, describes believers as "exiles" and "aliens" who nevertheless form part of the "household of God."[30] The tractate known as Hebrews similarly construes believers in Christ as "strangers and sojourners" while extending God's promise of land to the Israelites to followers of Christ in the form of a heavenly land.[31] According to the apostle Paul, who cast believers as Christ's imperial subjects, "Our citizenship is in heaven" (Phil. 3:20).[32] The author of Ephesians added that "you are no longer strangers and aliens, but you are citizens with the saints and also members of the household of God" (Eph. 2:19).

Not only did the earliest Christ followers form ethnically diverse communities and create networks across provincial borders and citizenship boundaries, but some also imagined themselves as resident aliens with respect to Israel. Christianity's success depended in large part on the Roman Empire's fluid provincial borders and the earliest communities' ability to provide noncitizens with a sense of belonging. The rub was that believers had to submit themselves to Christ and his transethnic empire to gain access to this glorious citizenship in heaven.

THE BORDER BETWEEN MATTHEW AND LUKE

In response to the worsening global refugee crisis, Pope Francis proclaimed in June 2014, "We believe that Jesus was a refugee, had to flee to save his life, with Saint Joseph and Mary, had to leave for Egypt." After Trump issued his "Muslim ban" in 2017, the renowned civil rights advocate Rev. Al Sharpton concurred with the pope in a tweet asking Christians to "remember to thank God for his son, Jesus a refugee who fled to Egypt."[33]

Republican influencers can't stand the idea that Jesus was a refugee. The hosts of *Fox and Friends* attacked Sharpton for his tweet, calling it inaccurate according to the Bible. As evidence that Sharpton was wrong and didn't know his Bible, they quoted tweets from random viewers saying that Jesus went to Egypt to pay his taxes. "He paid his taxes unlike you," one said, prompting the four racist anchors to suggest that Sharpton's ministerial credentials must have been a handout.

Paula White-Cain took a somewhat different position when defending the Trump administration's border separation policy and detention of immigrants. According to her, it's true that Jesus was a refugee because he lived in Egypt for three and a half years. "But it was not illegal," she insists. "If he had broken the law, then he would have been sinful and he would not have been our Messiah."[34]

White-Cain's view assumes that Jesus was sinless and that his period of refuge in Egypt therefore must have been legal (because "illegal" in her view is not only a type of person but a sinful type of person). She's right on just one count: if Jesus's family went to Egypt, this action would have been legal. But the reason is not that they went through some legal process of immigration, pausing while their lives were on the line to process their paperwork. It would have been legal because crossing provincial borders in the Roman Empire was like crossing state borders today. Jesus's family wouldn't have had to show papers.

The Twitter commentators cited as authorities on *Fox and Friends* didn't appeal to Jesus's sinlessness like White-Cain. Instead, they patched the story of the flight of Jesus's family to Egypt in Matthew together with the narrative in Luke that Jesus's family went to Bethlehem to pay their census taxes into a fiction that contradicts both sources.

Matthew and Luke are the only sources for narratives of Jesus's birth in the New Testament, and they differ significantly in their details. Luke explains that Jesus was born in Bethlehem (just across the border from Jerusalem, in modern Palestine) and that his parents had to register for the census there instead of Nazareth—the Galilean village about eighty miles away where they had been living—because Bethlehem was Joseph's hometown. Luke's gospel mentions nothing about Herod trying to kill Jesus or a flight to Egypt.

Matthew states that Jesus was born in Bethlehem but doesn't imply that his family had been in the Galilee beforehand and doesn't mention a census. In a dream, an angel appeared to Joseph to tell him to take his family and "flee to Egypt, and remain there until I tell you; for Herod is about to search for the child, to destroy him" (Matt. 2:13). After they escaped, Matthew says, Herod had all children two years or younger in and around Bethlehem killed. Jesus's family returned to Egypt only after an angel told Joseph that Herod had died. Joseph, however, was worried that Herod's son Archelaus, who became ruler of Judaea, would continue his father's quest to destroy Jesus. In Matthew, Joseph only ever took his family to Nazareth to avoid Archelaus, since Herod's other son, Antipas, ruled the Galilee. They remained refugees in Nazareth.

Little, if anything, in these stories is historically reliable. The historical Jesus was likely born in Nazareth. This is why Mark, the earliest New Testament gospel, doesn't mention his birth in Bethlehem. Matthew and Luke share the tradition that placed his birth in Bethlehem because this is where the Messiah descended from King David was supposed to be born according to certain interpretations of the Hebrew scriptures.[35]

Luke, moreover, misdates the census to a time when Herod was still alive. The Roman provincial census wasn't taken in Judaea until direct Roman rule was established there in 6 CE, after Archelaus was deposed and long after Herod's death in 4 BCE.[36]

Matthew's story of the "massacre of the innocents" taps into Jewish polemical traditions that Herod was a tyrant who killed "old and young."[37] Because Herod did execute three of his own sons on charges of treason, even the emperor Augustus supposedly joked that he'd rather be a pig in Judaea than a son of Herod.[38] But it is very unlikely that Herod, however maniacal he may have been, orchestrated a mass murder of young children without it leaving any other trace in our ancient sources. It would be especially shocking that Josephus, who spared no details when describing Herod's missteps, failed to mention this atrocity.

According to Matthew's narrative, Jesus's family were refugees, full stop. They were refugees in Egypt and refugees again in the Galilee. First, they fled their place of residence to escape a tyrant trying to kill Jesus, and then they immigrated to another place to avoid the possibility of a similar situation arising with the tyrant's son. Fortunately for Jesus's family, they weren't separated at any of the borders they crossed. They weren't put into detention cells.

But Matthew's story is fanciful. The author of this gospel likely invented this story to make Jesus into a New Moses. Just as Moses gave the Israelites the Torah on Mount Sinai, Matthew's Jesus gave his followers his interpretation of the Law in his Sermon on the Mount (Luke, who didn't place as much emphasis on Jesus as a New Moses, said that the Sermon was given on a plain). The Torah is more important to Jesus in Matthew than in any of the other gospels. "Do not think," Matthew's Jesus cautions, "that I have come to abolish the Law or the Prophets; I have come not to abolish but to fulfill."[39] Just as Moses traditionally gave the Israelites the five books of the Torah, Jesus's teaching in Matthew takes the form of five discrete discourses.[40]

Matthew also depicted Jesus's birth as miraculous just like Moses's. While the infant Moses was saved from a pharaoh who was trying to kill all the newborn Hebrew boys in Egypt, the infant Jesus was saved from a king trying to kill all the newborn boys in Bethlehem by fleeing to Egypt. The rabbis in Matthew's context emphasized the Law of Moses as the authoritative source of their teachings. Matthew responded by casting Jesus as a New Moses and his ethics as an authoritative interpretation of the Torah.

Republican influencers' patching together of Matthew and Luke to save Jesus from being a refugee doesn't work. Luke is clear that Joseph took his family to Bethlehem to pay the census taxes, not from Bethlehem to Egypt. Matthew is clear that Jesus fled Bethlehem to escape the king, not to pay taxes. These stories are incompatible.

Republican influencers sometimes bring teachings of Jesus into the immigration debate. For instance, the conservative Roman Catholic apologist Dave Armstrong cites Luke 11:21–22: "When a strong man, fully armed, guards his castle, his property is safe. But when one stronger than he attacks him and overpowers him, he takes away his armor in which he trusted and divides his plunder." Armstrong claims that, through this teaching, "Jesus explicitly endorses the perfectly permissible notion of self-defense and protection of what one owns (including one's house). This is clearly analogous to countries establishing sensible laws for entrance of immigrants."[41]

Luke 11:21–22 is a superb prooftext for protectionists because they can contort it to mean that people should bear arms to defend themselves from immigrant invaders. And it does seem to mean that when pried loose from its literary context. In both Luke and Mark, however, Jesus issues this teaching in the midst of his debate with Beelzebul, the ruler of the demons.[42] Jesus contends that he can defeat the powers of Beelzebul because he casts out demons by the "finger of God." He offers the strongman comparison as an allegory in which the armed strong man is Satan, protected by his demons, and the stronger attacker is Jesus, whose exorcisms take away Satan's armor and divide his kingdom of demons. According to Armstrong, then, Americans should be like Satan and guard themselves from Jesus!

Immigration is one of the only political issues where Republican influencers want to see more government intervention. Even Drollinger, who interprets Jesus as a prophet of Small Government, cites Romans 13:4 to support a government crackdown on illegal immigration: "For the authority does not bear the sword in vain!" The same verse that was repeatedly used to perpetuate American slavery is still serving the interests of racism.[43]

But it's not racist at all according to Drollinger, who protests too much: "To procedurally exclude *foreign* individuals who might be criminals, traitors, or terrorists, or who possess communicable diseases is not racist in the least! It is good stewardship to protect the citizens of a nation who have unmistakably pledged their allegiance to that nation and their fellow citizens!"[44] On the basis of his anachronistic imposition of modern understandings of legal immigration onto anti-immigrant sentiments in the Old Testament, Drollinger argues that it is racist only to exclude legal immigrants. It's not racist to exclude foreigners, as he interprets the Bible, because they *might* be criminals, traitors, terrorists, or disease carriers.

That assumption is the very definition of racism.

EYE FOR AN EYE, SWORD FOR A SWORD?

Rodney Howard-Browne, a member of Trump's Evangelical Advisory Board, posted new signs on his Florida church doors two days after a gunman armed with a semiautomatic rifle killed twenty-six people in a Baptist church in Sutherland Springs, Texas, in November 2017. The new "Warning" signs, an obvious publicity stunt, said, "Please know this is not a gun free zone— we are heavily armed—any attempt will be dealt with deadly force—yes we are a church and we will protect our people."[45] Howard-Browne responded to the massacre with the same ethic as Republican legislators in Texas: guns protect people from guns, especially in churches.

This progun ethic gels with what Trump considers his "favorite" Bible verse: "eye for an eye." The president admitted that it is "not a particularly nice thing," but he thinks that this teaching is important because it protects "us" from outsiders. "They're taking our jobs," he declaimed, "they're taking our money, and they're taking the health of our country." Trump implied that guns protect white people from immigrants, whom he has repeatedly described as violent criminals and invaders, echoing the hate speech of white nationalists and leading gun rights proponents like the NRA chief executive Wayne LaPierre.[46] Trump made this connection between guns and protection from invaders even more explicit by trying to relegate background checks for gun purchases to immigration reform in the wake of the El Paso shooting.[47]

Christian critics from both sides of the aisle were quick to censure Trump for glorifying the ancient Israelite law of retaliation (*lex talionis*) without even acknowledging that Jesus had upended it. Leviticus 24:19–20, like the legal codes of many other ancient cultures, stipulates that "anyone who maims another shall suffer the same injury in return: fracture for fracture, eye for eye, tooth for tooth; the injury inflicted is the injury to be suffered."

As part of his effort to script Jesus as a New Moses, Matthew recounts Jesus reforming this law in his Sermon on the Mount: "You have heard it said, 'An eye for an eye and a tooth for a tooth.' But I say to you, Do not resist an evildoer. But if anyone strikes you on the right cheek, turn the other also " (Matt. 5:38–39). Trump isn't so fond of that last part.

For progun Christian influencers like Howard-Browne, the right to bear arms is a "God-given" freedom that must be defended from the regulations of Big Government. Gun rights advocates tend to view any form of gun control as an attempt to restrict the individual's freedom. Many gun control advocates aren't pursuing a ban on guns, though. They want, instead, to ban semiautomatic assault rifles and to block people with violent criminal records or mental health conditions from purchasing guns.

Before the NRA was taken over by right-wing Second Amendment fundamentalists, some of its leaders actually supported gun control. The NRA was founded right after the Civil

War as a club for people interested in hunting or competitive shooting. It was a men's club that promoted guns as tokens of masculinity, often romanticizing manliness through problematic fantasies where rugged cowboys wielding guns brought law and order to the Western frontier by killing Indians and bandits.[48]

Still, the NRA didn't become a gun rights advocacy group until the 1970s. The assassinations of the 1960s, and especially the revelation that JFK's killer obtained his rifle through a mail-order ad in the NRA's magazine *American Rifleman,* prompted attempts to restrict access to guns. Five days after JFK's murder, the executive vice president of the NRA supported gun control legislation, saying, "We do not think that any sane American, who calls himself an American, can object to placing into this bill the instrument which killed the president of the United States."[49]

Gun rights hard-liners in the NRA disagreed, leading to a division in the leadership of the NRA. At an event known as the "Revolt at Cincinnati" in 1977, the NRA's hard-liners executed a coup that expelled the NRA's old guard from their positions of leadership.[50] From this point on, the NRA lobbied against all gun control legislation and became increasingly allied with the Christian Right and the Moral Majority.

Major Jessica Dawson, a professor of sociology at West Point, has analyzed language used in *American Rifleman* from 1975 to 2018 and observed that the organization's leaders have described the Second Amendment as a "God-given right" since the Revolt at Cincinnati but that its usage of this phrase dramatically increased after Obama's election in 2008. This surge coincided with the reactionary nationalism of the Tea Party and other white right-wing opponents of Obama. LaPierre even invoked the conspiracy theory that Obama wasn't born in America in his defense of gun rights in 2009: "The National Rifle Association will always defend that God-given birthright from every enemy out there, both foreign and domestic!"[51]

By describing their individualist interpretation of the Second Amendment as "God-given," the NRA denies that the government has any authority to regulate access to guns (or the multibillion-dollar firearms industry).[52] When Charlton Heston, DeMille's Moses, was president of the NRA from 1998 to 2003, he exploited his image as a cowboy-Moses to portray the Ten Amendments as God-given just like the Ten Commandments.[53]

Christian gun control opponents often note that Jesus's disciples were armed, according to the gospels. Larry Pratt, executive director emeritus of Gun Owners of America (a firearms lobby that is even more adamant about fighting gun control than the NRA) and former Republican member of the Virginia House of Delegates, claims that the founders deemed owning and carrying guns a God-given right just as Jesus did. Christ commanded his disciples to buy swords just before his crucifixion, according to Pratt, because he believed they had the right to defend themselves. He told them not to deploy their weapons only because it would interfere with his mission to redeem believers from sin through his death and resurrection.[54]

"It just boggles my mind," Falwell Junior says in agreement with Pratt's position, "that anybody would be against what Jesus told his disciples in Luke 22:36. He told them if they had to sell their coat to buy a sword to do it because he knew danger was coming and he wanted them to defend themselves."[55] Falwell Junior encourages the Evangelical students at his Liberty University to carry guns and practice their shooting skills at the campus shooting range.[56]

The arrest scene in the gospels that Pratt and Falwell Junior have interpreted as Jesus's support for the Second Amendment appears in all four gospels.[57] In Mark's version, when Judas arrives with an armed crowd of chief priests, scribes, and elders to arrest Jesus, "one of those who stood near drew his sword and struck the slave of the High Priest, cutting off his ear" (Mark 14:47). Although it is not certain, by describing the disciple who drew a sword as "one of those who stood near," Mark gives the impression that Jesus's whole group was armed. Jesus says to the crowd, "Have you come out with swords and clubs to arrest me as though I were a bandit?" He then prevents a brawl by saying, "Let the scriptures be fulfilled" (Mark 14:48–49) and complying with his arrest.

Matthew and Luke, who used Mark as a source, weren't as willing to present Jesus and his disciples as an armed mob. Matthew added that Jesus actually rebuked the disciple: "Put your sword back into its place; for all who take the sword will perish by the sword" (Matt. 26:52). Jesus then assures the defensive disciple that God could have sent twelve legions of angels if he wanted to resist his arrest but that then the scriptures would not be fulfilled.

Luke went even further to downplay the image of Jesus's group as an armed gang. Before the arrest, Jesus tells his disciples, "The one who has no sword must sell his cloak and buy one" (Luke 22:36). He says this, Luke emphasizes, so that the prophecy in Isaiah 53:12 will be fulfilled: "And he was counted among the lawless" (Luke 22:37). Once the disciples acquire two swords, Jesus decides that "it is enough"—enough for him to be counted among the outlaws as Isaiah prophesied. When a disciple cuts off the ear of the slave of the high priest during the ensuing arrest, Jesus says, "No more of this!" (Luke 22:51). Luke also adds the detail that Jesus healed the slave's ear, exemplifying his teaching to love your enemies.

John narrates a version of the story that isn't directly based on Mark but also offers a less violent image of Jesus's group than

Mark. John names the disciple who draws his sword as Simon Peter and the slave as Malchus. Like Matthew, John describes Jesus rebuking Peter—"Put your sword back into its sheath" (John 18:11)—so that his destiny may be fulfilled.

Historians and theologians of varied political positions have long debated whether the historical Jesus was a violent revolutionary like the different rebel groups that were present in first-century Judaea.[58] The fact that our earliest gospel, Mark, depicts Jesus's disciples as armed and doesn't depict Jesus clearly rebuking the disciple who attacked the high priest's slave supports the revolutionary hypothesis. Yet even in Mark, Jesus doesn't allow a violent clash to happen. Mark also doesn't explain whether the disciple who pulls his sword is holding it for self-defense.

The Greek word used for "sword" in these accounts, *machaira,* could just refer to the knife used to sacrifice lambs for Passover. Many ordinary Jews in Jerusalem would have carried these knives on Passover, the night of Jesus's arrest in Mark, Matthew, and Luke.[59] But it could also refer to a much more disastrous sword like that which Matthew's Jesus vows to wield when he will return to the earth in an apocalyptic fury (Matt. 10:34).[60]

We can't determine on the basis of our surviving sources whether the historical Jesus was, in fact, a violent revolutionary with motives similar to those of contemporaneous rebel groups in Judaea. What we can detect, however, is that the gospel writers were very careful to show that Jesus was *not* a rebellious bandit.[61] As we have seen, in Mark, Matthew, and Luke, Jesus turns this potential charge on the Temple leaders by calling the Temple a "cave of bandits." Differentiating the followers of Jesus from Jewish rebels against the Roman Empire was a key survival strategy for the churches in the postwar decades in which the gospels were written.

None of the gospels describes carrying a sword as an expression of the God-given right to self-defense. If we read only Mark, we might assume that Jesus and his disciples carried swords for self-defense. All three of the other gospels are clear that Jesus rejected the use of swords to defend him. Matthew and John do not resolve the question of whether Jesus rejected the use of weapons because he was opposed to violence or simply because they would interfere with him fulfilling his destiny. Luke, however, does imply that Jesus rejected the use of violence. He does so in two ways: by relating that Jesus healed the slave's ear and by discarding Mark's use of the fulfillment-of-destiny motif as Jesus's reason for calling off the disciple with the sword.

The divergent gospel narratives about Jesus's arrest do not amount to an adequate biblical support for the right to self-defense. Even if they did, they by no means serve as a God-given justification for the government relinquishing any control over background checks and the purchase of semiautomatic weapons. The disciple who tried to defend Jesus was not, according to the gospels, firing an AR-15 he had purchased with his hunting license.

•   •   •

When a nineteen-year-old white nationalist killed one person and injured three others by firing his legally obtained AR-15 rifle at a congregation of Jews celebrating Passover in their synagogue in Poway, California, in April 2019, he believed that he was exercising his God-given right to self-defense. He embodied a Far Right version of the Christian nationalism that the NRA and other right-wing organizations have relied on since the 1970s to protect the gun industry by demonizing outsiders.

Before his attack, the shooter posted a manifesto online that teems with toxic white nationalist ideas anchored by anti-Semitic interpretations of the New Testament.[62] He was eager to address potential objections to his actions. "How can you call yourself a Christian and do this?" he wrote. "Surely the Bible calls for you to love your enemies?"

After reproving people who supposedly twist the words of the Bible and ignore its historical context, he explains that "it is not loving towards your friend to let him be murdered. *It is not loving towards your enemy—the thief—to let him murder.* A child can understand the concept of self-defense. It is unlawful and cowardly to stand on the sidelines as the European people are genocided around you. I did not want to have to kill Jews. But they have given us no other option."[63]

In the mind of this deranged and deluded young man, the New Testament is divinely inspired historical proof that white Europeans must defend themselves against invasive Jews: murdering Jews before they have a chance to murder people of European ancestry *is* loving one's enemies.

The shooter's manifesto is a disturbing example of how right-wing interpretations of Jesus with no historical basis have gained credence in some circles as history. While his actions were radical, his beliefs do not stray far from widespread right-wing interpretations of the gospels. He interprets the interethnic communities of early Christ followers as xenophobic white Christians, and he derives from Jesus's teachings a reason for using weapons to defend himself from outsiders. In the process, he completely ignores the Jewishness of Jesus and his disciples and misunderstands the sociohistorical tensions involved in the emergence of Jesus's movement within Judaism. He also confuses protection with aggression.

The Second Amendment has from its origins been used to assert white supremacy over people who are falsely vilified as violent outsiders, whether they are Native Americans, African

Americans, Latinos, Muslims, or Jews. But it was not until the 1970s that gun lobbyists and the emergent Christian Right devised the theological and political fiction that the Second Amendment protects the God-given right of any individual to own any type of gun without any government oversight. This dangerous nationalist narrative only protects the gun industry and repeatedly puts marginalized communities at risk.

Nowhere in the gospels does Jesus say that the solution to sword violence is giving more people swords. If the gospel writers' Jesus were celebrating Passover in the Poway synagogue when the shooter raised his AR-15, would he have pulled out his own AR-15 to shoot the shooter? An eye for an eye?

Of course not. Luke's Jesus, at least, would have said, "No more of this!"

CHAPTER NINE

The End of the World

THE RAPTURE CHANGES EVERYTHING. That's the core message of the "prophecy expert" Tim LaHaye's numerous pop-apocalyptic books. The Left Behind series, composed by the sportswriter Jerry Jenkins from LaHaye's notes, have sold more than sixty million copies since 1995. The books are fictional novels, but they advance LaHaye's genuine interpretations of prophecies about the end of days. It is hard to overstate the influence of these books on the end-times expectations of American Christians, regardless of their denominational affiliation. Falwell described the first novel of the series as having a greater impact on Christianity "than that of any other book in modern times, outside the Bible."[1]

The end-times scenarios anticipated by LaHaye are called "premillennial" because they posit that Christ will return before the millennium, a thousand years in which Christ will reign over earth, leading up to the Last Judgment. When Christ returns, he will "rapture"—that is, take away from the earth— righteous Christian believers and leave the sinners and infidels behind to face their violent demise and eternal damnation.

By patching Jesus's description of a "great tribulation" during the end-times in Matthew 24:21 together with other texts, premillennial preachers have determined that there will be a period of tribulation on earth prior to Christ's millennial reign. But they disagree about when the rapture will occur in relation to the millennium. The prevailing view among Evangelicals, promoted by LaHaye, Lindsey, Graham, Falwell, and others, is that Christ will rapture believers prior to the period of tribulation and will then return with his raptured elect to reign over the earth.

The idea that Christ will soon come to inaugurate either the period of tribulation or the millennium itself positions modern believers on the brink of the Kingdom of God. Current affairs, whether cultural changes or political events, may thus be identified as signs of the end-times. In recent years, apocalyptic preachers among the Christian Right have used political rhetoric about the end-times to deny that climate change is caused by humans and to promote support for the state of Israel, among other things.

LaHaye neatly lays out both of these positions in his book *Global Warning: Are We on the Brink of World War III?*, coauthored by Ed Hindson, dean emeritus of Liberty University's School of Divinity.[2] The title is a play on "global warming"; *Global Warning* suggests that Al Gore and the UN have devised an elaborate scam to get the government to regulate carbon dioxide emissions. LaHaye and Hindson don't deny that there has been an uptick in famines, plagues, and earthquakes in recent history; instead, they use Jesus's warnings about the "birth pangs" of the end-times in Matthew 24–25 to cast these natural disasters as signs from God that the end is near.[3] Humans should not interfere with God's plan for the earth, the authors caution.

In a subsequent chapter, LaHaye and Hindson recognize the "restoration" of the state of Israel and the destruction of its Muslim opponents as a prerequisite for the end-times. "The decimation of Israel's enemies could open the opportunity for the rebuilding of the Jewish temple on the site of the Temple Mount in Jerusalem," they write, implying the destruction of the Muslim Dome of the Rock and Al-Aqsa Mosque. LaHaye and Hindson's Zionism is not pro-Judaism. "The manner in which God destroys Israel's enemies," they continue, "may open the hearts of the Jews to the truth of the gospel, which they will be responsible for disseminating to the world during the tribulation because Christians have been removed by the rapture."[4] If Jews don't accept Christ, they'll be wiped out just like Muslims.

Apocalyptic fantasies like LaHaye's appropriate the Bible's terrifying images of the Last Judgment to exhort readers to political action or inaction in the present. The biblical book that serves as the source of most modern end-times speculation, Revelation (aka "the Apocalypse"), similarly uses apocalyptic rhetoric as a political strategy, but it was written by a Jewish follower of Christ as a critique of the Roman Empire. And its author, John of Patmos, had never heard of the "pretribulation rapture."

APOCALYPTIC POLITICS IN THE NEW TESTAMENT WORLD

With their city in flames, crowds of Jews took refuge in a portico of the Jerusalem Temple, waiting for God to intervene to save them from the encroaching Roman soldiers. On that tragic day in 70 CE, Roman soldiers set fire to the portico from below and not a soul survived. According to the Jewish historian Josephus, these people were the victims of false prophets who had persuaded them that the Temple destruction was part of an end-times scenario in which God's angelic army would swoop in to rescue the righteous.[5]

Even if Josephus's story about the demise of these hopeful apocalypticists is not historically reliable, surviving texts show that there were Jews who would have understood the war with the Romans as the onslaught of the apocalypse. What is interesting about Josephus's account is his understanding of popular apocalyptic prophecies as causing people to wait and hope instead of flee or engage in armed resistance. Josephus has captured a fundamental dynamic of apocalyptic thinking: apocalyptic preachers persuade people that their world is so corrupt that there is nothing they can do to save it; they can only hope and pray that God will disrupt history to transform the world.

The word *apocalypse* derives from the Greek word *apocalypsis,* which means "revelation" or "unveiling." In ordinary English, the term is most often used hyperbolically as a label for some epic catastrophe. In more technical terms, though, it refers to a literary genre in which an angel (in most cases) communicates divine revelations about cosmic mysteries or the end of the world to a human recipient.[6]

The angels of these texts should be jarring to those of us accustomed to thinking of angels as sweet children cloaked in white sheets and crowned with garland halos, or as Precious Moments knickknacks collecting dust on a shelf. In the ancient apocalyptic imagination, angels are androgynous heavenly beings. They are God's holy warriors responsible for the redemption of the righteous and the violent destruction of the wicked. Apocalypses are military fantasies that position angels on God's front lines.

Many ancient and modern Christians have accepted apocalypses as true predictions of things to come. But the prophecies of the future contained in these texts were mostly written *after the fact* and then attributed to ancient heroes. For instance, the only literary apocalypse in the Hebrew Bible, Daniel, was written by a Jewish author around 164 BCE but attributed to a sixth-century visionary named Daniel. It was written after many of the events it prophesied, which is why they are correct. This veracity endows the author's political perspective, ethical pronouncements, and predictions of an imminent end of the world with legitimacy and authority.[7]

Apocalyptic discourse addresses a regular set of topics, whether these are expressed in the form of a literary apocalypse, a book written in another literary genre, or other media. Most strikingly, apocalyptic discourse envisions alternative worlds situated in different times (e.g., a new age) and/or different spaces (e.g., the heavens). It also tends to focus on topics such as dream visions, dramatic symbols, heavenly intermediaries like angels and messiahs, cosmic speculation, catastrophe, judgment, and the afterlife. Apocalyptic discourse also relies on two main theological themes, dualism (a rigid antagonism between forces of good and evil) and determinism (God's control over history).[8]

Apocalyptic discourse is political discourse.[9] It aims to convince people that a cosmic struggle between the forces of good and evil is unfolding in historical events. Certain individuals and groups, so it goes, are aligned with the forces of evil, and the text provides insights into how one can join the ranks of the righteous who will be saved in the end-times.

A development of classical prophecy, apocalyptic discourse first emerged among the Israelites with prophets like Ezekiel, Zechariah, and Joel in the wake of the destruction of the first Jerusalem Temple by the Babylonians. Whereas earlier prophets like Amos and Jeremiah prophesied God's role in transforming the present social order, the prophets who experienced foreign conquest and rule had a more fatalistic view of history. They envisioned much more dramatic transformations of the world than their prophetic forebears, but they didn't yet imagine the resurrection or eternal life for the righteous.[10]

The apocalypse genre didn't become widespread among Jewish authors until the periods in which Israel was subject to Hellenistic and Roman rulers. In response to the repressive rule of the Seleucid monarch Antiochus IV Epiphanes, Jewish authors wrote apocalypses that envisaged the eternal liberation of the Jews and the destruction of the Seleucid Empire and its collaborators. The author of the book of Daniel attributed to Daniel a vision of four beasts that represent the empires of the Babylonians, Persians, Medes, and Macedonians. Out of the fourth beast comes a little horn that is responsible for desecrating the Jerusalem Temple. This horn is a coded reference to Antiochus IV.

Like all apocalyptic discourses, Daniel uses carefully encoded language and symbols to offer critical commentary on a current political situation—namely, the perceived harshness of the religious and economic policies of Antiochus IV.[11] After accurately "prophesying" events up to the reign of Antiochus IV, the book of Daniel offers a vision of a heavenly messiah "like a Son of Man"—probably originally understood to be the archangel Michael—who would establish an everlasting kingdom, deliver the holy ones, and initiate the resurrection of the dead.

The book of Daniel encourages its audience to accept the teachings of the Wise (11:33–35)—a persecuted group that probably included the author of Daniel. It urges people to accept a political view that rejects collaboration with the Seleucids, but it doesn't exhort people to engage in active resistance. The Apocalypse of Weeks, a text written at the same time, envisions the righteous as participants in the destruction of the wicked at the Last Judgment (I joke with my students that this text's vision of judgment is like Daniel's if rewritten by Tarantino as a revenge fantasy). But even this text doesn't urge readers to take any political action prior to God's intervention in history.[12] Like the Jews left waiting for God on the Temple Mount in 70 CE, the audiences of these apocalypses are instructed that it is too late for their actions to change the world. Only God can improve their well-being.

Jewish authors began to use apocalyptic discourse to critique Roman rule shortly after the Roman general Pompey first conquered Judaea in 63 BCE. The Psalms of Solomon, a noncanonical collection of eighteen psalms attributed to King Solomon, prophesied (after the fact) Pompey's conquest and death. Another text known as the Testament of Moses prophesied (after the fact) Herod's tyrannical rule and the rise of a corrupt priestly ruling class in the first century CE. After the Temple destruction, apocalypses called 4 Ezra and 2 Baruch used their revered ancient namesakes and the setting of the Babylonian destruction of the First Temple to reflect on the Romans destroying the Second Temple and reassure their audiences that, as before, God would redeem his people and destroy their imperial overlords.

The only full-blown literary apocalypse in the New Testament is the book of Revelation, but most of the New Testament texts dabble in apocalyptic discourse. Many historians agree that Jesus himself was likely an apocalyptic preacher, although they dispute over whether he understood himself as the Messiah or whether this idea was developed by his followers after his death.[13] With subtle differences, Mark, Matthew, and Luke each present Jesus's life, ministry, death, and resurrection as the beginnings of the gradual emergence of the Kingdom of God—

as a "mustard seed" that will continue to grow.[14] John takes this "realized" approach to the end-times farther than the other gospels, focusing on a believer's ability to transcend history through the knowledge of God offered by Jesus rather than through a militaristic end-times scenario in which Jesus returns.[15]

Modern premillennial Christians claim that the Bible envisions an end-times schema that includes the rapture. This rapture is not in the Bible. Its proponents have devised their rapture theology by patching together texts from Ezekiel, Daniel, Matthew, and Revelation and then reading them in light of verses from 1 Thessalonians.

With the letter known as 1 Thessalonians, the apostle Paul was responding to concerns among the Thessalonian believers that some people in their community had died but Christ had not yet returned. Paul assured them that Christ's return was still imminent and that the dead would still participate in the resurrection: "For the Lord himself, with a cry of command, with the archangel's call and with the sound of God's trumpet, will descend from heaven, and the dead in Christ will rise first. Then we who are alive, who are left, will be caught up in the clouds together with them to meet the Lord in the air" (1 Thess. 4:16–17).

The Greek word translated here as "caught up" is the basis for what premillennialists interpret as the rapture. Our English word *rapture* derives from the Latin verb *rapere* (seize, carry off), which is used to translate the Greek verb *harpazō* (seize, carry off) in 1 Thessalonians 4:17. Note, however, that Paul never indicates that this meeting with the Lord in the air is a separate event from the Second Coming in which Christ establishes his dominion. On the contrary, Paul's description of Christ's descent being heralded by the militaristic cry of command, archangel's call, and trumpet blast depicts this descent in the same way that other Jewish texts from this time portray the Messiah ushering in the Kingdom of God.[16]

As the New Testament scholar and Lutheran minister Barbara Rossing explains in her book *The Rapture Exposed,* the pretribulation rapture is a modern idea that fuses this problematic interpretation of 1 Thessalonians with speculative interpretations of cryptic prophecies from other biblical texts.[17] The Anglo-Irish Protestant minister John Nelson Darby (1800–1882) was the first to systematize and popularize a premillennial rapture theology in which Christ returns twice—first to rapture his church to heaven and a second time, after a seven-year tribulation, to establish God's kingdom on earth. Darby's infatuation with the end-times was at least in part a response to growing fears of Protestant decline during a period of Catholic resurgence in Ireland.[18]

Through at least six preaching tours, Darby exported his ideas about the rapture and God's ordering of time according to intervals, or "dispensations," to North America. In this new setting, Darby's rapture theology fueled the pessimism of Evangelicals who were leery of social and cultural change in the aftermath of the Civil War.[19]

In the face of a rapidly changing world, these early proponents of premillennial dispensationalism urged listeners to sit tight until God comes. They distinguished themselves in this way from postmillennialists, who believed that humans should actively contribute to building the Kingdom of God on earth.[20]

Especially since the emergence of the Christian Right, premillennial preachers have also advocated human action on certain issues—namely, providing political and financial support for the state of Israel, where Christian Zionists believe exiled Jews will gather as the end-times begin to unfold. While this endorsement of political action contradicts the usual deterministic emphasis of premillennialism, it illustrates our key point about apocalyptic discourse: it is, more than anything else, an idiom of political persuasion.

RED DRAGON OR GREEN DRAGON?

"I do not know how many future generations we can count on before the Lord returns." When James Watts said these words in 1981, he wasn't staking a position on climate change. Since he was Ronald Reagan's newly appointed Evangelical Secretary of the Interior and a major opponent of regulations to prevent climate change, however, his words were instantly construed by environmentalists as a justification for his environmental apathy. Why sink resources into preventing climate change if Christ will soon return to bring an end to this world?

Recent studies have found that conservative Evangelicals' environmental apathy isn't as strictly tied to expectations of the end-times as their progressive detractors have assumed.[21] When interviewed, Evangelical climate change skeptics appeal more often to divine determinism—"God controls the weather"—than to the imminent destruction of the earth in the end-times as a foundation for rejecting scientific theories of anthropogenic (human-induced) climate change.

To be clear, 97 percent of the international scientific community asserts that humans are causing irreparable harm to the earth through their toxic levels of carbon emissions.[22] In September 2019, one hundred scientists from across the world contributed to a report by the UN's Intergovernmental Panel on Climate Change. The report documents how unchecked greenhouse gas emissions are increasing global temperatures and, as a result, melting glaciers and raising ocean levels.[23] Like their detractors, environmental activists are prone to presenting this evidence of climate change in apocalyptic terms in order to motivate action. This is why the Bulletin of the Atomic Scientists, a watchdog for nuclear mobilization and anthropogenic climate change, has kept its infamous Doomsday Clock set at two minutes to midnight since 2018.[24] Unlike apocalyptic discourses of climate change denial, however, the basic presuppositions of even the most radical and apocalyptic forms of environmentalism are supported by observable data analyzed by scientists over time.[25] Also, and this can't be emphasized enough, the nuclear scientists who use apocalyptic rhetoric want to stop the Doomsday Clock from striking midnight, not welcome some impending divine destruction of the earth.[26]

The Christian Right refuses to accept these scientists' evidence and warnings. Polls show that white Evangelicals are much more likely to deny climate change than people affiliated with other religious groups. Only 28 percent of white Evangelicals accept that climate change is a consequence of human activities according to a 2014 Pew Research Center poll. Meanwhile, 41 percent of white mainline Protestants, 56 percent of black Protestants, and 77 percent of Hispanic Catholics attribute climate change to human activity.[27]

Right-wing Christian influencers often dismiss climate change as a secular theory that, like evolution, denies God's control over nature. This paranoia about environmental science being a form of pagan nature worship suits the Christian Right's "embattled mentality"—their identity as defenders of a traditional culture against the abominations of modernity.[28]

Climate change denial is not a traditional Christian position, though. It is a political position that has been curated by Republican influencers in recent history. During the 1970s and '80s, Evangelicals became increasingly concerned with environmentalism—with "stewardship" of God's creation, or what is sometimes called "climate care."[29] By the 1990s, the Evangelical Left started to form environmentalist organizations like the Evangelical Environmental Network (founded in 1993).

There was a huge backlash among the Evangelical Right, eager as ever to decry transgressions against the free market. The leading voice of the climate change denial movement was E. Calvin Beisner, who widely promoted climate change denial in the 1990s. Beisner worked with a conservative think tank known as the Acton Institute to form the Interfaith Council for Environmental Stewardship, whose "Cornwall Declaration on Environmental Stewardship" (2000) was a major benchmark in the climate change denial movement. Signed by right-wing Protestant, Catholic, and Jewish faith leaders, this document advances a theology of "ecological stewardship" that rejects government action to curtail global warming. "We aspire to a world," the declaration states, "in which widespread economic freedom—which is integral to private, market economies—makes sound ecological stewardship available to ever greater numbers."[30]

Beisner and the pro–free market organization he helped to form, the Cornwall Alliance for the Stewardship of Creation (formerly the Interfaith Stewardship Alliance), are the beneficiaries of corporate oil money. Beisner holds positions of influence within the Acton Institute and the antienvironmental Committee for a Constructive Tomorrow, both of which receive funding from ExxonMobil, Chevron, and other corporate oil magnates like the Koch brothers and the Scaife family.[31]

The Cornwall Alliance and its political allies remain persistent in their attempts to influence the political allegiances of Christians. They regularly compete with the environmentalist

Evangelical Climate Initiative, which was formed in 2006, for the votes of Evangelicals.[32] In 2010, the Cornwall Alliance kicked off a campaign called Resisting the Green Dragon. It paints secular and Christian environmentalists with the same brush as a pagan "Green Religion" whose adherents idolize nature.

The Resisting the Green Dragon campaign has widely disseminated climate change denial propaganda among Christian churches and schools. Some of the most influential figures of the Christian Right appear in its twelve-part DVD series, which identifies environmentalism with Satan. By conflating environmentalism with the evils of Big Government and globalization, these videos instigate fears of a one-nation totalitarian government of the sort familiar to viewers from the pop apocalypticism of Lindsey, LaHaye and Jenkins, and televangelists like Pat Robertson.[33]

Apocalyptic discourse thus provides the language and symbols for the Christian Right's climate change skepticism. It is used to assert God's control over creation but also to color their liberal opponents as forces of evil. Its paradoxical message is that human activity doesn't change the climate, but human political activity—namely voting against environmentalism—can help slay the Green Dragon of environmentalism. As Falwell once massaged this paradox, if Christian conservatives are politically active, then "God can bless the country and before the rapture ... we can stay a free nation."[34]

The Cornwall Alliance's Green Dragon is an allusion to the dragon of the book of Revelation, but that dragon is red and it has seven heads and ten horns. Throughout history, Christians have interpreted this apocalypse's prophecies as relevant to their own times and imminent future, yet the book was written by a visionary named John from the island of Patmos to churches in seven cities in western Asia Minor (Turkey). John prefaced his apocalypse with seven discrete letters to these churches (chapters 1–3). The letters betray his interest in persuading members of these churches to avoid participation in certain Roman religious practices, like eating food that had been sacrificed to the Roman gods and divine emperors.

John's apocalypse is a vivid critique of the Roman Empire and especially its exploitative accumulation of wealth and its use of emperor worship as a strategy of political legitimation.[35] The book's Red Dragon is Satan, but this dragon is not alone in assaulting the churches. According to John's visions, the Red Dragon gave power, a throne, and authority to a Sea Beast, which represents the Roman Empire and its emperors.[36]

This Sea Beast bears the number 666, which modern conservatives have attributed to everyone from Hitler to Obama. In its original context, the 666 most likely referred to the emperor Nero. Transliterated into Hebrew letters, which also represent numbers, the name "Neron Caesar" adds up to 666. Some of our earliest manuscripts record the number as 616, which follows the alternative Hebrew transliteration of "Nero Caesar."[37]

The book itself was probably written two to three decades after Nero's tumultuous reign, during the rule of Domitian in the 90s CE. Even at this time, Nero's contested reputation— Was he the champion of the masses or an extravagant tyrant?— made him a convenient symbol for hopes of a political revolution and critiques of Roman imperial rule. In the decades after Nero's death in 68 CE, some Roman and Jewish authors believed that this controversial emperor would somehow return to redeem or destroy Rome, depending on whether the author admired Nero.[38] A Jewish apocalypse written in the early second century CE, for instance, slanders Nero as an evil serpent that pretended to be equal to God. This text even claims that Nero never died, as many were led to believe, but instead fled to Persia where he was preparing an army to sack Rome.[39] Revelation 13:3 assumes this same critical version of the legend about Nero's return when describing the Sea Beast recovering from a mortal wound that seemed to be a death blow.

Another monster, the Land Beast, is responsible for persuading people to worship the image of the Sea Beast and for causing anyone who engages in commerce to bear the mark of the Sea Beast.[40] In John's political critique, the Land Beast represents the priests and officials who promoted emperor worship. Because meat left over from sacrificing animals during emperor worship would enter local markets, Jews and Christians debated whether or not it was acceptable to eat.[41] Both in his letters to the churches and in his claim that participating in commerce is collusion with the Sea Beast, John insists that eating food sacrificed to the Roman emperors is a form of idolatry.

Like most apocalypses, Revelation fantasizes about the end of the earth occasioning the destruction of these alleged forces of evil. The book is rife with images of cosmic destruction like plagues, famines, and earthquakes. In its final chapters, Revelation explains that John "saw a new heaven and a new earth, for the first heaven and the first earth had passed away, and the sea was no more" (Rev. 21:1).

In quite the reverse of the rapture scenario, John envisions God and his heavenly Jerusalem descending to earth in Revelation 21:2–3. This has led some Christian environmentalist interpreters to emphasize transformation over destruction, implying that there will be continuity between the old earth and the new earth.[42] While the text does indeed allow for some continuity between the old earth and the new heaven on earth, much as continuity is implied by the resurrection of the dead, it is clear that the scale of destruction will be immeasurable.[43]

Revelation envisions God supplanting the old earth with a new heaven on earth, but the book nowhere endorses humans neglecting the earth during the interim before its end. On the contrary, John's condemnation of the Roman Empire includes a critique of the empire's dominion over the environment. John's critique is especially attuned to the Roman Empire's use of the sea to increase the wealth of the rich and powerful. After depicting Rome as a Sea Beast and as the Whore of Babylon "seated on many waters" (Rev. 17:1), John imagines shipmasters, seafarers, and sailors crying out after Rome's destruction, "Alas, alas, the great city, where all who had ships at sea grew rich by her wealth! For in one hour she has been laid waste" (Rev. 18:19).

Romans used the sea, as John specified already in 18:12–13, to attain profits through trade in cargoes that included natural resources like gold, silver, iron, marble, ivory, wood, animals, and humans—that is, slaves. John revealed to the members of his churches, all situated near the coast of a Roman province deeply invested in the exploitation of natural resources and their sale through maritime trade, that God would destroy Rome for the way that it had exploited his creation to make the rich richer.[44]

The way that the Roman Empire used the sea to facilitate the creation of wealth was so unjust, according to Revelation's visions, that God would destroy the sea forever. There would be a new heaven and earth, but the sea would be "no more" (Rev. 21:1).

When modern climate change skeptics recast the Red Dragon as a Green Dragon, they imply that environmentalism is a form of idolatry like that promoted by the forces of the Red Dragon in Revelation. Yet they are quick to overlook the fact that the earth is lauded for saving the mother of the Messiah (likely a symbol for Israel or the church) from the Red Dragon after the archangel Michael and his angelic army threw him out of heaven. On earth, the Red Dragon tried to wipe out the woman with a flood, but "the earth came to the help of the woman; it opened its mouth and swallowed the river that the dragon had poured from his mouth" (Rev. 12:16).

This positive view of the earth undermines common images in Roman propaganda in which the emperor is viewed as dominating the earth and sea.[45] John's apocalypse doesn't explain whether people should attempt to protect the earth before its cataclysmic end, but it leaves little doubt that certain powerful humans are responsible for corrupting the earth through their greed and hubris.

The actions of John's Red Dragon, Sea Beast, and Land Beast don't even remotely resemble those of environmentalists, the so-called Green Dragon. If anything, they come much closer to resembling the desires of the corporate-backed Cornwall Alliance, recklessly exploiting the natural resources of the land and sea to increase the wealth of the rich and powerful.

APOCALYPTIC FRENEMIES

Each year, thousands of US Christians travel to the Holy Land on tours run by Christian Zionists.[46] For enthusiastic premillennialists, these tours cast Israel as the Jewish Promised Land and the site of the Last Judgment.

Christian Zionists' understandings of Zion are based on interpretations of the Old Testament. Certain scriptural texts written during the Babylonian Exile imagined Zion—whether understood as the whole Land of Israel or just Jerusalem—as the site of Israel's future restoration and God's judgment against

Israel's oppressors. Parts of Isaiah even predict that Gentiles will gather in Jerusalem to recognize the supremacy of Israel's God prior to Israel's redemption. During the Second Temple period, Jews and Christ followers developed Isaiah's vision of restoration into apocalyptic scenarios in which faithful Gentiles congregated in Jerusalem to worship God in the run-up to the end-times.[47] Christian Zionist tours capitalize on these notions of Zion as the place where Christians unite with Israel as a prerequisite for the messianic age, but with an anti-Semitic twist: the rapture.

Harold Willmington, a self-proclaimed end-times expert, used to lead such tours of the Holy Land for an organization run by Jerry Falwell. Willmington was deeply concerned to make sure that Jews would understand what happened to Christians after the rapture and would know what they had to do to be saved too. So, on one of his tours, he stashed a plastic-wrapped Protestant Bible in a cave in the Valley of Petra, where Jews would take refuge during the tribulation according to fanciful interpretations of certain verses in the prophets.[48] Inside the Bible, he inscribed a note: "Attention to all of Hebrew background: This Bible has been placed here on October 14, 1974, by the students and Dean of the Thomas Road Bible Institute in Lynchburg, Va., U.S.A. We respectfully urge its finder to prayerfully and publicly read the following Bible chapters. They are: Daniel 7 and 11; Matthew 24; II Thessalonians 2; Revelation 12 and 13."[49] Willmington's time capsule for Jews left behind after the rapture urges them to accept Christ or face persecution and death. He wasn't the first or the last to stash away a Bible with a "Rapture for Dummies" note for Jews. Willmington intended for his actions to recall those of one of the earliest American proponents of premillennial dispensationalism, William E. Blackstone (1841–1935), who spent thousands of dollars hiding countless copies of the New Testament in the caves of Petra so that Jews might wise up and avoid the eternal hellfire.[50]

Many factors have motivated Christian Zionism historically and continue to do so today, but the most significant and enduring of these is the apocalyptic expectation that Jews will be assembled in Zion when Jesus returns.[52] Blackstone was an influential early proponent of American Zionism, but specifically Christian Zionism. In his book *Jesus is Coming* (1878), he is adamant that God's Word says that Jews should be returned to Israel. Israel, after all, is "God's sun dial," by which Christians can understand "our place in chronology, our position in the march of events." In 1891, he wrote the Blackstone Memorial, a petition that called for support for a Jewish homeland in Palestine (so that the stage would be set for Christian salvation). It was signed by more than four hundred influencers, including the future president William McKinley and corporate moguls like John D. Rockefeller and J. P. Morgan.[51]

One of America's best-known Christian Zionists in more recent history is John Hagee, an Evangelical pastor and proponent of the Prosperity Gospel who has written widely selling books like *Jerusalem Countdown* (2006).[53] Hagee is notorious for declaring that the Harry Potter series is a roadmap to witchcraft and has convinced him that the Antichrist will soon arrive, since Harry's "forehead is marked with the lightning bolt of the Hitler SS."[54] He is also infamous for arguing that the Holocaust was God's way of pushing Jews back toward the land of Israel.[55]

Despite such outrageous statements, Hagee is revered by many for his work as the head of America's largest pro-Israel organization, Christians United for Israel (CUFI), which boasts seven million members.[56] Hagee's "church," John Hagee Ministries, and other organizations whose leaders are involved with

Figure 18. Ivanka Trump (President Trump's daughter and adviser) and her husband Jared Kushner stand beside Israeli prime minister Benjamin Netanyahu in the front row of the dedication ceremony for the US Embassy in Jerusalem on May 14, 2018, while the US ambassador to Israel, David Friedman, speaks. Two right-wing Evangelical pastors spoke at the event, Robert Jeffress and John Hagee. Credit: Wikimedia Commons (U.S. Embassy, Jerusalem).

CUFI have donated millions of dollars in support of Israel's settlements in the West Bank. Some of these organizations even send Evangelicals to volunteer at the settlements.[57]

Hagee's organization is at the center of a coalition between right-wing American politicians and right-wing Israeli politicians. Hagee was invited to give a speech at the May 2018 dedication ceremony for the US Embassy in Jerusalem. The relocation of the embassy from Tel Aviv to Jerusalem was a physical expression of the Trump administration's recognition of Jerusalem as Israel's capital, a political maneuver aimed at satisfying Trump's Evangelical base (figure 18).[58] Who better to commemorate this move than the man who had become the face of Christian Zionism?

"We stand reminding the dictators of the world that the United States of America and Israel are forever united," Hagee asserted. "Let every Islamic terrorist hear this message: Israel lives.... Let it echo down the marble halls of the presidential palace in Iran: Israel lives."[59]

Hagee disguises a desired alliance between Christians and Jews against Muslims as an alliance between the US and Israel against Islamic terrorism, echoing Pence's own speech to the Israeli Knesset on the relocation of the embassy a few months earlier. In that speech, Pence hitched the state of Israel's settler colonialism to America's, saying, "My country's very first settlers also saw themselves as pilgrims, sent by Providence, to build a new Promised Land." He then proceeded, adopting problematic apocalyptic dualisms of "right over wrong [and] good over evil," to spin America's recognition of Jerusalem as the Jews' "sacred city" into a defense against radical Islamic terrorism. Pence proclaimed that whereas ISIS sought to create an Islamic caliphate, Trump, through his dedication to the state of Israel, would "prove the emptiness of its apocalyptic promises."[60]

Pence claimed that the apocalyptic expectations of Muslim fundamentalists were wrong but those of Christian fundamentalists were right. Even more, America's recognition of Jerusalem as the Jewish capital rightly fulfilled the apocalyptic promises to Jews and Christians. "It was the faith of the Jewish people," the vice president pronounced, "that gathered the scattered fragments of a people and made them whole again; that took the language of the Bible and the landscape of the Psalms and made them live again. And it was faith that rebuilt the ruins of Jerusalem and made them strong again."

Pence, Hagee, and other Christian Zionists who have publicly presented support for Israel as a biblical mandate condemn any criticism of Israel's aggressive policy of creating and expanding Israeli settlements in the West Bank, ruthlessly demolishing Palestinians' homes, as "anti-Semitism."[61] Trump's repeated attacks on the Muslim Democratic congresswoman Ilhan Omar for critiquing Israel promote this problematic conflation of anti-Zionism with anti-Semitism. Tellingly, Trump targets Omar and other women of color in Congress but not white anti-Zionist politicians like Rep. Betsy McCollum, who has stood up for Palestinian rights against American pro-Israel lobbies for more than a decade.[62] At CUFI's July 2019 summit devoted to countering anti-Semitism, Pence also targeted Omar, saying, "Anti-Semitism has no place in the Congress of the United States ... and anyone who slanders the historic alliance between the U.S. and Israel should not be sitting on the Foreign Affairs Committee in the House of Representatives."[63]

Christian Zionists are often keen to label Islam and anti-Zionism as anti-Semitism, but their theology is itself highly anti-Semitic. If someone told you that they thought a Jew should be tortured or slaughtered, wouldn't you consider this anti-Semitism? How is it any different when Christian Zionists profess that Jews who do not convert to Christianity will be annihilated in the end-times, or will spend eternity being tortured in hell? In the powerful words of Rabbi Alissa Wise, "There's hardly a more anti-Semitic notion than that."[64]

American Christian Zionism is as anti-Jewish as it is anti-Muslim. As Rabbi Wise has observed, the Christian Right has contorted what anti-Semitism means so that it now refers to any idea or statement that clashes with the right-wing agenda. Christian Zionists' apocalyptic rhetoric about defending Jews by supporting Israel is a smokescreen used "to shield actual neo-Nazis, bona-fide racists and their enablers from criticism."[65] Instead of interrogating the rise of virulent anti-Semitism and white nationalism among the Far Right, Christian Zionists preoccupy themselves with slandering Muslims and progressives as anti-Semites.

Theologies of the rapture have enabled certain premillennialists to attribute special significance to the chosen-ness of those Christians deemed righteous. At the same time, these theologies allow that others to whom God has extended his promises— namely, the sinful Christians and Jews left behind—will have a chance to repent after witnessing the trials wrought by the Antichrist. As we have seen, this pretribulation rapture scenario is a modern invention without solid biblical foundations.

Regardless of particular beliefs about if and when the rapture will occur, it is clear that New Testament texts anticipate end-times schemas in which Christ, the angels, and in some cases the saints and martyrs will judge the living and the dead. The timetable of apocalypses like Revelation can be interpreted in many different ways, but one point is certain: those who do not confess their loyalty to Christ won't fare well.

Modern Christians understand those who are saved at Judgment as "Christian" and those who are damned as not "Christian," but Revelation never uses the term *Christian*. The book of Revelation was written during a period in which different communities that followed Christ were negotiating their identities with respect to Judaism, not to mention Greco-Roman religious practices. Many who accepted Christ during the period in which the New Testament texts were written would have considered themselves as part of the people of Israel, and some would have identified themselves, in ethnic and religious terms, as Jewish. The label "Christian" didn't become widespread until the second century CE, when self-identifying "Christian" apologists wearied themselves trying to explain how Christians' beliefs and practices were distinct from Jews'.[66]

If we approach Revelation without a preconceived notion of Christianity and Judaism as two separate and established religions, its author's prejudices take a different shape. John's letters to the churches at Smyrna and Philadelphia both denounce "those who say that they are Jews and are not, but are a synagogue of Satan" (Rev. 2:9, with slightly different wording in 3:9). The synagogue of Satan is traditionally understood as a label for all Jews, but this interpretation doesn't account for John's claim that they say they are Jews but are not. Why would an author care about people masquerading as Jews if he identified as a Christian and thought all Jews would be damned for rejecting Christ?

Building on significant contributions by other scholars, the eminent Princeton historian Elaine Pagels has recently made a compelling argument that John's churches and those he maligns as the "synagogue of Satan" were Jewish followers of Christ. This explains why John never uses the term *Christian,* why he cares so much about people identifying as "Jews," and why his apocalypse is laden with symbols pertaining to Jewish Temple worship.[67]

From Paul's letters and Acts of the Apostles, we know that there were divisions among the early followers of Christ regarding how much of the Jewish Law should be followed by Gentile members of the churches. Paul thought that Gentiles should not have to follow the entirety of the Jewish Law: they didn't need to keep a kosher diet, and men didn't need to get circumcised (a high price for initiation for the Gentile men to whom Paul preached!). Acts of the Apostles makes it seem as if there was a rapprochement between Paul's group and the Jerusalem church represented by the apostle Peter and James, the brother of Jesus. Gentiles didn't need to keep kosher or get circumcised, but they did have to follow certain stipulations based on the Torah. They were expected "to abstain only from things polluted by idols and from fornication and from whatever has been strangled and from blood" (Acts 15:20). Sometimes called the Noahide laws, these are laws that ancient Jews believed God set out in a covenant through Noah with all humans, not just the Jews.[68]

In his own letters, Paul gives no hint that he assented to this compromise with Peter (Cephas) and James. "When Cephas came to Antioch, I opposed him to his face," Paul states in Galatians 2:11. He accuses Peter of hypocrisy for not abstaining from food sacrificed to idols himself but expecting Gentiles to do so. According to Paul's own words, he didn't accept the conditions of Peter and James. To make this point clear, Paul explains in 1 Corinthians that Gentiles don't have to avoid food sacrificed to "idols" so long as they recognize that the food was sacrificed to *false* "idols," not gods, since there is only one God (1 Cor. 8–10).

Paul proclaims that Gentile converts are still part of Israel even if they don't keep these aspects of the Jewish law that Peter and James think they should. Paul doesn't seem to have expected Gentiles to give up their own ethnic and civic identities, but he insists that they should, in some sense, count themselves among Israel. He speaks of Gentiles as children of the promise God made with Abraham, as branches grafted onto a tree that represents Israel, and even as "the Israel of God."[69] One thing that Gentiles must forsake when they become part of Israel, however, is the belief in other gods. "You know that when you were Gentiles, you were enticed and led astray to idols that could not speak," Paul explains in 1 Corinthians 12:2, shortly after describing the Israelites of Moses's day as "our ancestors" (1 Cor. 10:1).[70]

Paul urges Gentiles to think of themselves as Israel even though they don't need to abide by the restrictions advocated by Peter and James. Gentiles don't need to abstain from food sacrificed to idols. They don't have to abide by the Noahide prohibition against eating meat that hasn't been prepared by removing its blood in a ritually acceptable fashion. And they may not have been expected to abstain from all of the forms of sexual impurity that are prescribed for Israelites and "resident aliens" in Leviticus—for instance, the commandment against having sex with a woman during her menstruation.[71]

John of Patmos disagreed with Paul's teachings in the strongest terms. He explains in his letters to the churches at Pergamum and Thyatira what he understands as being led astray by Satan, and thus what he likely considers the transgression of those he calls the "synagogue of Satan." He accuses some among the churches in these cities of adhering to teachings of false prophets like Balaam and Jezebel, who "put a stumbling block before the people of Israel, so that they would eat food sacrificed to idols and practice fornication" (Rev. 2:14; see also 2:20).

John agreed with the Jerusalem church, against Paul, that Gentiles must abstain from meat sacrificed to idols and from fornication, as defined by the Noahide laws. When he rails against "those who say they are Jews and are not" as a "synagogue of Satan," he implies that they are guilty of the same practices. The synagogue of Satan is, as Pagels has argued, a reference to Christ followers who obeyed the teachings of Paul.[72] Upholding the perspective of the Jerusalem church, John chastises these Pauline followers of Christ for considering themselves part of the people of Israel when they didn't follow these laws.

Modern Christian Zionists interpret Revelation to mean that any sinful Christian, Jew, Muslim, or other pagan who doesn't accept Christ will suffer eternal damnation. But these modern Christians follow the teachings of Paul. And most don't ensure that their meat is butchered in a ritually acceptable fashion. One has to wonder, if John of Patmos were alive today, might he identify these modern Christian Zionists as representatives of the synagogue of Satan?

. . .

Apocalyptic discourse is a mode of political persuasion that advances fantasies about the end-times to affect political allegiances in the present. Through vivid scenes of horrific violence and gore, punctuated by perplexing symbols, apocalyptic preachers describe history and society as the unfolding of a cosmic struggle between good and evil. They evoke images of terror to influence behaviors, lend legitimacy to certain types of people, and condemn other types of people to eternal damnation.

Most of the authors of the New Testament writings expected Jesus to return during their lifetimes to bring about the end of the world, but none of them appealed to the rapidly approaching end-times as a license for accelerating the earth's destruction. Right-wing climate change skeptics use the pretense of God being in control of the earth to justify humans taking control of the earth, abusing its resources for the benefit of the rich and powerful. They portray environmentalists, including Christian environmentalists, as an apocalyptic Green Dragon attempting to impose a totalitarian government on them. Yet their promarket, limited-government approach to the environment helps rich fossil fuel executives to increase their wealth. They endorse some of the same practices of economic exploitation that John of Patmos condemned in his apocalypse.

If there is one location on earth that right-wing Christians are eager to protect from destruction, it is Israel, the stage of the end-times. Christian Zionists conflate supporting the state of Israel with opposing Islamic terrorism. Much of the time they confuse geopolitics with ethnicity and religion by neglecting to distinguish between the state of Israel and all Jews, as well as between Islamic terrorism and all Muslims.

The primary reason that Christian Zionists support Israel is that they believe Jews must return to Zion before Christ returns. By the same apocalyptic logic, however, they anticipate the eternal damnation of Jews when Christ does return. Some premillennialists are confident that the Jews who are left behind after the church is raptured will come to their senses and accept Christ. If they don't, though, the raptured church will join Christ in judging them as unworthy of salvation. When Christian Zionists pay lip service to rooting out anti-Semitism, they miss the beams in their own eyes.

Revelation, the most comprehensive narrative of the endtimes in the Bible, is a violent and dangerous book. It imagines the destruction of anyone who doesn't accept Christ. John took a special interest in vilifying the economically exploitative Roman Empire and those who followed Paul's assimilationist form of Judaism. Revelation is not a Christian book that condemns Jews but a book that a Jewish follower of Christ wrote, at least in part, to denounce other followers of Christ who didn't adhere to the same interpretations of the Torah as he did.

It is crucial that ancient visions like those contained in Revelation be interpreted as products of specific historical circumstances. If they aren't, they can too easily be used to sanctify hatred toward whoever happen to be the interpreter's most reviled opponents—toward liberals or conservatives; toward Christians, Jews, or Muslims; or even toward Potterheads.

Afterword

"Truth isn't truth." Rudy Giuliani's infamous defense of Trump has been touted by critics as the defining statement of the age of Trump.[1] Together with Kellyanne Conway's description of Trump's demonstrably false boast about the size of the crowd at his 2016 inauguration as an "alternative fact" and the president's own vilification of journalism that criticizes him as "fake news," Giuliani's words exemplify the "post-truth" politics of our times. With emotional appeals garnering recognition as "truths," random Twitter users being quoted like experts on the twenty-four-hour news cycle, and media outlets that trade in conspiracy theories filling the internet with hateful lies, Americans are facing a scourge of misinformation. How is anyone supposed to know right from wrong and fact from fiction anymore?

It's easier than ever for a problematic biblical interpretation to gain traction as a sacred truth amid right-wing politicians' barrage of post-truth communications. These post-truth claims to knowledge are sometimes misunderstood as inclusive because they reject singular ways of knowing and allow instead for multiple interpretations. Yet the right-wing politicians and pundits who depend on "alternative facts" rarely concede that an opposing view might also be true. Instead, they aggressively flaunt their facts as the *only* facts and their biblical interpretations as the *only* true meanings of God's word.

Republican influencers rely on this post-truth political culture to simplify complexity, avoid engagement, and silence opposition. They evade substantiating their arguments with evidence derived through responsible engagement with reliable sources. Instead, they use their positions of political influence to dodge critical inquiry and create confusion. In lieu of marshaling evidence, they either repeat their claims or cut off the conversation. "Next question!"

In this book, I have attempted to expose and debunk the Christian Right's biblical gaslighting on a number of contemporary political issues. I've described their interpretations of Jesus's politics as products of a hermeneutics of hate, where social prejudices inform biblical interpretations that in turn justify these same social prejudices. To disrupt this problematic cycle, I've examined modern historical sources to show when and how Republican interpretations originated, and I've investigated a wide range of ancient sources to determine what the New Testament texts could have meant in their original historical contexts.

Throughout the book, I've strived to be transparent about how I use my sources—how I translate them; when, why, and by whom I think they were written; and how I reconstruct their theological and political biases. I've used long-established historical methods to subject the New Testament texts to the same critical scrutiny with which historians approach other influential ancient texts, whether Homer's *Iliad*, Plato's *Republic*, or Augustine's *City of God*.

Even still, other professional historians of early Christianity won't agree with all of my arguments about Jesus and the gospels. This is because there isn't a single way of interpreting a text, even when its original language and literary and historical contexts are taken into account. This disagreement is productive. It is more important, I think, to engage in this critical dialogue about ways in which these ancient words can be responsibly interpreted in light of their ancient contexts than to try to lock down exact meanings.

While multiple interpretations of texts may contribute to historical knowledge, some interpretations are more responsible than others. Irresponsible interpretations are those that disregard the contexts in which a text acquires meaning—the author's social-historical context, the literary context of a verse or passage in a book, and the interpreter's own social-historical context. When these parameters aren't seriously taken into account, a text can too easily be interpreted as support for the interpreter's own agenda.

I am, of course, also susceptible to reading the ancient texts through the lens of my own experiences and predispositions. By framing my interpretations in light of the historical context of the New Testament—to what was even *thinkable* in the New Testament world—I have tried to destabilize my own interpretive biases as much as possible. Readers will find that the ancient understandings of Jesus that I have reconstructed in this book often do not fit neatly with a progressive agenda.

The New Testament contains a diverse set of ancient perspectives on the meaning of Jesus's life and teachings. In certain cases, these ancient sources should strike modern readers as surprisingly progressive on particular social issues (e.g., Luke). In other cases, their violent and exclusionary politics should send shivers down our spines (e.g., Revelation). As Iowa State University professor Hector Avalos has argued, a responsible modern interpreter should be willing to recognize the good and the bad in the New Testament's ethics.[2] These writings are, after all, relics from ancient cultures that didn't value human equality and democracy in the same way that modern Americans do—or should.

The New Testament gospels were written long before the modern emergence of the categories and ideas on which many interpretations—whether politically conservative or liberal—depend. They were written before anyone recognized "religion" as a distinct sphere of social life, before the development of free-market capitalism, before "homosexual" was a distinct sexual orientation, before fetal personhood was legally disputed, before legal immigration documents were required to move to a new place, before there was state welfare, before guns (and "God-given rights" to guns) were invented, before modern industrial technologies enabled humans to cause irreparable damage to the earth, and before there was a modern independent state of Israel.

These texts were written before "Christianity."

So many modern interpretations of Jesus's life, teachings, and death are just that, *modern*. To some degree this is inevitable, but if we truly want to understand why these texts were written and how their authors and earliest audiences might have understood them, we need to use critical and responsible methods of historical interpretation that constrain our own predispositions. As catchy as the famous hymn by Dale Evans is, "The Bible Tells Me So" isn't a compelling argument for anything. The Bible can't speak for itself. It must be interpreted, and it is in this process of interpretation that modern prejudices are too often granted divine authority.

There is much that modern Americans can learn from the New Testament, regardless of their religion, race, or political inclination. The key is to approach the text with an open mind, exercising awareness of the process of interpretation and reveling in the opportunity to learn from, and be challenged by, the diverse ideas, hopes, anxieties, and prejudices of ancient persons who lived in a world quite different from our own.

Notes

INTRODUCTION

Epigraphs: Donald Trump, interview by Cal Thomas, June 10, 2016), www.newsadvance.com/opinion/columnists/thomas_cal/cal-thomas-an-interview-with-donald-trump/article_7aa5441a-2da8–11e6-bc3f-132aed b6ee3f.html, and Jesse Byrnes, "Trump: Kerry Probably Hasn't Read the Bible," *Hill,* February 24, 2016, https://thehill.com/blogs/blog-briefing-room/news/270610-trump-kerry-probably-hasnt-read-the-bible.

1. For an introduction to hermeneutics, see Jens Zimmermann, *Hermeneutics: A Very Short Introduction* (Oxford: Oxford University Press, 2015). For theological hermeneutics, see the essays in John Webster, Kathryn Tanner, and Iain Torrance, eds., *The Oxford Handbook of Systematic Theology* (Oxford: Oxford University Press, 2009). For a centrist study of New Testament ethics that articulates a sophisticated theory of hermeneutics, see Richard B. Hays, *The Moral Vision of the New Testament: Community, Cross, New Creation: A Contemporary Introduction to New Testament Ethics* (New York: HarperOne, 1996).

2. Phyllis Trible, *Texts of Terror: Literary-Feminist Readings of Biblical Narratives* (Philadelphia: Fortress, 1984).

3. "Toni Morrison: Nobel Lecture," Nobel Prize website, November 7, 1993, www.nobelprize.org/prizes/literature/1993/morrison/lecture/.

4. Deborah Jian Lee, *Rescuing Jesus: How People of Color, Women, and Queer Christians Are Reclaiming Evangelicalism* (Boston: Beacon, 2016). On the increasing dissension among Republican Christians over social and political issues, see Angela Denker, *Red State Christians: Understanding the Voters Who Elected Donald Trump* (Minneapolis, MN: Fortress, 2019); Robert P. Jones, *The End of White Christian America* (New York: Simon and Schuster, 2016).

5. *The West Wing,* Season 2, Episode 3 ("The Midterms"), written by Aaron Sorkin (2000).

6. Rodney A. Werline, "Work, Poverty, and Welfare," in *The Bible in Political Debate: What Does It Really Say?*, ed. Frances Flannery and Rodney A. Werline (London: Bloomsbury, 2016), 75.

7. John J. Collins, *What Are Biblical Values? What the Bible Says on Key Ethical Issues* (New Haven, CT: Yale University Press, 2019), 8; see also his *The Bible after Babel: Historical Criticism in a Postmodern Age* (Grand Rapids, MI: Eerdmans, 2005).

8. The ancient words often translated as "Jew" (e.g., *Ioudaios* in Greek texts) can also be translated as "Judaean." I prefer this latter translation because it makes it clear that a person who identified with (or was identified by) this label would be associated with the geographical region of "Judaea," which was particularly significant in the period following the First Jewish Revolt (see my *"Iudaea Capta* vs. Mother Zion: The Flavian Discourse on Judaeans and Its Delegitimation in 4 Ezra," *Journal for the Study of Judaism* 49 (2018): 498–550, esp. 500n9). Scholars continue to debate whether "Jew" or "Judaean" should be preferred (see Adele Reinhartz et al., "Jew or Judean: Have Scholars Erased the Jews from Antiquity?," *Marginalia,* August 2014, https://marginalia.lareviewofbooks.org/jew-judean-forum/). I have chosen to discuss "Jews" in this book, in contrast with some of my other writings, in order to simplify complications that arise when moving back and forth between the ancient texts and modern interpretations. I do, however, point out places where the geographical-ethnic aspect of Jewish identity deserves more emphasis than it has typically received.

9. The only uses of the term *Christian* in the New Testament appear in Acts 11:26 and 26:28 and 1 Peter 4:16. Most likely, the term was originally applied by outsiders. On the gradual formation of a distinctive

Christian identity, see, among others, Judith Lieu, *Christian Identity in the Jewish and Graeco-Roman World* (Oxford: Oxford University Press, 2004). Followers of Christ probably embraced the term in part to differentiate themselves from Jews, who were the victims of considerable prejudice after the First Jewish Revolt. See Marius Heemstra, *The Fiscus Judaicus and the Parting of the Ways* (Tübingen: Mohr Siebeck, 2010). Paula Fredriksen provides a full historical reconstruction of the Jewish origins of the Jesus movement in *When Christians Were Jews: The First Generation* (New Haven, CT: Yale University Press, 2018).

10. For historical-critical introductions to the New Testament, see L. Michael White, *From Jesus to Christianity: How Four Generations of Visionaries and Storytellers Created the New Testament and Christian Faith* (San Francisco: Harper San Francisco, 2004); Bart D. Ehrman, *The New Testament: A Historical Introduction to the Early Christian Writings* (Oxford: Oxford University Press, 2004); Harry O. Maier, *New Testament Christianity in the Roman World* (Oxford: Oxford University Press, 2019).

11. Mark is the only one of the gospels that historians will sometimes date during or earlier than the First Jewish Revolt (66–70 CE) rather than after the Temple destruction. Recent scholarship has made a strong case, however, for dating Mark after 70 CE; John S. Kloppenborg, "*Evocatio Deorum* and the Date of Mark," *Journal of Biblical Literature* 124, no. 3 (2005): 419–50; Stephen Simon Kimondo, *The Gospel of Mark and the Roman-Jewish War of 66–70 CE: Jesus' Story as a Contrast to the Events of the War* (Eugene, OR: Pickwick, 2018). For an authoritative historical analysis of the First Jewish Revolt, which technically continued after the Temple destruction of 70 CE until the last rebels were defeated in 74 CE, see Steve Mason, *A History of the Jewish War: AD 66–74* (Cambridge: Cambridge University Press, 2016).

12. See Karl Galinsky, introduction to *Memory in Ancient Rome and Early Christianity*, ed. Karl Galinsky (Oxford: Oxford University Press, 2016), 1–42. On memory in the Jesus tradition, see Chris Keith, *Jesus' Literacy: Scribal Culture and the Teacher from Galilee* (London: T&T Clark, 2011); Alan Kirk, *Memory and the Jesus Tradition* (London: Bloomsbury, 2018).

13. Catherine Hezser, *Jewish Literacy in Roman Palestine* (Tübingen: Mohr Siebeck, 2001), 496.

14. Bart D. Ehrman, *Forged: Writing in the Name of God—Why the Bible's Authors Are Not Who We Think They Are* (New York: Harper Collins, 2011).

15. L. Michael White, *Scripting Jesus: The Gospels in Rewrite* (New York: HarperOne, 2010). See also Bart Ehrman, *Jesus, Interrupted: Revealing the Hidden Contradictions in the Bible (and Why We Don't Know about Them)* (New York: HarperCollins, 2009). Richard Bauckham's defense of the gospels as eyewitness testimony in *Jesus and the Eyewitnesses: The Gospels as Eyewitness Testimony* (Grand Rapids, MI: Eerdmans, 2006) seeks to establish miracles as historical. James Crossley has shown that Bauckham's methodology advances conservative Christian, neoliberal assumptions that would not be recognized as valid in any other field of historical inquiry (*Jesus in an Age of Neoliberalism: Quests, Scholarship and Ideology* [London: Routledge, 2014], chap. 7).

16. See my *Revelations of Ideology: Apocalyptic Class Politics in Early Roman Palestine* (Leiden: Brill, 2018) and *Class and Power in Roman Palestine: The Socioeconomic Setting of Judaism and Christian Origins* (Cambridge: Cambridge University Press, 2019).

1. A PORTRAIT OF REPUBLICAN JESUS

1. Anne Lamott, *Bird by Bird: Some Instructions on Writing and Life* (New York: Anchor Books, 1995), 22 (she attributes this quip to "my priest friend Tom").

2. E.g., R. S. Sugirtharajah, *Jesus in Asia* (Cambridge, MA: Harvard University Press, 2018); Mustafa Akyol, *The Islamic Jesus: How the King of the Jews Became a Prophet of the Muslims* (New York: St. Martin's, 2017).

3. Stephen Prothero, *American Jesus: How the Son of God Became a National Icon* (New York: Farrar, Straus and Giroux, 2004), 8.

4. Sean McCloud has analyzed this phenomenon of two churches in the same tradition having very different "class theologies" in *Divine Hierarchies: Class in American Religion and Religious Studies* (Chapel Hill: University of North Carolina Press, 2007).

5. Steven P. Miller, *The Age of Evangelicalism: America's Born-Again Years* (Oxford: Oxford University Press, 2014), 7.

6. On the idea of Big Government and its Republican detractors, see, among others, Jeff Madrick, *The Case for Big Government*, 2nd ed. (Princeton, NJ: Princeton University Press, 2010).

7. I discuss this fake history of the founding fathers further in chapters 2, 3, and 4.

8. Bill O'Reilly and Martin Dugard, *Killing Jesus: A History* (New York: Holt, 2013), 2.

9. O'Reilly and Dugard, *Killing Jesus*.

10. O'Reilly and Dugard, *Killing Jesus*, 273.

11. O'Reilly and Dugard furnish a lengthy footnote in which they discuss the four canonical gospels as the sources of their "facts, quotes, and stories about Jesus" (*Killing Jesus*, 22). They relate the traditional position that the authors of the gospels were their namesakes, ignoring the position of the majority of critical scholars that this was not the case (among others: Bart Ehrman, *Jesus, Interrupted: Revealing the Hidden Contradictions in the Bible (and Why We Don't Know about Them)* [New York: HarperCollins, 2009]). They even cite the traditional understanding of Luke as a physician as proof of his credibility as a source for that gospel's description of Jesus sweating blood (*Killing Jesus*, 222)—a detail that might not have even been in the original gospel according to manuscript evidence. O'Reilly and Dugard also emphasize the reliability of John as a source since he was an "eyewitness" (22). Again, this clashes with scholarly research, which recognizes John as the latest and most problematic of the gospels as a historical source.

12. Candida Moss, "Five Things Bill O'Reilly Flubs in 'Killing Jesus,'" CNN Belief Blog, October 4, 2013, http://religion.blogs.cnn .com/2013/10/04/five-things-bill-oreilly-gets-wrong-in-killing-jesus/; Candida Moss, "The Gospel According to Bill O'Reilly," *Daily Beast*, September 27, 2013, www.thedailybeast.com/the-gospel-according-to-bill-oreilly. Moss also appeared on *The O'Reilly Factor* to refute the historical claims of *Killing Jesus*.

13. As far as scholarly sources are concerned, the authors have devoted a section at the end of the book (O'Reilly and Dugard, *Killing Jesus*, 275–80) to discussing their sources—or, rather, making it appear that they are conversant in scholarship. The sources they highlight

include a few reputable scholarly works on the Roman army and Jews alongside outdated and conservative Christian books on Jesus. On O'Reilly and Dugard's fake history across their Killing series, see Matthew Stevenson, "Killing Bill O'Reilly: The Disgraced Broadcaster's Distortions of History," *Harper's Magazine,* July 2017, https://harpers.org/archive/2017/07/killing-bill-oreilly/.

14. O'Reilly and Dugard, *Killing Jesus,* 272. Steven Green has documented how George Washington has been, from his own time to today, "transformed from being simply pious into possessing a faith that was evangelical or religiously orthodox" (*Inventing a Christian America: The Myth of the Religious Founding* [Oxford: Oxford University Press, 2015], 206).

15. On Fox News as Republican propaganda, see Yochai Benkler, Rob Faris, and Hal Roberts, *Network Propaganda: Manipulation, Disinformation, and Radicalization in American Politics* (Oxford: Oxford University Press, 2018), esp. chap. 5; Nicole Hemmer, *Messengers of the Right: Conservative Media and the Transformation of American Politics* (Philadelphia: University of Pennsylvania Press, 2016); Howard Kurtz, *Media Madness: Donald Trump, the Press, and the War over the Truth* (New York: Simon and Schuster, 2018); Jane Mayer, "The Making of the Fox News White House," *New Yorker,* March 4, 2019, www.newyorker.com/magazine/2019/03/11/the-making-of-the-fox-news-white-house.

16. Khadijah Costley White, *The Branding of Right-Wing Activism: The News Media and the Tea Party* (Oxford: Oxford University Press, 2018); Anthony DiMaggio, *The Rise of the Tea Party: Political Discontent and Corporate Media in the Age of Obama* (New York: New York University Press, 2011), 108–9; Paul Street and Anthony R. Dimaggio, *Crashing the Tea Party: Mass Media and the Campaign to Remake American Politics* (London: Routledge, 2015), 53, 137. I discuss the Tea Party's role in shaping the Republican Jesus in chapter 4.

17. O'Reilly and Dugard, *Killing Jesus,* 68 (their emphasis).

18. O'Reilly and Dugard, *Killing Jesus,* 59, 253n.

19. Jeffrey M. Berry and Sarah Sobieraj, *The Outrage Industry: Political Opinion Media and the New Incivility* (Oxford: Oxford University Press, 2016), 47–50. O'Reilly has now written two books on the Nazis, *Hitler's Last Days* and *Killing the SS* (with Dugard), which are as problematic as *Killing Jesus* and the rest of the books in the series.

20. O'Reilly and Dugard, *Killing Jesus*, 88 (see also 68, 137, and throughout).

21. O'Reilly and Dugard, *Killing Jesus*, 83.

22. O'Reilly and Dugard, *Killing Jesus*, 82. James S. McLaren addresses Josephus's biased representation of Judas in "Constructing Judaean History in the Diaspora: Josephus's Accounts of Judas," in *Negotiating Diaspora: Jewish Strategies in the Roman Empire*, ed. John M. G. Barclay (London: T&T Clark, 2004), 90–108.

23. Nadav Sharon, *Judea under Roman Domination: The First Generation of Statelessness and Its Legacy* (Atlanta, GA: SBL, 2017); James M. Scott, *BACCHIUS IUDAEUS: A Denarius Commemorating Pompey's Victory over Judea* (Göttingen: Vandenhoeck and Ruprecht, 2015); Tony Keddie, *Class and Power in Roman Palestine: The Socioeconomic Setting of Judaism and Christian Origins* (Cambridge: Cambridge University Press, 2019).

24. O'Reilly and Dugard, *Killing Jesus*, 12, 152.

25. Peter Richardson, *Herod: King of the Jews and Friend of the Romans* (Columbia: University of South Carolina Press, 1996); Géza Vermes, *The True Herod* (London: Bloomsbury, 2014); Adam Marshak, *The Many Faces of Herod the Great* (Grand Rapids, MI: Eerdmans, 2015); Nikos Kokkinos, *The Herodian Dynasty: Origins, Role in Society and Eclipse* (Sheffield: Sheffield Academic, 1998).

26. Exod. 20:4; Deut. 5:8. See Steven Fine, *Art and Judaism in the Greco-Roman World: Toward a New Jewish Archaeology* (Cambridge: Cambridge University Press, 2005), 69–81.

27. On these cultural negotiations, see my "*Triclinium* Trialectics: The *Triclinium* as Contested Space in Early Roman Palestine," *Harvard Theological Review* 113 (2020): 63–88.

28. O'Reilly and Dugard, *Killing Jesus*, 108–9.

29. James H. Kim On Chong-Gossard, "Who Slept with Whom in the Roman Empire? Women, Sex, and Scandal in Suetonius' *Caesares*," in *Private and Public Lies: The Discourse of Despotism and Deceit in the Graeco-Roman World*, ed. Andrew J. Turner, James H. Kim On Chong-Gossard, and Frederik Juliaan Vervaet (Leiden: Brill, 2010), 295–330.

30. Robin Meyers, *Why the Christian Right Is Wrong: A Minister's Manifesto for Taking Back Your Faith, Your Flag, Your Future* (San Francisco: Jossey-Bass, 2006), 63–71.

31. O'Reilly and Dugard, *Killing Jesus*, 226–27 (my emphasis).

32. O'Reilly and Dugard, *Killing Jesus*, 123.

33. O'Reilly and Dugard, *Killing Jesus*, 204.

34. Pamela Eisenbaum, *Paul Was Not a Christian: The Original Message of a Misunderstood Apostle* (New York: HarperOne, 2009), chap. 7.

35. O'Reilly and Dugard rightly convey the scholarly view that there was no middle class in the Roman Empire and Jewish society of Jesus's time (*Killing Jesus*, 144), but they wrongly assume that everybody fit neatly into the "unclean" and working classes, on the one hand, or the aristocracy on the other. The Pharisees are depicted as wealthy and powerful throughout the book (159, 201, etc.); this is correct for some Pharisees, but many were what scholars have described as "middlers" or "subelites" in place of the classification "middle class" (Tony Keddie, *Revelations of Ideology: Apocalyptic Class Politics in Early Roman Palestine* [Leiden: Brill, 2018], 80–86, 242–45).

36. O'Reilly and Dugard, *Killing Jesus*, 130. Moss has similarly noted the irony of O'Reilly and Dugard relying on anti-Catholic tropes in their depiction of the Pharisees ("Five Things").

37. Seán Freyne, *Galilee, from Alexander the Great to Hadrian, 323 B.C.E. to 135 C.E.: A Study of Second Temple Judaism* (Notre Dame, IN: University of Notre Dame Press, 1980); Halvor Moxnes, "The Construction of Galilee as a Place for the Historical Jesus," *Biblical Theology Bulletin* 31 (2001): 26–37, 64–77; Mark A. Chancey, *The Myth of a Gentile Galilee: The Population of Galilee and New Testament Studies* (Cambridge: Cambridge University Press, 2004).

38. Lee I. Levine, *The Ancient Synagogue: The First Thousand Years* (New Haven, CT: Yale University Press, 2000), 45–80; Jodi Magness, *The Archaeology of the Holy Land: From the Destruction of Solomon's Temple to the Muslim Conquest* (Cambridge: Cambridge University Press, 2012), 286–92; Eric M. Meyers and Mark A. Chancey, *Archaeology of the Land of the Bible*, vol. 3, *Alexander to Constantine* (New Haven, CT: Yale University Press, 2012), 203–38.

39. O'Reilly and Dugard, *Killing Jesus*, 91.

40. O'Reilly and Dugard, *Killing Jesus*, 90. Also on 131: "His family is not the wealthiest in town; nor is he the smartest among them."

41. O'Reilly and Dugard, *Killing Jesus*, 126.

42. O'Reilly and Dugard, *Killing Jesus,* 136.

43. O'Reilly and Dugard, *Killing Jesus,* 159.

44. Ernest Renan, *Histoire générale et système comparé des langues semitiques,* 5th ed. (Paris: Imprimerie Imperiale, 1855), 4, cited in Heschel, *Aryan Jesus,* 35. Although Renan's ranking of races proved quite problematic, he sought, unlike his intellectual heirs, to distinguish the Ashkenazi Jews of central Europe from the Semitic race. They were originally Turkic refugees, he argued, who converted to Judaism and then migrated into the Rhineland. Renan also sought to dismantle French theories of nationalism based on race, though those theories prevailed and became the basis of global white nationalist thought today. See Thomas Chatterton Williams, "The French Origins of 'You Will Not Replace Us': The European Thinkers behind the White-Nationalist Rallying Cry," *New Yorker,* November 27, 2017, www.newyorker.com/magazine/2017/12/04/the-french-origins-of-you-will-not-replace-us.

45. Ernest Renan, *The Life of Jesus* (London: Trübner, 1867), 51, 74–76, and throughout); originally published as *Vie de Jésus* (Paris: Michel Lévy frères, 1863). Robert Priest chronicles the book's enormous popularity and the controversy it caused when it was first published in *The Gospel According to Renan: Reading, Writing, and Religion in Nineteenth-Century France* (Oxford: Oxford University Press, 2015).

46. Renan, *Life of Jesus,* 96.

47. Renan, *Life of Jesus,* 66–67.

48. Renan, *Life of Jesus,* 206–7. See Susannah Heschel, *The Aryan Jesus: Christian Theologians and the Bible in Nazi Germany* (Princeton, NJ: Princeton University Press, 2008), 34–38; Shawn Kelley, *Racializing Jesus: Race, Ideology, and the Formation of Modern Biblical Scholarship* (London: Routledge, 2002), 84–87; Halvor Moxnes, *Jesus and the Rise of Nationalism: A New Quest for the Nineteenth Century Historical Jesus* (London: Tauris, 2012), chap. 5.

49. O'Reilly and Dugard, *Killing Jesus,* 71–72.

50. Images of Christ by Hofmann were very popular in the US before being supplanted by the more masculine images of Christ by Warner Sallman, the artist who painted the ubiquitous *Head of Christ.* John D. Rockefeller Jr. was among the conservative businessmen who

purchased Hofmann's paintings. See Stephen Prothero, *American Jesus: How the Son of God Became a National Icon* (New York: Farrar, Straus and Giroux, 2004), 115–19, 276; Erika Doss, "Making a 'Virile, Manly Christ': The Cultural Origins and Meanings of Warner Sallman's Religious Imagery," in *Icons of American Protestantism: The Art of Warner Sallman,* ed. David Morgan (New Haven, CT: Yale University Press, 1996), 61–94.

51. Henry Louis Gates Jr., *Stony the Road: Reconstruction, White Supremacy, and the Rise of Jim Crow* (New York: Penguin, 2019), 73–75.

52. Mark 11:15–19; Matt. 21:12–17; Luke 19:45–58; John 2:13–22.

53. O'Reilly and Dugard, *Killing Jesus,* 119–26, 190–96. The authors mainly follow John for the earlier encounter and the Synoptic gospels (Mark, Matthew, and Luke) for the latter.

54. John 2:16.

55. O'Reilly and Dugard, *Killing Jesus,* 121, 124. On the terms used in the gospels, see my "Beyond the 'Den of Robbers': The Dialectics of Sacred and Profane Finances in Early Roman Jerusalem," in *Dialectics of Religion in the Roman World,* ed. Francesca Mazzilli and Dies van der Linde (forthcoming).

56. O'Reilly and Dugard, *Killing Jesus,* 122.

57. O'Reilly and Dugard, *Killing Jesus,* 123.

58. O'Reilly and Dugard think that some of the Temple priests and money changers' profits are somehow channeled back to Rome: "The Temple priests and their Roman masters get most of the profit through taxation and money changing" (*Killing Jesus,* 122). Candida Moss has noted that there is no evidence to support this assumption ("Five Things" and "Gospel According to Bill O'Reilly").

59. O'Reilly and Dugard, *Killing Jesus,* 122.

60. See chapter 5.

61. O'Reilly and Dugard, *Killing Jesus,* 270. Islamophobia and a racist view of Arabs as violent also shows up in the book through the characterization of Herodias, the Nabatean wife of Antipas, and her daughter Salome as Arabs, and of Antipas as living in fear of "attack from Arabia" (106, 107n.). The book also depicts the army in Judaea as a mix of "Arab, Samarian, and Syrian forces" (165). They are correct that the military forces in Judaea would have consisted largely of locals from the province of Syria, but this mix included Jews (Christopher B.

Zeichmann, *The Roman Army and the New Testament* (Lanham, MD: Lexington/Fortress, 2018). Both the book and the movie also depict Herodias and Salome through an Orientalist lens as violent, lustful Arabs plotting to kill John the Baptist (*Killing Jesus*, 150–52).

62. Sam Thielman, "How Fox Ate National Geographic," *Guardian*, November 14, 2015, www.theguardian.com/media/2015/nov/14/how-fox-ate-national-geographic.

63. "The Costumes: Killing Jesus," YouTube, March 11, 2015, www.youtube.com/watch?v=tM2rz-8ylWg.

64. David Dennis Jr., "Ridley Scott's Explanation for Whitewashing His Exodus Movie Is Infuriating," *Medium*, November 26, 2014, https://medium.com/@DavidDWrites/ridley-scotts-explanation-for-whitewashing-his-exodus-movie-is-infuriating-8d36bd555ada.

65. Mike Fillon, "The Real Face of Jesus," *Popular Mechanics*, January 23, 2015, www.popularmechanics.com/science/health/a234/1282186/.

66. See Craig A. Evans, *Jesus and His World: The Archaeological Evidence* (Louisville, KY: Westminster John Knox, 2012), 148–52; Joan E. Taylor, *What Did Jesus Look Like?* (London: T&T Clark, 2018).

67. Jonathan Merritt, "Why a Muslim Actor Plays Jesus in Bill O'Reilly's 'Killing Jesus,'" Religion News Service, March 23, 2015, https://religionnews.com/2015/03/23/muslim-actor-plays-jesus-bill-oreillys-killing-jesus-tv-special/.

68. "Joe Doyle on Playing Judas," YouTube, March 13, 2015, www.youtube.com/watch?v=IQvs2XIId_s.

69. Nancy Kang provides a critical perspective on race in some of Scott's films in "'Good Badmen': Reading Race in American Gangster, Black Rain, and Body of Lies," in *The Culture and Philosophy of Ridley Scott*, ed. Adam Barkman, Ashley Barkman, and Nancy Kang (Lanham, MD: Lexington, 2013), 23–44. As Kang notes, following Richard A. Schwartz (*The Films of Ridley Scott* [Westport, CT: Praeger, 2001]), Scott's movies espouse "liberal values marbled through with neo-classically conservative ideals" (24).

70. Brian Locke, "White and 'Black' versus Yellow: Metaphor and *Blade Runner*'s Racial Politics," *Arizona Quarterly: A Journal of American Literature, Culture, and Theory* 65 (2009): 115. See also David Desser, "Race,

Space and Class: The Politics of the SF Film from *Metropolis* to *Blade Runner*," in *Retrofitting "Blade Runner": Issues in Ridley Scott's "Blade Runner" and Philip K. Dick's "Do Androids Dream of Electric Sheep?,"* ed. Judith Kerman, 2nd ed. (Madison: University of Wisconsin Press, 1997), 110–23.

71. Scholars searching for the "historical Jesus" have often reconstructed a Jesus whose politics match their own. Ironically, leading liberal (i.e., moderate left-leaning) historians have also sometimes depicted Jesus as an opponent of Judaism while focusing on construing him as a multiculturalist opponent of empire. See Kelley, *Racializing Jesus,* chaps. 5–6; James Crossley, *Jesus and the Chaos of History: Redirecting the Life of the Historical Jesus* (Oxford: Oxford University Press, 2015); James Crossley, *Jesus in an Age of Neoliberalism: Quests, Scholarship and Ideology* (London: Routledge, 2014), esp. chaps. 5–6.

2. EARLY MODERN HERALDS

1. Mark 10:25; Matt. 19:24; Luke 18:25.

2. Peter Brown, *Through the Eye of a Needle: Wealth, the Fall of Rome, and the Making of Christianity in the West, 350–550 AD* (Princeton, NJ: Princeton University Press, 2012).

3. One of the key texts for this perspective is 1 Tim. 6:10, where "the love of money" (as opposed to wealth itself) is described as "a root of all kinds of evil."

4. Martin E. Marty, *Martin Luther: A Life* (New York: Penguin, 2004), 29.

5. Scott H. Hendrix, *Martin Luther: Visionary Reformer* (New Haven, CT: Yale University Press, 2016), 89–91; Alec Ryrie, *Protestants: The Faith That Made the Modern World* (New York: Viking, 2017), 15–39.

6. Hendrix, *Martin Luther,* 58. See Luther, Ninety-Five Theses, nos. 27–28. For an English translation of the Ninety-Five Theses with commentary, see Timothy J. Wengert, *Martin Luther's Ninety-Five Theses: With Introduction, Commentary, and Study Guide* (Minneapolis, MN: Fortress, 2015).,

7. Bernhard Lohse, *Martin Luther: An Introduction to His Life and Work* (Philadelphia: Fortress, 1986), 42.

8. Wengert, *Martin Luther's Ninety-Five Theses*, no. 1. I have adapted Wengert's translations slightly.

9. Andrew Pettegree, *Brand Luther: 1517, Printing, and the Making of the Reformation* (New York: Penguin, 2015).

10. James M. Stayer, *The German Peasants' War and Anabaptist Community of Goods* (Montreal: McGill-Queen's Press, 1991).

11. For the nuances of Luther's theology of predestination and free will, especially in comparison to Calvin's, see Robert Kolb, *Bound Choice, Election, and Wittenberg Theological Method: From Martin Luther to the Formula of Concord* (Grand Rapids, MI: Eerdmans, 2005); Joel R. Beeke, *Debated Issues in Sovereign Predestination: Early Lutheran Predestination, Calvinian Reprobation, and Variations in Genevan Lapsarianism* (Göttingen: Vandenhoeck and Ruprecht, 2017), 13–24.

12. B. R. Rees, *Pelagius: Life and Letters* (Rochester, NY: Boydell, 1998).

13. See Eric L. Jenkins, *Free to Say No? Free Will and Augustine's Evolving Doctrines of Grace and Election* (Cambridge: Clarke, 2013), for the nuances in Augustine's discussions of free will.

14. Keith D. Stanglin and Thomas H. McCall, *Jacob Arminius: Theologian of Grace* (Oxford: Oxford University Press, 2012).

15. Arminius, *Declaration of Sentiments* 2.20, from W. Stephen Gunter, *Arminius and His Declaration of Sentiments: An Annotated Translation with Introduction and Theological Commentary* (Waco, TX: Baylor University Press, 2012), 135.

16. McCloud, *Divine Hierarchies*, 7.

17. Gerald O. McCulloh, "The Influence of Arminius on American Theology," in *Man's Faith and Freedom: The Theological Influence of Jacobus Arminius*, ed. Gerald O. McCulloh (New York: Abingdon, 1962), 64–87.

18. Paul E. Johnson, *A Shopkeeper's Millennium: Society and Revivals in Rochester, New York, 1815–1837*, rev. ed. (New York: Hill and Wang, 2004); Sean McCloud, *Divine Hierarchies: Class in American Religion and Religious Studies* (Chapel Hill: University of North Carolina Press, 2007), 112–18.

19. Max Weber, *The Protestant Ethic and the Spirit of Capitalism*, trans. Stephen Kalberg, 3rd ed. (Los Angeles: Roxbury, 2002).

20. Roland Boer and Christina Petterson, *Idols of Nations: Biblical Myth at the Origins of Capitalism* (Minneapolis, MN: Fortress, 2014), 46.

21. James Fulcher, *Capitalism: A Very Short Introduction* (Oxford: Oxford University Press, 2004), 2.

22. Joyce Appleby, *The Relentless Revolution: A History of Capitalism* (New York: Norton, 2010), 27–55; James R. Fichter, *So Great a Profit: How the East Indies Trade Transformed Anglo-American Capitalism* (Cambridge, MA: Harvard University Press, 2010); Emily Erikson, *Between Monopoly and Free Trade: The English East India Company, 1600–1757* (Princeton, NJ: Princeton University Press, 2014).

23. David Harvey, *A Brief History of Neoliberalism* (Oxford: Oxford University Press, 2005), 20.

24. The philosopher Michele Foucault famously described neoliberalism in terms of "state phobia" in *The Birth of Biopolitics: Lectures at the Collège de France, 1978–79*, trans. Graham Burchell (New York: Picador, 2008), 187.

25. Lawrence Baines, *Privatization of America's Public Institutions: The Story of the American Sellout* (New York: Lang, 2019).

26. Adam Kotsko provides a timely and incisive interrogation of the political theology of neoliberalism in *Neoliberalism's Demons: On the Political Theology of Late Capital* (Stanford, CA: Stanford University Press, 2018).

27. Martine Julia van Ittersum, "The Long Goodbye: Hugo Grotius' Justification of Dutch Expansion Overseas, 1615–1645," *History of European Ideas* 36 (2010): 386–411; Martine Julia van Ittersum, *Profit and Principle: Hugo Grotius, Natural Rights Theories and the Rise of Dutch Power in the East Indies, 1595–1615* (Leiden: Brill, 2006).

28. Jan Rohls, "Calvinism, Arminianism and Socinianism in the Netherlands until the Synod of Dort," in *Socinianism and Arminianism: Antitrinitarians, Calvinists, and Cultural Exchange in Seventeenth-Century Europe,* ed. Martin Mulsow and Jan Rohls (Leiden: Brill, 2005), 3–48; Jan Paul Heering, *Hugo Grotius as Apologist for the Christian Religion: A Study of His Work "De Veritate Religionis Christianae," 1640* (Leiden: Brill, 2004); Henk Nellen, *Hugo Grotius: A Lifelong Struggle for Peace in Church and State, 1583–1645*, trans. J. C. Grayson (Leiden: Brill, 2014).

29. Harm-Jan van Dam, "*De Imperio Summarum Potestatum circa Sacra*," in *Hugo Grotius, Theologian: Essays in Honour of G. H. M. Posthumus Meyjes,* ed. Henk J. M. Nellen and Edwin Rabbie (Leiden: Brill, 1994), 19–40.

30. Hugo Grotius, *The Rights of War and Peace, in Three Books,* trans. Jean Barbeyrac (Clark, NJ: Lawbook Exchange, 2004) 2.20.46–51. Notably, Grotius disputes common interpretations of Luke 14:23 (Jesus's parable of the great banquet) to support his argument that belief cannot be compelled.

31. Boer and Petterson, *Idols of Nations,* 10.

32. Grotius, *Commentary on the Law of Prize and Booty,* ed. Martine Julia Van Ittersum, trans. John Clarke (Indianapolis: Liberty, 2006), 33–34, quoted in Boer and Petterson, *Idols of Nations,* 35.

33. Hugo Grotius, *The Freedom of the Seas, or, the Right Which Belongs to the Dutch to Take Part in the East Indian Trade,* trans. Ralph van Deman Magoffin (Union, NJ: Lawbook Exchange, 2001), 16. See Jonathan Ziskind, "International Law and Ancient Sources: Grotius and Selden," *Review of Politics* 35 (1973): 555.

34. Nellen, *Hugo Grotius,* 231.

35. Van Ittersum, *Profit and Principle,* 105–88.

36. Hugo Grotius, *Ad Matthaeum,* 22:17, in *Opera omnia theologica, in tres tomos divisa. Ante quidem per partes, nunc autem conjunctim et accuratius edita* (Amsterdam: Blaeu, 1679), vol. 2–1, 202b, lines 4–33. See Dirk van Miert, *The Emancipation of Biblical Philology in the Dutch Republic, 1590–1670* (Oxford: Oxford University Press, 2018), 155–56.

37. Marco Barducci, *Hugo Grotius and the Century of Revolution, 1613–1718: Transnational Reception in English Political Thought* (Oxford: Oxford University Press, 2017), 194.

38. Barbara Arneil, *John Locke and America: The Defence of English Colonialism* (Oxford: Clarendon, 1996); William Uzgalis, "John Locke, Racism, Slavery, and Indian Lands," in *The Oxford Handbook of Philosophy and Race,* ed. Naomi Zack (Oxford: Oxford University Press, 2017), 21–30; Nagamitsu Miura, *John Locke and the Native Americans: Early English Liberalism and Its Colonial Reality* (Newcastle: Cambridge Scholars, 2013).

39. See further Carville Earle, *The American Way: A Geographical History of Crisis and Recovery* (Oxford: Rowman and Littlefield, 2005), chap. 9.

40. Locke's understanding of the human condition wavered between the views of the Arminians and those of the Socinians. The Socinians were an originally Polish offshoot of the Reformed Church

that came under the influence of an Italian Anabaptist named Fausto Sozzini after he was driven out of Italy by the Inquisition in the late 1500s. They rejected absolute predestination like the Arminians but also rejected Original Sin and the orthodox doctrine of the Trinity (some were later called Unitarians). In *The Reasonableness of Christianity,* Locke's presentation of Jesus isn't trinitarian—Jesus isn't defined as coequal, consubstantial, coeternal, or any other theological co-jargon with God the Father. But Locke doesn't explicitly reject the Trinity either. We must, therefore, settle for understanding Locke as an English Protestant with a palate for Arminian and Socinian ideas. See John Marshall, "Locke, Socinianism, 'Socinianism,' and Unitarianism," in *English Philosophy in the Age of Locke,* ed. Michael Alexander Stewart (Oxford: Oxford University Press, 2000), 111–82; John Marshall, *John Locke: Resistance, Religion, and Responsibility* (Cambridge: Cambridge University Press, 1994), esp. 53; Sarah Mortimer, *Reason and Religion in the English Revolution: The Challenge of Socinianism* (Cambridge: Cambridge University Press, 2010); Boer and Petterson, *Idols of Nations,* 51.

41. Kim Ian Parker, *The Biblical Politics of John Locke* (Waterloo: Wilfrid Laurier University Press, 2006), 32. Note that Parker is a promoter of liberalism and uncritical about Locke's motives, as noted by Boer and Petterson (*Idols of Nations,* 48n5).

42. Yechiel Leiter, *John Locke's Political Philosophy and the Hebrew Bible* (Cambridge: Cambridge University Press, 2018), esp. 367–80.

43. Boer and Petterson point out that he does acknowledge the curse of hard labor in an unpublished note and rightly imply that it was not published for a reason (*Idols of Nations,* 68).

44. John Locke, *Second Treatise of Civil Government* 5.26, in *Two Treatises of Government and a Letter concerning Toleration,* ed. Ian Shapiro (New Haven, CT: Yale University Press, 2003).

45. Boer and Petterson, *Idols of Nations,* 72–81.

46. Locke, *Second Treatise* 5.32, quoted in Boer and Petterson, *Idols of Nations,* 77.

47. Adam Smith, *An Inquiry into the Nature and Causes of the Wealth of Nations* 1.1.1 (Oxford: Oxford University Press, 1979).

48. John Locke, *A Paraphrase and Notes on the Epistles of St. Paul to the Galatians, 1 and 2 Corinthians, Romans, Ephesians,* in *The Works of John Locke, Esq: In Three Volumes,* vol. 3, 5th ed. (London: S. Birt et al., 1751), 310.

49. Denise A. Spellberg, *Thomas Jefferson's Qur'an: Islam and the Founders* (New York: Knopf, 2013), 65–79, 111–13.

50. Marshall, *John Locke,* 447–48.

51. John Locke, *The Reasonableness of Christianity, as Delivered in the Scriptures,* in *Delphi Complete Works of John Locke (Illustrated),* sec. 151. Also quoted in Parker, *Biblical Politics,* 63.

52. McCulloh, "Influence of Arminius."

53. Allen Jayne, *Jefferson's Declaration of Independence: Origins, Philosophy, and Theology* (Lexington: University Press of Kentucky, 2015), 41–61; Renée Jeffery, *Hugo Grotius in International Thought* (New York: Palgrave Macmillan, 2006), 77–78.

54. Isaac Kramnick and R. Laurence Moore, *The Godless Constitution: The Case against Religious Correctness* (New York: Norton, 1996), 92.

55. Spellberg, *Thomas Jefferson's Qur'an.*

56. Most recently, see Andrew L. Seidel, *The Founding Myth: Why Christian Nationalism Is Un-American* (New York: Sterling, 2019). See also Kramnick and Moore, *Godless Constitution;* David Sehat, *The Myth of American Religious Freedom* (Oxford: Oxford University Press, 2011); Amanda Porterfield, *Conceived in Doubt: Religion and Politics in the New American Nation* (Chicago: University of Chicago Press, 2010); Steven K. Green, *Inventing a Christian America: The Myth of the Religious Founding* (Oxford: Oxford University Press, 2015).

57. Kramnick and Moore, *Godless Constitution,* 17 (10–15 percent); Sehat, *Myth of American Religious Freedom,* 5 (17 percent); Richard Hofstadter, *Anti-Intellectualism in American Life* (New York: Vintage, 1962), chaps. 3–4.

58. Kramnick and Moore, *Godless Constitution,* 34.

59. Jayne, *Jefferson's Declaration of Independence,* 37. Near the end of his life, Jefferson wrote about his religious convictions that "I am in a sect by myself, as far as I know." See Stephen Prothero, *American Jesus: How the Son of God Became a National Icon* (New York: Farrar, Straus and Giroux, 2004), 32.

60. Kramnick and Moore, *Godless Constitution*, 84–85. On Smith's liberalism and political theology, see Boer and Petterson, *Idols of Nations*, 87–130.

61. Quoted in F. W. Gibbs, *Joseph Priestley: Adventurer in Science and Champion of Truth* (London: Nelson, 1965), 249.

62. Mark Beliles, ed., *The Selected Religious Letters and Papers of Thomas Jefferson* (Charlottesville, VA: America Publications, 2013), 113.

63. Thomas Jefferson, *The Jefferson Bible: The Life and Morals of Jesus of Nazareth* (Mineola, NY: Dover, 2012).

64. For the text of the Declaration of Independence and Constitution, with commentary, see Richard Beeman, *The Penguin Guide to the United States Constitution: A Fully Annotated Declaration of Independence, U.S. Constitution and Amendments, and Selections from the Federalist Papers* (New York: Penguin, 2010).

65. Beeman, *Penguin Guide*.

66. Kramnick and Moore, *Godless Constitution*, 26–45. See further Pauline Maier, *Ratification: The People Debate the Constitution, 1787–1788* (New York: Simon and Schuster, 2011), and the essays in Daniel L. Dreisbach and Mark David Hall, eds., *Faith and the Founders of the American Republic* (Oxford: Oxford University Press, 2014).

67. Kramnick and Moore, *Godless Constitution*, 43.

68. Woody Holton, *Unruly Americans and the Origins of the Constitution* (New York: Hill and Wang, 2007).

69. Ray Raphael, *Founding Myths: Stories That Hide Our Patriotic Past* (New York: New Press, 2014), 145–56.

70. Quoted in Michael Kranish, *Flight from Monticello: Thomas Jefferson at War* (Oxford: Oxford University Press, 2010), 264.

71. Quoted in Kranish, *Flight from Monticello*, 264. On Jefferson against religious taxation, see also Daniel L. Dreisbach, *Thomas Jefferson and the Wall of Separation between Church and State* (New York: New York University Press, 2002).

72. Robin L. Einhorn, *American Taxation, American Slavery* (Chicago: University of Chicago Press, 2006).

73. Richard Samuelson, "Jefferson and Religion: Private Belief, Public Policy," in *The Cambridge Companion to Thomas Jefferson*, ed. Frank Shuffelton (Cambridge: Cambridge University Press, 2009), 146.

74. Margo J. Anderson, *The American Census: A Social History,* 2nd ed. (New Haven, CT: Yale University Press, 2015), chap. 1.

3. A CORPORATE ASSAULT ON THE NEW DEAL

1. Frances FitzGerald, *The Evangelicals: The Struggle to Shape America* (New York: Simon and Schuster, 2017), 26; Nathan O. Hatch, *The Democratization of American Christianity* (New Haven, CT: Yale University Press, 1989).

2. FitzGerald, *Evangelicals,* 31.

3. According to a 2014 poll by the Pew Research Center: "Religious Landscape Study," www.pewforum.org/religious-landscape-study/.

4. Randall Balmer, *Evangelicalism in America* (Waco, TX: Baylor University Press, 2016), xi–xii.

5. Paul E. Johnson, *A Shopkeeper's Millennium: Society and Revivals in Rochester, New York, 1815–1837,* rev. ed. (New York: Hill and Wang, 2004); Ira L. Mandelker, *Religion, Society, and Utopia in Nineteenth-Century America* (Amherst: University of Massachusetts Press, 2009), 34–36.

6. Jonathan P. Herzog, *The Spiritual-Industrial Complex: America's Religious Battle against Communism in the Early Cold War* (Oxford: Oxford University Press, 2011), 35. According to the 1936 US Census of Religious Bodies, Christian church membership overall increased 2 percent between 1926 and 1936, considerably less than in previous decades. The Southern Baptist churches lost 23 percent, and the Methodist Episcopal churches lost 14 percent; however, Roman Catholics grew 7 percent and the Church of Jesus Christ of Latter-day Saints grew 25 percent.

7. For recent histories of the Great Depression and New Deal, see Jason Scott Smith, *A Concise History of the New Deal* (Cambridge: Cambridge University Press, 2014); Michael Hiltzik, *The New Deal* (New York: Simon and Schuster, 2012).

8. Mark 11:15–19; Matt. 21:12–17; Luke 19:45–58; and John 2:13–22. For a full discussion of this episode and its interpretation by Republicans, see chap. 6.

9. See further Christine Wicker, *The Simple Faith of Franklin Delano Roosevelt: Religion's Role in the FDR Presidency* (Washington, DC: Smithso-

nian, 2017). The speech is available online: https://en.wikisource.org /wiki/Franklin_Roosevelt%27s_First_Inaugural_Address.

10. Christopher H. Evans, *The Social Gospel in American Religion: A History* (New York: New York University Press, 2017).

11. Jacob H. Dorn, "'In Spiritual Communion': Eugene V. Debs and the Socialist Christians," *Journal of the Gilded Age and Progressive Era* 2 (2003): 303–25. See further, Ernest Freeberg, *Democracy's Prisoner: Eugene V. Debs, the Great War, and the Right to Dissent* (Cambridge, MA: Harvard University Press, 2008).

12. Both quoted in Kevin M. Kruse, *One Nation under God: How Corporate America Invented Christian America* (New York: Basic Books, 2015), 5–6.

13. Quotations from Kruse, *One Nation*, 6. On the corporate influence on the development of the Christian Right in the mid-twentieth century, see, in addition to Kruse's excellent book, see Herzog, *Spiritual-Industrial Complex;* Kim Phillips-Fein, *Invisible Hands: The Businessmen's Crusade against the New Deal* (New York: Norton, 2009); Matthew Avery Sutton, *American Apocalypse: A History of Modern Evangelicalism* (Cambridge, MA: Harvard University Press, 2014); Amanda Porterfield, *Corporate Spirit: Religion and the Rise of the Modern Corporation* (Oxford: Oxford University Press, 2018), chap. 7.

14. Kruse, *One Nation*, 7. I've discussed the capitalist interpretations of Jesus by New Testament scholars during this period in Keddie, *Revelations of Ideology*, 11–24. See also James Crossley, *Jesus in an Age of Neoliberalism: Quests, Scholarship and Ideology* (London: Routledge, 2014), esp. chap. 4.

15. Quoted in Kruse, *One Nation*, 12.

16. Quoted in Kruse, *One Nation*, 12. See further Eckard V. Toy, "Spiritual Mobilization: The Failure of an Ultraconservative Ideal in the 1950's," *Pacific Northwest Quarterly* 61 (1970): 77–86.

17. Kruse, *One Nation*, 14–19. See also Phillips-Fein, *Invisible Hands*, 70–77.

18. Michael J. McVicar, *Christian Reconstruction: R. J. Rushdoony and American Religious Conservatism* (Chapel Hill: University of North Carolina Press, 2015), 51.

19. James W. Fifield Jr., *The Single Path* (Englewood Cliffs: Prentice-Hall, 1957), 80.

20. Fifield, *Single Path,* 102.

21. Brian Doherty, *Radicals for Capitalism: A Freewheeling History of the Modern American Libertarian Movement* (New York: PublicAffairs, 2007), 271–74; McVicar, *Christian Reconstruction,* 51.

22. Quotations from Richard J. Callahan, Kathryn Lofton, and Chad Seales, "Allegories of Progress: Industrial Religion in the United States," *Journal of the American Academy of Religion* 78 (2010): 14–19. The healing of the man with the withered hand appears in Mark 3:1–6; Matt. 12:9–13; Luke 6:6–11.

23. Bethany Moreton, *To Serve God and Wal-Mart: The Making of Christian Free Enterprise* (Cambridge, MA: Harvard University Press, 2009). See also Lake Lambert III, *Spirituality, Inc.: Religion in the American Workplace* (New York: New York University Press, 2009).

24. D. Michael Lindsay, "Is the National Prayer Breakfast Surrounded by a 'Christian Mafia'? Religious Publicity and Secrecy within the Corridors of Power," *Journal of the American Academy of Religion* 74 (2006): 390–419.

25. Jeff Sharlet, *The Family: The Secret Fundamentalism at the Heart of American Power* (New York: HarperCollins, 2008); Jeff Sharlet, *C Street: The Fundamentalist Threat to American Democracy* (New York: Little, Brown, 2010).

26. Quotations from Kruse, *One Nation,* 40, 42.

27. Kruse, *One Nation,* 46.

28. Quotations from Kruse, *One Nation,* 49. See further Angela M. Lahr, *Millennial Dreams and Apocalyptic Nightmares: The Cold War Origins of Political Evangelicalism* (Oxford: Oxford University Press, 2007), 54–55, 84.

29. Herzog, *Spiritual-Industrial Complex,* 6–7. See also T. Jeremy Gunn, *Spiritual Weapons: The Cold War and the Forging of an American National Religion* (Westport, CT: Praeger, 2009).

30. See Ellen W. Schrecker, *The Age of McCarthyism: A Brief History with Documents* (Boston: Bedford/St. Martin's, 2016); Ellen W. Schrecker, *Many Are the Crimes: McCarthyism in America* (Princeton, NJ: Princeton University Press, 1999).

31. Herzog, *Spiritual-Industrial Complex,* 48–49; Carolyn C. Jones, "Seeing Taxation in the Mid-Twentieth Century: US Tax Compliance," in *The Leap of Faith: The Fiscal Foundations of Successful Government*

in Europe and America, ed. Sven H. Steinmo (Oxford: Oxford University Press, 2018), 214–15.

32. Quoted in Herzog, *Spiritual-Industrial Complex,* 51.

33. Quoted in Harold Ivan Smith, *Eleanor: A Spiritual Biography: The Faith of the 20th Century's Most Influential Woman* (Louisville, KY: Westminster John Knox, 2017), 166.

34. Herzog, *Spiritual-Industrial Complex,* 86–87.

35. Herzog, *Spiritual-Industrial Complex,* 88.

36. Donald Crosby, *God, Church, and Flag: Senator Joseph R. McCarthy and the Catholic Church, 1950–1957* (Chapel Hill: University of North Carolina Press, 2011).

37. John Cooney, *The American Pope: The Life and Times of Francis Cardinal Spellman* (New York: Times, 1984), 109.

38. Quoted in Allan J. Lichtman, *White Protestant Nation: The Rise of the American Conservative Movement* (New York: Grove, 2008), 200.

39. Eisenhower hesitantly joined a Presbyterian church one year into his presidency (Kruse, *One Nation,* 57, 73). The inaugural address is online at https://en.wikisource.org/wiki/Dwight_Eisenhower%27s_First_Inaugural_Address.

40. Kruse, *One Nation,* ix. Eisenhower appropriated this crusade language from Billy Graham (60).

41. Herzog, *Spiritual-Industrial Complex,* 101.

42. Kruse, *One Nation,* 77.

43. The phrase *Judeo-Christian values,* though ostensibly inclusive, has been used since the mid-twentieth century as a political tool by the Christian Right. It advances a supersessionist understanding of Judaism and is exclusionary toward other religions. See further Shalom Goldman, "What Do We Mean by 'Judeo-Christian'?" *Religion Dispatches,* February 15, 2011, www.religiondispatches.org/what-do-we-mean-by-judeo-christian/.

44. Herzog, *Spiritual-Industrial Complex,* 102.

45. Herzog, *Spiritual-Industrial Complex,* 101–8; Kruse, *One Nation,* chap. 4.

46. According to the Guinness World Records: "List of Highest-Grossing Films," 2017, https://en.wikipedia.org/wiki/List_of_highest-grossing_films.

47. Kruse, *One Nation,* 147; Martin A. Kayman, "'Iconic' Texts of Law and Religion: A Tale of Two Decalogues," in *Visualizing Law and Authority: Essays on Legal Aesthetics,* ed. Leif Dahlberg (Berlin: De Gruyter, 2012), 13–22. As of March 14, 2019, 194 granite monuments of the Ten Commandments commissioned by the Fraternal Order of Eagles had been identified: Jefferson Madison Center for Religious Liberty, "Where Are the Eagles Ten Commandments Monuments?" August-September 2019, www.eaglesmonuments.com/.

48. Avi Selk, "A Satanic Idol Goes to the Arkansas Capitol Building," *Washington Post,* August 17, 2018, www.washingtonpost.com/news/acts-of-faith/wp/2018/08/17/a-satanic-idols-3-year-journey-to-the-arkansas-capitol-building/?noredirect=on&utm_term=.131ef7b244c1.

49. Seth Dowland, *Family Values and the Rise of the Christian Right* (Philadelphia: University of Pennsylvania Press, 2015), 25–26, 30–31. Kruse, *One Nation,* 180–81, 192–93. On the Supreme Court's role in defining religion and religious freedom, see Winnifred Fallers Sullivan, *The Impossibility of Religious Freedom: New Edition,* rev. ed. (Princeton, NJ: Princeton University Press, 2018); Winnifred Fallers Sullivan, *Paying the Words Extra: Religious Discourse in the Supreme Court of the United States* (Cambridge, MA: Harvard University Press, 1994).

50. John Fea, *Believe Me: The Evangelical Road to Donald Trump* (Grand Rapids, MI: Eerdmans, 2018), 115–52. The use of this court metaphor to describe the political influence of the emergent Christian Right was famously set forth by the progressive Christian theologian Reinhold Niebuhr in his essay "The King's Chapel and the King's Court," which appeared in *Christianity and Crisis* on August 4, 1969.

51. Joel A. Carpenter, *Revive Us Again: The Reawakening of American Fundamentalism* (Oxford: Oxford University Press, 1997), chap. 12.

52. Darren Dochuk, "'Heavenly Houston': Billy Graham and Corporate Civil Rights in Sunbelt Evangelicalism's 'Golden Buckle,'" in *Billy Graham: American Pilgrim,* ed. Andrew S. Finstuen, Anne Blue Wills, and Grant Wacker (Oxford: Oxford University Press, 2017), 161–95, esp. 181, 186.

53. Billy Graham, "The Economics of the Apocalypse," sermon delivered in Honolulu in 1974, https://billygraham.org/audio/the-economics-of-the-apocalypse/.

54. Steven P. Miller, *Billy Graham and the Rise of the Republican South* (Philadelphia: University of Pennsylvania Press, 2009), 28.

55. Quoted in Curtis J. Evans, "A Politics of Conversion: Billy Graham's Political and Social Vision," in Finstuen, Wills, and Wacker, *Billy Graham*, 153–54.

56. Quoted in Michael G. Long, *Billy Graham and the Beloved Community: America's Evangelist and the Dream of Martin Luther King, Jr.* (New York: Palgrave Macmillan, 2006), 24. See also the essays in Michael G. Long, ed., *The Legacy of Billy Graham: Critical Reflections on America's Greatest Evangelist* (Louisville, KY: Westminster John Knox, 2008). Curtis J. Evans has noted that Graham's misgivings about the civil rights movement stemmed from his aversion to government intervention and, I'd add, his Protestant theological aversion to law; "A Politics of Conversion," 153–55.

57. Dowland, *Family Values*, 6–7.

58. Quoted in Sutton, *American Apocalypse*, 336.

59. As documented in meticulous detail by Long in *Billy Graham*.

60. Dov Grohsgal and Kevin M. Kruse, "How the Republican Majority Emerged," *Atlantic*, August 6, 2019, www.theatlantic.com/ideas/archive/2019/08/emerging-republican-majority/595504/; Daniel K. Williams, *God's Own Party: The Making of the Christian Right* (Oxford: Oxford University Press, 2010), chap. 5.

61. Richard Hofstadter, *The Paranoid Style in American Politics, and Other Essays* (1965; repr., New York: Vintage, 2008); Christian Smith, *American Evangelicalism: Embattled and Thriving* (Chicago: University of Chicago Press, 1998).

62. Grant Wacker has documented Graham's ambivalent and fluctuating views on the Vietnam War, in particular, in *America's Pastor: Billy Graham and the Shaping of a Nation* (Cambridge, MA: Harvard University Press, 2014), chap. 6.

63. Quoted in Sutton, *American Apocalypse*, 331.

64. Kruse, *One Nation*, 249–57.

65. Kruse, *One Nation*, 251.

66. Quoted in Kruse, *One Nation*, 263. See further, David E. Settje, *Faith and War: How Christians Debated the Cold and Vietnam Wars* (New York: New York University Press, 2011), 132–38; Gunn, *Spiritual Weapons*,

chap. 8. On Nixon's acknowledgment of his Quaker background whenever politically expedient, see H. Larry Ingle, *Nixon's First Cover-Up: The Religious Life of a Quaker President* (Columbia: University of Missouri Press, 2015).

67. Ingle, *Nixon's First Cover-Up*, 263–74.

68. Williams, *God's Own Party*, chaps. 8–9.

69. Eric R. Crouse, *The Cross and Reaganomics: Conservative Christians Defending Ronald Reagan* (Lanham, MD: Lexington, 2013), 44. On Falwell's politics, see further Michael Sean Winters, *God's Right Hand: How Jerry Falwell Made God a Republican and Baptized the American Right* (New York: HarperCollins, 2012).

70. Paul S. Boyer, *When Time Shall Be No More: Prophecy Belief in Modern American Culture* (Cambridge, MA: Belknap Press, 1992); Lahr, *Millennial Dreams*.

4. TEA AND PROSPERITY IN THE AGE OF TRUMP

1. Gregory A. Smith and Jessica Martínez, "How the Faithful Voted: A Preliminary 2016 Analysis," Pew Research Center, November 9, 2016, www.pewresearch.org/fact-tank/2016/11/09/how-the-faithful-voted-a-preliminary-2016-analysis/. On Evangelical support for Trump, see John Fea, *Believe Me: The Evangelical Road to Donald Trump* (Grand Rapids, MI: Eerdmans, 2018); Stephen Mansfield, *Choosing Donald Trump: God, Anger, Hope, and Why Christian Conservatives Supported Him* (Grand Rapids, MI: Baker, 2017). See also the apologetic account of Stephen E. Strang, *God and Donald Trump* (Lake Mary, FL: FrontLine, 2017), which Fea puts into context in *Believe Me*, 132.

2. "The Religion of Donald Trump," *Boston Globe*, September 14, 2015, www.bostonglobe.com/news/nation/2015/09/14/trumpsidebar/kLTBdwJosIkO4FXfZCzPyL/story.html. At a rally in Jacksonville, Florida, on October 24, 2015, Trump said a bit more about how he thinks of his Christianity in contrast to his opponent Ben Carson's: "I'm Presbyterian. That's down the middle of the road, folks. I mean, Seventh-Day Adventist, I just don't know about." Sean Sullivan, "Donald Trump Seeks a Sharp Contrast with Ben Carson's Seventh-Day

Adventist Faith," *Washington Post,* October 24, 2015, www.washingtonpost
.com/news/post-politics/wp/2015/10/24/donald-trump-seeks-a-sharp-a-
contrast-with-ben-carsons-seventh-day-adventist-faith/?noredirect=
on&utm_term=.faa622fb2ada.

3. Q&A at the Family Leadership Summit, Ames, Iowa, July 18,
2015. See Daniel Burke, "The Guilt-Free Gospel of Donald Trump,"
CNN.com, October 24, 2016, www.cnn.com/2016/10/21/politics/trump-
religion-gospel/index.html.

4. Donald J. Trump, *Great Again: How to Fix Our Crippled America,*
rev. ed. (New York: Threshold, 2016), 130. The 2015 original edition had
the title *Crippled America: How to Make America Great Again.*

5. Bryan T. Gervais and Irwin L. Morris, *Reactionary Republicanism:
How the Tea Party in the House Paved the Way for Trump's Victory* (Oxford:
Oxford University Press, 2018); Theda Skocpol and Vanessa William-
son, *The Tea Party and the Remaking of Republican Conservatism,* 2nd ed.
(Oxford: Oxford University Press, 2016); Ronald P. Formisano, *The Tea
Party: A Brief History* (Baltimore: Johns Hopkins University Press, 2012);
Abby Scher and Chip Berlet, "The Tea Party Movement," in *Under-
standing the Tea Party Movement,* ed. Nella Van Dyke and David S.
Meyer (London: Routledge, 2016), 99–124.

6. Benjamin L. Carp, *Defiance of the Patriots: The Boston Tea Party and
the Making of America* (New Haven, CT: Yale University Press, 2010),
chap. 1.

7. David Brody, *The Teavangelicals: The Inside Story of How the Evangelicals and the Tea Party Are Taking Back America* (Grand Rapids, MI:
Zondervan, 2012), 17.

8. Joshua Green, *Devil's Bargain: Steve Bannon, Donald Trump, and the
Nationalist Uprising* (New York: Penguin, 2017).

9. Formisano, *Tea Party,* 71; Skocpol and Williamson, *Tea Party,*
102–4; Jeff Nesbit, *Poison Tea: How Big Oil and Big Tobacco Invented the Tea
Party and Captured the GOP* (New York: Dunne, 2016).

10. Daniel Schulman, *Sons of Wichita: How the Koch Brothers Became
America's Most Powerful and Private Dynasty* (New York: Grand Central,
2014); Jane Mayer, *Dark Money: The Hidden History of the Billionaires
behind the Rise of the Radical Right* (New York: Anchor, 2017); Nancy

MacLean, *Democracy in Chains: The Deep History of the Radical Right's Stealth Plan for America* (New York: Penguin, 2017).

11. Gordon Lafer, *The One Percent Solution: How Corporations Are Remaking America One State at a Time* (Ithaca, NY: Cornell University Press, 2017); Alex Hertel-Fernandez, *State Capture: How Conservative Activists, Big Businesses, and Wealthy Donors Reshaped the American States and the Nation* (Oxford: Oxford University Press, 2019).

12. Gervais and Morris, *Reactionary Republicanism,* 3; Formisano, *Tea Party,* 42.

13. Gervais and Morris, *Reactionary Republicanism,* 5.

14. Gervais and Morris, *Reactionary Republicanism,* chaps. 7–9.

15. Brody, *Teavangelicals.* For historical analysis, see FitzGerald, *Evangelicals,* chap. 17.

16. Scott Clement and John C. Green, "The Tea Party and Religion," Pew Research Center, February 23, 2011, www.pewforum.org/2011/02/23/tea-party-and-religion/.

17. Gervais and Morris, *Reactionary Republicanism.*

18. Daniel K. Williams, *God's Own Party: The Making of the Christian Right* (Oxford: Oxford University Press, 2010), 189.

19. Fea, *Believe Me,* 165–78. According to a 2010 American Values Survey, 55 percent of Tea Partiers agreed that the US "has always been and is currently a Christian nation" (Formisano, *Tea Party,* 54).

20. John Nichols, "The Nation: American History 101 for Bachmann," NPR, July 6, 2011, www.npr.org/2011/07/06/137645109/the-nation-american-history-101-for-bachmann.

21. Osha Gray Davidson, "Michele Bachmann Salutes the Upside to Slavery," Forbes, July 8, 2011, www.forbes.com/sites/oshadavidson/2011/07/08/michele-bachmann-salutes-the-upside-to-slavery/#75565oc157fd.

22. On the birther controversy, see Charles J. Sykes, *How the Right Lost Its Mind* (New York: St. Martin's, 2017), 120–22.

23. Julie J. Ingersoll, *Building God's Kingdom: Inside the World of Christian Reconstruction* (Oxford: Oxford University Press, 2015), chap. 9.

24. Ryan Lizza, "Leap of Faith: The Making of a Republican Front-Runner," *New Yorker,* August 15, 2011, www.newyorker.com/magazine/2011/08/15/leap-of-faith-ryan-lizza.

25. Lizza, "Leap of Faith."

26. Sean Wilentz, "Confounding Fathers: The Tea Party's Cold War Roots," *New Yorker,* October 18, 2010, www.newyorker.com /magazine/2010/10/18/confounding-fathers.

27. W. Cleon Skousen, *The Five Thousand Year Leap* (Washington, DC: National Center for Constitutional Studies, 1981), 42–47.

28. W. Cleon Skousen, *Days of the Living Christ* (Salt Lake City, UT: Ensign, 1992), e.g., chap. 31 on the Parable of the Pounds.

29. W. Cleon Skousen, *The Making of America: The Substance and Meaning of the Constitution* (Washington, DC: National Center for Constitutional Studies, 1985).

30. Colin Woodard, *American Character: A History of the Epic Struggle between Individual Liberty and the Common Good* (New York: Viking, 2016), 229–31.

31. Skocpol and Williamson, *Tea Party,* 30.

32. Kate Bowler, *Blessed: A History of the American Prosperity Gospel* (Oxford: Oxford University Press, 2013), 7.

33. Mansfield, *Choosing Donald Trump,* 22–23, 73. Trump discusses how much he learned from Peale in *Great Again,* 130.

34. Carol V. R. George, *God's Salesman: Norman Vincent Peale and the Power of Positive Thinking* (1993; repr., Oxford: Oxford University Press, 2019), 165–69; Christopher Lane, *Surge of Piety: Norman Vincent Peale and the Remaking of American Religious Life* (New Haven, CT: Yale University Press, 2016).

35. Jonathan P. Herzog, *Spiritual-Industrial Complex: America's Religious Battle against Communism in the Early Cold War* (Oxford: Oxford University Press, 2011), 34.

36. Quoted in George, *God's Salesman,* 168; Mansfield, *Choosing Donald Trump,* 83.

37. Lane, *Surge of Piety.*

38. Bowler, *Blessed,* 57.

39. Norman Vincent Peale, *The Power of Positive Thinking* (1952; repr., New York: Fireside, 2003), 64.

40. Mansfield, *Choosing Donald Trump,* 84.

41. Andrew S. Finstuen, *Original Sin and Everyday Protestants: The Theology of Reinhold Niebuhr, Billy Graham, and Paul Tillich in an Age of Anxiety* (Chapel Hill: University of North Carolina Press, 2009), 33.

42. Quoted in Finstuen, *Original Sin*, 21.

43. Mansfield, *Choosing Donald Trump*, 76; Tamara Keith, "Trump Crowd Size Estimate May Involve 'the Power of Positive Thinking,'" NPR, January 22, 2017, www.npr.org/2017/01/22/510655254/trump-crowd-size-estimate-may-involve-the-power-of-positive-thinking.

44. Mansfield, *Choosing Donald Trump*, 81.

45. Fea, *Believe Me*, 134.

46. Mansfield, *Choosing Donald Trump*, 87–97.

47. Mark 5:25–34; Matt. 9:20–22; Luke 8:43–48. See Paula White, *Move On, Move Up: Turn Yesterday's Trials into Today's Triumphs* (New York: FaithWords, 2008), 287–89.

48. White, *Move On, Move Up*, 343.

49. On Trump Tower condo, see Fea, *Believe Me*, 136. On Paula White and BET, see Karen Alea Ford, "The Distorted Gospel of Paula White," *Slot*, January 19, 2017, https://theslot.jezebel.com/the-distorted-gospel-of-paula-white-1791346160.

50. Mansfield, *Choosing Donald Trump*, 94.

51. Mansfield, *Choosing Donald Trump*, 95–96. See also Julia Duin, "She Led Trump to Christ: The Rise of the Televangelist Who Advises the White House," *Washington Post*, November 14, 2017, www.washingtonpost.com/lifestyle/magazine/she-led-trump-to-christ-the-rise-of-the-televangelist-who-advises-the-white-house/2017/11/13/1dc3a830-bb1a-11e7-be94-fabb0f1e9ffb_story.html?utm_term=.76178104903a.

52. Laurie Goodstein, "Billy Graham Warned against Embracing a President. His Son Has Gone Another Way," *New York Times*, February 26, 2018, www.nytimes.com/2018/02/26/us/billy-graham-franklin-graham-trump.html; Eliza Griswold, "Franklin Graham's Uneasy Alliance with Donald Trump," *New Yorker*, September 11, 2018, www.newyorker.com/news/dispatch/franklin-grahams-uneasy-alliance-with-donald-trump.

53. Sarah Pulliam Bailey, "How Donald Trump Is Bringing Billy Graham's Complicated Family Back into White House Circles,"

Washington Post, January 12, 2017, www.washingtonpost.com/news/acts-of-faith/wp/2017/01/12/how-donald-trump-is-bringing-billy-grahams-complicated-family-back-into-white-house-circles/?noredirect=on&utm_term=.44e3a716c927.

54. Fea, *Believe Me*, 118–23.

55. Bailey, "Bringing Billy Graham's Complicated Family Back."

56. Harriet Sherwood, "Christian Leader Jerry Falwell Urges Trump Support: 'He's a Moral Person,'" *Guardian*, October 9, 2018, www.theguardian.com/us-news/2018/oct/09/christian-leader-jerry-falwell-urges-trump-support-hes-a-moral-person.

57. Sarah Pulliam Bailey, "Jerry Falwell Jr.: 'If More Good People Had Concealed-Carry Permits, Then We Could End Those' Islamic Terrorists," *Washington Post*, December 5, 2015, www.washingtonpost.com/news/acts-of-faith/wp/2015/12/05/liberty-university-president-if-more-good-people-had-concealed-guns-we-could-end-those-muslims/?utm_term=.58174212f22f.

58. According to Liberty's website: "Liberty University Quick Facts," 2020, www.liberty.edu/aboutliberty/index.cfm?PID=6925.

59. Fea, *Believe Me*, 141–42.

60. Fea, *Believe Me*, 140–41.

61. Editorial Board, "Liberty University Shows It Takes Sports More Seriously Than Sexual Assault," *Washington Post*, December 8, 2016: www.washingtonpost.com/opinions/liberty-university-shows-it-takes-sports-more-seriously-than-sexual-assault/2016/12/08/083b6906-bb36-11e6-91ee-1adddfe36cbe_story.html?utm_term=.21aa87d8a915.

62. Laurel Powell, "A New Trump Plan Could Encourage Religious Colleges to Reject Trans Students," *Medium*, December 12, 2018, https://medium.com/transequalitynow/a-new-trump-plan-could-encourage-religious-colleges-to-reject-trans-students-ddf33666eade.

63. Fea, *Believe Me*, 142.

64. Fea, *Believe Me*, 143–45.

65. Lindsay Ellis, "Liberty U. Senior Official Accepted Bag of Money for Helping Trump in Online Polls, Report Says," *Chronicle of Higher Education*, January 17, 2019, www.chronicle.com/article/Liberty-U-Senior-Official/245506.

66. According to the official website of Capitol Ministries: "Ministries," 2019, https://capmin.org/ministries/. On Trump and Pence handpicking the attendees, see Strang, *God and Donald Trump*, 29.

67. Eric Kelderman and Dan Bauman, "Who Is the Master at Master's University and Seminary?" *Chronicle of Higher Education*, November 29, 2018, www.chronicle.com/article/Fear-Intimidation/245206.

68. According to her biography page on the website of Capitol Ministries: "Danielle Drollinger: Biography," 2019, https://capmin .org/who-we-are/administration/danielle-drollinger-biography/.

69. Strang, *God and Donald Trump*, 30.

70. Official sponsors are listed on the Capitol Ministries website: "White House Cabinet Sponsors," 2019, https://capmin.org/ministries /washington-dc/white-house-cabinet-sponsors/.

71. Trump, *Great Again*, 130. He has also said this at rallies, e.g., at a rally in Mobile, Alabama, on August 23, 2015 (Carol Pogash, ed., *Quotations from Chairman Trump* [New York: Rosetta, 2016], 17).

72. Owen Amos, "Inside the White House Bible Study Group," BBC News, April 8, 2018, www.bbc.com/news/world-us-canada-43534724.

73. Katherine Stewart, "The Museum of the Bible Is a Safe Space for Christian Nationalists," *New York Times*, January 6, 2018, www .nytimes.com/2018/01/06/opinion/sunday/the-museum-of-the-bible-is-a-safe-space-for-christian-nationalists.html. The response was posted on the website of Capitol Ministries: "Fake News: The New York Times Gets It Wrong," January 8, 2018, https://capmin.org/response_media/fake-news-the-new-york-times-gets-it-wrong/.

74. Ralph Drollinger, "Clarifying the Continual Confusion about the Separation of Church and State," Capitol Ministries, April 28, 2017, https://capmin.org/clarifying-continual-confusion-separation-church-state/. A methodologically flawed textbook that has become influential among conservative Christians similarly patches together a number of garbled and decontextualized biblical texts to proclaim "significant Christian influence on Government" as a biblical mandate; see Wayne A. Grudem, *Politics According to the Bible: A Comprehensive Resource for Understanding Modern Political Issues in Light of Scripture* (Grand Rapids, MI: Zondervan, 2010), especially chaps. 2–3.

75. Kashmira Gander, "White House Bible Study Led by Pastor Who Is Anti-gay, Anti-women and Anti-Catholic," *Newsweek,* April 11, 2018,www.newsweek.com/white-house-bible-group-led-pastor-anti-gay-anti-women-anti-catholic-881860; Von Lucas Wiegelmann, "Meet the Preacher Who Teaches the Bible to the US Cabinet," *Welt,* October 29, 2017, www.welt.de/kultur/article170140247/Meet-the-preacher-who-teaches-the-Bible-to-the-US-Cabinet.html.

76. Allison Kaplan Sommer, "Trump Cabinet Is Undergoing a 'Spiritual Awakening' Thanks to Bible Group, Boasts Evangelical Pastor,"*Haaretz,*August1,2017,www.haaretz.com/us-news/.premium-pastor-trump-cabinet-undergoes-spiritual-awakening-due-to-bible-group-1.5438404.

77. Ralph Drollinger, "The Bible as an Aid to TST—Terrorist Sensitivity Training," Capitol Ministries, June 2, 2014, https://lobelog.com/is-mike-pompeo-as-islamophobic-as-his-spiritual-adviser/.

78. Ralph Drollinger, "Government and Economics: Free Markets and Regulation," Capitol Ministries, October 21, 2013, https://capmin.org/government-and-economics-free-markets-and-regulation/.

79. Candida R. Moss and Joel S. Baden, *Bible Nation: The United States of Hobby Lobby* (Princeton, NJ: Princeton University Press, 2017). For the forgeries, see Candida Moss, "Bible Museum's Dead Sea Scrolls Turn Out to Be Forgeries," *Daily Beast,* October 22, 2018, www.thedailybeast.com/bible-museums-dead-sea-scrolls-turn-out-to-be-forgeries?ref=scroll; Richard Luscombe, "'Dead Sea Scrolls Fragments' at Museum of the Bible Are All Fakes, Study Says," *Guardian,* March 16, 2020, www.theguardian.com/books/2020/mar/16/dead-sea-scrolls-fragments-at-museum-of-the-bible-are-all-fakes-study-says.

80. Cavan Concannon, "Theo-Politics, Archaeology, and the Ideology of the Museum of the Bible" in *The Museum of the Bible: A Critical Introduction* (Lanham, MD: Lexington/Fortress, 2019), ed. Jill Hicks-Keeton and Cavan Concannon, 101–20; Mark A. Chancey, "Museum of the Bible's Politicized Holy Land Trip," in Keeton and Concannon, *Museum of the Bible,* 275–94.

81. Moss and Baden, *Bible Nation,* 8–11.

82. As Moss and Baden have shown, the museum "does not appeal to its evangelical bona fides in order to leverage itself. Arguably, it

doesn't have to: the involvement of the Green family and the celebrity pastor Rick Warren already telegraph that the museum has Protestant roots. Instead, the museum emphasizes its academic credentials" (*Bible Nation*, 143).

83. Stewart, "Museum of the Bible."

84. Katherine Stewart, "Betsy DeVos and God's Plan for Schools," *New York Times,* December 13, 2016, www.nytimes.com/2016/12/13/opinion /betsy-devos-and-gods-plan-for-schools.html.

85. Isa. 44:28; 45:1–3, 13. Mansfield, *Choosing Donald Trump,* 148–51; Fea, *Believe Me,* 144–45.

86. For critiques of Trump from the Christian Left, see the essays in Miguel A. De La Torre, ed., *Faith and Resistance in the Age of Trump* (Maryknoll, NY: Orbis, 2017).

5. FAMILY VALUES

1. Quoted in Darren E. Grem, *The Blessings of Business: How Corporations Shaped Conservative Christianity* (Oxford: Oxford University Press, 2016), 72.

2. On *Christianity Today* as an opponent of the *Christian Century,* see Kenneth W. Shipps, "*Christianity Today*," in *The Conservative Press in Twentieth-Century America,* ed. Ronald Lora and William Henry Longton (Westport, CT: Greenwood, 1999), 171–80. On Pew's patronage, see Grem, *Blessings of Business,* 70–81. On the Pew family and oil executives' influence on the rise of conservatism, see Darren Dochuk, *Anointed with Oil: How Christianity and Crude Made Modern America* (New York: Basic, 2019).

3. Dennis P. Hollinger, "American Individualism and Evangelical Social Ethics: A Study of *Christianity Today,* 1956–1976" (PhD diss., Drew University, 1981), 202, quoted in Shipps, "*Christianity Today*," 176.

4. Rosemary Radford Ruether, *Christianity and the Making of the Modern Family* (Boston: Beacon, 2000).

5. On the history and ideology of the family values movement, see Seth Dowland, *Family Values and the Rise of the Christian Right* (Philadelphia: University of Pennsylvania Press, 2015). For accounts of Dobson's Focus on the Family, see Dan Gilgoff, *The Jesus Machine: How James Dobson, Focus on the Family, and Evangelical America Are Winning the Culture*

War (New York: St. Martin's, 2007); Hilde Løvdal Stephens, *Family Matters: James Dobson and Focus on the Family's Crusade for the Christian Home* (Tuscaloosa: University of Alabama Press, 2019).

6. Ralph Drollinger, "Clarity Regarding Same Sex Marriage," Capitol Ministries, January 23, 2018, https://capmin.org/clarity-regarding-same-sex-marriage/; "God's View on Babies—Inside and Outside the Womb," Capitol Ministries, March 19, 2019, https://capmin.org/gods-view-on-babies-inside-and-outside-the-womb/.

7. Chrys Ingraham, *White Weddings: Romancing Heterosexuality in Popular Culture* (New York: Routledge, 1999).

8. *Digest* 50.16.195 (Ulpian). Translation adapted from Jane F. Gardner and Thomas Wiedemann, eds., *The Roman Household: A Sourcebook* (London: Routledge, 1991), 4.

9. L. Michael White, "Paul and *Pater Familias*," in *Paul in the Greco-Roman World: A Handbook*, ed. J. Paul Sampley, rev. ed. (London: Bloomsbury, 2016), 171–203.

10. Craig A. Williams, *Roman Homosexuality*, 2nd ed. (Oxford: Oxford University Press, 2010), 280–86. On Roman marriage law, see Susan Treggiari, *Roman Marriage: Iusti Coniuges from the Time of Cicero to the Time of Ulpian* (Oxford: Clarendon, 1991).

11. Michael L. Satlow, *Jewish Marriage in Antiquity* (Princeton, NJ: Princeton University Press, 2001), 98, 191–92.

12. *P.Yad.* 10, line 5, in *The Documents from the Bar Kochba Period in the Cave of Letters* (1989; repr., Jerusalem, 2002); all further citations to this papyrus are from this translation. Cf. *P.Mur.* 20, line 3, in *Les grottes de Murabba'ât*, ed. P. Benoît, J. T. Milik, et R. de Vaux (Oxford: Clarendon Press, 1961). See Satlow, *Jewish Marriage*, 85–86.

13. *P.Yad.* 10. Satlow, *Jewish Marriage*, 98–99; Jacobine G. Oudshoorn, *The Relationship between Roman and Local Law in the Babatha and Salome Komaise Archives: General Analysis and Three Case Studies on Law of Succession, Guardianship and Marriage* (Leiden: Brill, 2007), 379–98. The marriage contract makes the patriarchal assumption throughout that it's the husband's duty to protect the wife, but we know on the basis of Babatha's own possessions that the marriage would have also helped Judah financially—perhaps even more than Babatha.

14. On marriage ages across the empire, see Peter Garnsey and Richard P. Saller, *The Roman Empire: Economy, Society and Culture*, 2nd ed. (Oakland: University of California Press, 2015), 159. On marriage ages among Jews, see Satlow, *Jewish Marriage*, 105–9. On average life expectancy, see Garnsey and Saller, *Roman Empire*, 161.

15. John J. Collins, "Marriage, Divorce, and Family in Second Temple Judaism," in *Families in Ancient Israel*, ed. Leo G. Perdue et al. (Louisville, KY: Westminster John Knox, 1997), 109.

16. Collins, "Marriage, Divorce, and Family," 115–21.

17. Sabine R. Huebner, *The Family in Roman Egypt: A Comparative Approach to Intergenerational Solidarity and Conflict* (Cambridge: Cambridge University Press, 2013); Treggiari, *Roman Marriage*, 72–73.

18. Keith Hopkins, "Contraception in the Roman Empire," *Comparative Studies in Society and History* 8 (1965): 124–51.

19. Maureen Carroll, *Infancy and Earliest Childhood in the Roman World: "A Fragment of Time"* (Oxford: Oxford University Press, 2018), 147–51.

20. The ceremony marking the child's acceptance into the family is known as the *Dies Lustricus* and took place on the eighth day for boys and ninth for girls. Plutarch, *Roman Questions* 288b–e; Macrobius, *Saturnalia* 1.16.36.

21. *P.Oxy.* IV 744 (17 BCE, Egypt), in *The Oxyrhynchus Papyri*, gen. ed. Bernard P. Grenfell and Arthur S. Hunt (London: Egypt Exploration Fund, 1904).

22. Soranus, *Gynecology* 1.60, trans. Owsei Temkin, *Soranus' Gynecology* (Baltimore: Johns Hopkins University Press, 1991). See further Konstantinos Kapparis, *Abortion in the Ancient World* (London: Duckworth, 2002), 16–18, 78–81.

23. Aristotle, *History of Animals* 7.583b.14–23.

24. Véronique Dasen, "Becoming Human: From the Embryo to the Newborn Child," in *The Oxford Handbook of Childhood and Education in the Classical World*, ed. Judith Evans Grubbs and Tim Parkin (Oxford: Oxford University Press, 2013), 19.

25. Tara Mulder, "Ancient Medicine and Fetal Personhood," *Eidolon*, October 26, 2015, https://eidolon.pub/ancient-medicine-and-the-straw-man-of-fetal-personhood-73eed36b945a.

26. Richard B. Hays, *The Moral Vision of the New Testament: Community, Cross, New Creation: A Contemporary Introduction to New Testament Ethics* (New York: HarperOne, 1996), 446–47. Another biblical text commonly cited as proof of fetal personhood is Jer. 1:5, "Before I formed you in the womb I knew you." This text should probably be understood metaphorically, but even if we take it literally, it doesn't specify at what point during gestation God "formed" the fetus (and similarly with Ps. 139:13–15). Even more importantly, when Jeremiah expresses his wish that he never had a life, he speaks of being "killed" from the womb (Jer. 20:14–18). The Hebrew word used for "killed" here is never used anywhere in the Bible for instances of "murder"—that is, for the intentional and unjustified homicide of a human that is forbidden by the Ten Commandments. See Richard Elliott Friedman and Shawna Dolansky, *The Bible Now* (Oxford: Oxford University Press, 2011), 43–52.

27. E.g., Gen. 2:7; 6:17; 7:15, 22. See Friedman and Dolansky, *Bible Now*, 52–53. The Mishnah further explains that a fetus becomes a person only when the greater part of its head or body (if a breech birth) has emerged from its mother's body; Mishnah Niddah 3:5. See John J. Collins, *What Are Biblical Values? What the Bible Says on Key Ethical Issues* (New Haven, CT: Yale University Press, 2019), 54.

28. Kapparis, *Abortion*, 176–94.

29. Strabo, *Geography* 17.824; Tacitus, *Histories* 5.5; Josephus, *Against Apion* 2.202. For a survey of ancient Jewish perspectives on abortion, see Julian Barr, *Tertullian and the Unborn Child: Christian and Pagan Attitudes in Historical Perspective* (New York: Routledge, 2017), 76–81.

30. Musonius Rufus 12 (*Concerning Sexual Pleasures*), excerpted in Jennifer Larson, ed., *Greek and Roman Sexualities: A Sourcebook* (London: Bloomsbury, 2012), 176.

31. David M. Halperin, *One Hundred Years of Homosexuality: And Other Essays on Greek Love* (New York: Routledge, 2012), 15.

32. Michel Foucault, *The History of Sexuality*, vol. 1, *An Introduction*, trans. Robert Hurley (New York: Vintage, 1990).

33. *CIL* (*Corpus Inscriptionum Latinarum*, gen. ed. Theodor Mommsen [Berlin, 1862—]) IV 2210, 3932, translated by Thomas Hubbard in *Homosexuality in Greece and Rome: A Sourcebook of Basic Documents* (Berkeley: University of California Press, 2003), 422. Sarah Levin-

Richardson provides critical insights into the sex culture reflected in the archaeological evidence from Pompeii in *The Brothel of Pompeii: Sex, Class, and Gender at the Margins of Roman Society* (Cambridge: Cambridge University Press, 2019).

34. See the classic study of Roman toxic masculinity by Amy Richlin, *The Garden of Priapus: Sexuality and Aggression in Roman Humor*, rev. ed. (New York: Oxford University Press, 1992).

35. For a general overview, see Williams, *Roman Homosexuality*.

36. Musonius Rufus 12, excerpted in Larson, *Greek and Roman Sexualities*, 175.

37. 1 Cor. 5–7. For discussions of references (and potential references) to same-sex sex in Rom. 1:26–27 and 1 Cor. 6:9, see Dale B. Martin, *Sex and the Single Savior: Gender and Sexuality in Biblical Interpretation* (Louisville, KY: Westminster John Knox, 2006), 37–54; Sarah Ruden, *Paul among the People: The Apostle Reinterpreted and Reimagined in His Own Time* (New York: Image, 2010).

38. The argument I am presenting here has been made at length, with careful attention to the difficult Hebrew in these verses and sustained engagement with recent scholarship, in Friedman and Dolansky, *Bible Now,* chap. 1. See also Jonathan L. Jackson, "Culture Wars, Homosexuality, and the Bible," in *The Bible in Political Debate: What Does It Really Say?,* ed. Frances Flannery and Rodney Alan Werline (London: Bloomsbury, 2016), 87–100; Collins, *What Are Biblical Values?,* 70–74.

39. Lev. 18:18. See Friedman and Dolansky, *Bible Now,* 14.

40. Middle Assyrian Law A 20, cited and discussed in Friedman and Dolansky, *Bible Now,* 31.

41. For a survey of sources, see William Loader, *Making Sense of Sex: Attitudes towards Sexuality in Early Jewish and Christian Literature* (Grand Rapids, MI: Eerdmans, 2013).

42. Even condemnations of lesbian sex in the Roman world were based on the idea that a male penetrator was a prerequisite for "natural" sex. See Bernadette J. Brooten, *Love between Women: Early Christian Responses to Female Homoeroticism* (Chicago: University of Chicago Press, 1996).

43. Lauren Berlant, *The Queen of America Goes to Washington City: Essays on Sex and Citizenship* (Durham, NC: Duke University Press, 1997).

44. Neil J. Young, *We Gather Together: The Religious Right and the Problem of Interfaith Politics* (Oxford: Oxford University Press, 2016), 101. See also Jackson, "Culture Wars," 22.

45. Quoted in Young, *We Gather Together*, 103.

46. Daniel K. Williams, *Defenders of the Unborn: The Pro-life Movement before Roe v. Wade* (Oxford: Oxford University Press, 2016), 85.

47. Quotations from Dowland, *Family Values*, 115–16.

48. Adam Rogers, "'Heartbeat Bills' Get the Science of Fetal Heartbeats All Wrong," *Wired*, May 14, 2019, www.wired.com/story /heartbeat-bills-get-the-science-of-fetal-heartbeats-all-wrong/.

49. Chris Cameron, "Trump Repeats a False Claim That Doctors 'Execute' Newborns," *New York Times*, April 28, 2019, www.nytimes.com /2019/04/28/us/politics/trump-abortion-fact-check.html.

50. Tara C. Jatlaoui et al., "Abortion Surveillance—United States, 2015," *Morbidity and Mortality Weekly Report Surveillance Summaries* 67–13 (November 3, 2018): 1–45, www.cdc.gov/mmwr/volumes/67/ss/ss6713a1 .htm#suggestedcitation.

51. Earlier texts by Christ followers, such as the Epistle of Barnabas (19:5) and Apocalypse of Peter (8), described abortion as murder. But they didn't supply extensive medical justifications for prohibiting abortion the way Tertullian would. See Barr, *Tertullian*, 82–95.

52. Tertullian, *On the Soul* 26.4–9. See Barr, *Tertullian*, 103–6.

53. Tertullian, *On the Apparel of Women* 1.1. On Tertullian's contradicting arguments about when a fetus becomes a human being, see Barr, *Tertullian*.

54. A second-century CE infancy gospel known as the Proto-Gospel of James claims that Mary was twelve when she married Joseph (8.3–9.12) and sixteen when she became pregnant (12.9).

55. Emily McFarlan Miller, "Conservatives Defend Roy Moore— Invoking Joseph, Mary and the Ten Commandments," Religion News Service, November 10, 2017, https://religionnews.com/2017/11/10 /conservatives-defend-roy-moore-invoking-joseph-mary-and-the-ten-commandments/.

56. Joseph A. Fitzmyer, *The Gospel According to Luke (I–IX)* (New York: Doubleday, 1970), 363.

57. Pseudo-Plutarch, *Doctrines of the Philosophers* 5.15.907. See Dasen, "Becoming Human," 19; Kapparis, *Abortion*, 41–44.

58. Fitzmyer, *Gospel According to Luke*, 364.

59. E.g., John P. Meier, *A Marginal Jew*, vol. 2, *Mentor, Message, and Miracles* (New York: Doubleday, 1994); Joel Marcus, *John the Baptist in History and Theology* (Columbia: University of South Carolina Press, 2018).

60. François Bovon, *Luke 1: A Commentary on the Gospel of Luke 1:1–9:50* (Minneapolis, MN: Fortress, 2002), 58–59.

61. Ruth Graham, "Yep, the Purple Teletubby Was Gay," *Slate*, December 7, 2017, https://slate.com/technology/2017/12/jerry-falwell-and-tinky-winky-the-gay-teletubby.html; Nick Wing, "Christian Extremists Praise Anti-LGBT Violence after Orlando Because Every Religion Has Radicals," June 22, 2016, www.huffingtonpost.ca/entry/christian-extremists-orlando-shooting_n_576ad4f7e4b0c0252e7805ba.

62. Quoted in Anthony Michael Petro, *After the Wrath of God: AIDS, Sexuality, and American Religion* (Oxford: Oxford University Press, 2015), 28.

63. Jerry Falwell, *Listen, America!* (New York: Doubleday, 1980), 183.

64. Tim LaHaye, *What Everyone Should Know about Homosexuality*, 4th ed. (Wheaton, IL: Living Books, 1978 [originally published as *The Unhappy Gays: What Everyone Should Know about Homosexuality*]), 203. See further Thomas L. Long, "Apocalyptus Interruptus: Christian Fundamentalists, Sodomy, and the End," in *Gender and Apocalyptic Desire*, ed. Brenda E. Brasher and Lee Quinby (New York: Routledge, 2014).

65. Quoted in Gilgoff, *Jesus Machine*, 147.

66. Michelangelo Signorile, "Mike Pence's Beliefs Are Clear: Same-Sex Marriage Leads to 'Societal Collapse,'" *HuffPost*, February 16, 2018, www.huffpost.com/entry/opinion-signorile-mike-pence-adam-rippo_n_5a8473dfe4b0058d55654e9e.

67. Michelangelo Signorile, "President Trump's Anti-LGBT Agenda Is Louder Than His Pride Message," *Daily Beast*, May 31, 2019, www.thedailybeast.com/president-trumps-anti-lgbt-agenda-is-louder-than-his-pride-message.

68. Stoyan Zaimov, "Franklin Graham Tells Target to Respect 'Genders That God Created' after Store Opts for Gender-Neutral

Sections," *Christian Post,* August 12, 2015, www.christianpost.com/news /franklin-graham-tells-target-to-respect-genders-that-god-created-after-store-opts-for-gender-neutral-sections.html.

69. J. Andrew Overman, *Matthew's Gospel and Formative Judaism: The Social World of the Matthean Community* (Minneapolis, MN: Fortress, 1990); Anthony J. Saldarini, *Matthew's Christian-Jewish Community* (Chicago: University of Chicago Press, 1994); John Kampen, *Matthew within Sectarian Judaism: An Examination* (New Haven, CT: Yale University Press, 2019).

70. Jesus's instructions on divorce and remarriage are also presented in the Sermon on the Mount (Matt. 5:31–32), which characterizes Jesus as a New Moses. The Greek word that is usually interpreted as adultery in these passages is *porneia,* which can refer to types of sexual immorality ranging from adultery to rape and incest.

71. Mishnah Gittin 9:10. See Saldarini, *Matthew's Christian-Jewish Community,* 150; Ulrich Luz, *Matthew 8–20: A Commentary* (Minneapolis, MN: Fortress, 2001), 488.

72. Jennifer Wright Knust, *Unprotected Texts: The Bible's Surprising Contradictions about Sex and Desire* (New York: HarperOne, 2011), 69–77.

73. 1 Cor. 7:10–16.

74. Jennifer Glass and Philip Levchak, "Red States, Blue States, and Divorce: Understanding the Impact of Conservative Protestantism on Regional Variation in Divorce Rates," *American Journal of Sociology* 119 (2014): 1002–46.

75. Taryn Hillin, "You May Be Surprised How Many Born-Again Christians Use Ashley Madison," *HuffPost,* June 4, 2014, www .huffingtonpost.ca/entry/infidelity-and-religion_n_5447526.

76. Jack Rogers, *Jesus, the Bible, and Homosexuality: Explode the Myths, Heal the Church,* rev. ed. (Louisville, KY: Westminster John Knox, 2009), 130–31.

77. *Digest* 50.16.128 (Ulpian); Mathew Kuefler, *The Manly Eunuch: Masculinity, Gender Ambiguity, and Christian Ideology in Late Antiquity* (Chicago: University of Chicago Press, 2001), 32–34.

78. Kuefler, *Manly Eunuch,* 63.

79. Pliny the Elder, *Natural History* 11.110.

80. Lucian, *Eunuch* 6.

81. Philo of Alexandria, *On Dreams* 2.184. See also Philo, *On the Special Laws* 1.324–25; Josephus, *Jewish Antiquities* 4.290–91.

82. Kuefler, *Manly Eunuch*, 33.

83. Mishnah Yevamot 8:4–6. See Jack Collins, "Appropriation and Development of Castration as a Symbol and Practice in Early Christianity," in *Castration and Culture in the Middle Ages,* ed. Larissa Tracy (Cambridge: Brewer, 2013), 74–78; Luz, *Matthew 8–20, 501*.

84. Matthew might be influenced here by the prophecy in Isa. 56:3–5, which implies that in the future kingdom eunuchs will be shown to be fertile regardless of whether they can produce children (Knust, *Unprotected Texts*, 68–69).

85. See also Mark 12:18–27; Luke 20:27–39; 1 Cor. 15:35–58. Candida Moss discusses attempts by male Christian leaders to interpret these New Testament teachings about resurrected bodies toward more traditional gender norms in subsequent centuries: *Divine Bodies: Resurrecting Perfection in the New Testament and Early Christianity* (New Haven, CT: Yale University Press, 2019), 69–71.

86. Wayne A. Meeks, *In Search of the Early Christians: Selected Essays* (New Haven, CT: Yale University Press, 2002), 3–54.

87. Dale B. Martin, *The Corinthian Body* (New Haven, CT: Yale University Press, 1999), 230–32.

88. Gospel of Thomas 114, ed. and trans. J. K. Elliott, *The Apocryphal New Testament: A Collection of Apocryphal Christian Literature in an English Translation Based on M. R. James* (Oxford: Oxford University Press, 1993). Most historians date the text between the mid-first century CE and the mid-second century CE.

89. Tertullian, *On Female Fashion* 1.2, trans. S. Thelwall, in *Ante-Nicene Fathers: Translations of the Writings of the Fathers Down to A.D. 325,* ed. Alexander Roberts and James Dondalson, vol. 4 (Buffalo, NY: Christian Literature Publishing, 1885).

90. Acts 8 also highlights the positive example of a eunuch for followers of Christ. See Brittany E. Wilson, *Unmanly Men: Refigurations of Masculinity in Luke-Acts* (Oxford: Oxford University Press, 2015).

91. Matt. 12:48; Mark 3:33. See also Luke 8:19–21; 14:25–26.

92. Matt. 8:22. See also Luke 9:57–62.

93. See further, David Wheeler-Reed, *Regulating Sex in the Roman Empire: Ideology, the Bible, and the Early Christians* (New Haven, CT: Yale University Press, 2017).

6. CHARITY

1. Gary Scott Smith, *Religion in the Oval Office: The Religious Lives of American Presidents* (Oxford: Oxford University Press, 2015), 203.

2. "Remarks on Private Sector Initiatives at a White House Luncheon for National Religious Leaders (April 13, 1982)," in *Public Papers of the Presidents of the United States: Ronald Reagan, 1982* (Washington, DC: US Government Printing Office, 1982), 454. Nick Spencer has shown that the Samaritan was also a regular feature in Margaret Thatcher's neoliberal rhetoric during this era; see *The Political Samaritan: How Power Hijacked a Parable* (London: Bloomsbury, 2017).

3. Kathryn Edin and H. Luke Shaefer, *$2.00 a Day: Living on Almost Nothing in America* (Boston: Houghton Mifflin Harcourt, 2015), 16; Joe Soss, Richard C. Fording, and Sanford F. Schram, *Disciplining the Poor: Neoliberal Paternalism and the Persistent Power of Race* (Chicago: University of Chicago Press, 2011), 33; Tamura Lomax, *Jezebel Unhinged: Loosing the Black Female Body in Religion and Culture* (Durham, NC: Duke University Press, 2018), 69–73.

4. Edin and Shaefer, *$2.00 a Day*, 1–33.

5. "The 104th Congress: The Republican Leader; Excerpts from Gingrich's Speech on Party's Agenda for the 104th Congress," *New York Times,* January 5, 1995, www.nytimes.com/1995/01/05/us/104th-congress-republican-leader-excerpts-gingrich-s-speech-party-s-agenda-for.html.

6. William J. Clinton, "Remarks to the Progressive National Baptist Convention in Charlotte, North Carolina (Aug. 9, 1995)," American Presidency Project, www.presidency.ucsb.edu/documents/remarks-the-progressive-national-baptist-convention-charlotte-north-carolina. See further Smith, *Religion,* 353–55.

7. Edin and Shaefer, *$2.00 a Day,* 17–33.

8. Marian Wright Edelman, "Say No to This Welfare Reform,"

Washington Post, November 3, 1995, www.washingtonpost.com/archive /opinions/1995/11/03/say-no-to-this-welfare-reform/761831e4–5327–4e40– 8aae-44b43a9fee41/; Personal Responsibility, Work Opportunity, and Medicaid Restructuring Act of 1996, *Congressional Record,* vol. 142, no. 106 (July 18, 1996), www.congress.gov/104/crec/1996/07/18/CREC-1996–07–18-pt1-PgS8070.pdf.

9. "Near poverty" represents "individuals who are less than 50% above the official poverty line" (Rubin Patterson and Giselle Thompson, "Transnational Factors Driving U.S. Inequality and Poverty," in *The Routledge Handbook of Poverty in the United States,* ed. Stephen Haymes, Maria Vidal de Haymes, and Reuben Jonathan Miller [New York: Routledge, 2014], 33, 41).

10. Cicero, *On His House* 89.

11. Dionysius of Halicarnassus, *Roman Antiquities* 7.20, quoted in Paul Erdkamp, "The Food Supply of the Capital," in *The Cambridge Companion to Ancient Rome,* ed. Paul Erdkamp (Cambridge: Cambridge University Press, 2013), 269. *Alimenta* are sometimes described as a Roman form of welfare, but the program was not formalized until the second century CE, only pertained to Italy, and had a negligible impact.

12. Aristotle, *Rhetoric* 1361a42–1361b3; *Nicomachean Ethics* 4.1.7; Seneca the Younger, *On Benefits* 4.3.1–2. On contradictions in Seneca's view, see Thomas R. Blanton IV, *A Spiritual Economy: Gift Exchange in the Letters of Paul of Tarsus* (New Haven, CT: Yale University Press, 2017), chap. 3.

13. There is a great deal of scholarship on Greco-Roman benefaction. For an insightful recent study, see Arjan Zuiderhoek, *The Politics of Munificence in the Roman Empire: Citizens, Elites and Benefactors in Asia Minor* (Cambridge: Cambridge University Press, 2009). On civic benefaction in early Christian sources, see Bruce W. Winter, *Seek the Welfare of the City: Christians as Benefactors and Citizens* (Grand Rapids, MI: Eerdmans, 1994).

14. Plautus, *Trinummus* 339, cited in Anneliese R. Parkin, "'You Do Him No Service': An Exploration of Pagan Almsgiving," in *Poverty in the Roman World,* ed. Margaret Atkins and Robin Osborne (Cambridge: Cambridge University Press, 2006), 65–66. See also Roman Garrison, *Redemptive Almsgiving in Early Christianity* (Sheffield: Sheffield Academic Press, 1993), 38–45.

15. Gregg Gardner, *The Origins of Organized Charity in Rabbinic Judaism* (Cambridge: Cambridge University Press, 2015).

16. Daniel (Theodotion's Greek version) 4:27 (NETS, adapted), discussed in Garrison, *Redemptive Almsgiving*, 52. See further Gary A. Anderson, *Charity: The Place of the Poor in the Biblical Tradition* (New Haven, CT: Yale University Press, 2013).

17. Gardner, *Origins of Organized Charity*, 31–32; Tony Keddie, *Class and Power in Roman Palestine: The Socioeconomic Setting of Judaism and Christian Origins* (Cambridge: Cambridge University Press, 2019), 179.

18. Pseudo-Diogenes, *Epistles* 33.3, ed. Abraham J. Malherbe, *The Cynic Epistles: A Study Edition* (Atlanta: Scholars, 1977), 141. For further discussion of ancient Roman views of poverty, see the essays in Margaret Atkins and Robin Osborne, eds., *Poverty in the Roman World* (Cambridge: Cambridge University Press, 2006). For early Christian perspectives, see Helen Rhee, *Loving the Poor, Saving the Rich: Wealth, Poverty, and Early Christian Formation* (Grand Rapids, MI: Baker, 2012).

19. See the varying assessments in Walter Scheidel and Steven J. Friesen, "The Size of the Economy and the Distribution of Income in the Roman Empire," *Journal of Roman Studies* 99 (2009): 69–91; Steven J. Friesen, "Poverty in Pauline Studies: Beyond the So-Called New Consensus," *Journal for the Study of the New Testament* 26 (2004): 323–61; Bruce Longenecker, *Remember the Poor: Paul, Poverty, and the Greco-Roman World* (Grand Rapids, MI: Eerdmans, 2010); Timothy A. Brookins, "Economic Profiling of Early Christian Communities," in *Paul and Economics: A Handbook*, ed. Thomas R. Blanton IV and Raymond Pickett (Minneapolis, MN: Fortress, 2017), 57–88.

20. In 2017 (the latest available data), the official poverty rate was 12.3 percent, based on poverty thresholds of $12,488 for a single person and $24,858 for a family of four with two children under eighteen. Kayla Fontenot, Jessica Semega, and Melissa Kollar, "Income and Poverty in the United States: 2017," US Census Bureau, September 12, 2018, www.census.gov/library/publications/2018/demo/p60–263.html). See also Patterson and Thompson, "Transnational Factors."

21. Peter Garnsey, *Cities, Peasants and Food in Classical Antiquity: Essays in Social and Economic History* (Cambridge: Cambridge University Press, 1998), 213.

22. Stephen Caliendo, *Inequality in America: Race, Poverty, and Fulfilling Democracy's Promise* (New York: Routledge, 2018); Peter Edelman, *Not a Crime to Be Poor: The Criminalization of Poverty in America* (New York: New Press, 2017).

23. Erich S. Gruen, *Rethinking the Other in Antiquity* (Princeton, NJ: Princeton University Press, 2011); Frank M. Snowden Jr., *Before Color Prejudice: The Ancient View of Blacks* (Cambridge, MA: Harvard University Press, 1991).

24. William V. Harris, ed., *Popular Medicine in Graeco-Roman Antiquity: Explorations* (Leiden: Brill, 2016).

25. Kyle Harper, *The Fate of Rome: Climate, Disease, and the End of an Empire* (Princeton, NJ: Princeton University Press, 2017), chap. 3.

26. Galen, *On Mixtures* 1.4.531; Seneca, *On Clemency* 1.25.4, quoted in Harper, *Fate of Rome*, 87–88.

27. Harper, *Fate of Rome*, 87.

28. Rosemary Margaret Luff, *The Impact of Jesus in First-Century Palestine* (Cambridge: Cambridge University Press, 2019), 114–44.

29. Mary Douglas, *Collected Works*, vol. 2, *Purity and Danger* (London: Routledge, 2013). It is worth noting that the modern concept of hygiene, though informed by scientific knowledge, has been heavily influenced by Protestant Christianity and capitalist ideology; see Kathryn Lofton, *Consuming Religion* (Chicago: University of Chicago Press, 2017), 82–104.

30. E. P. Sanders, *Judaism: Practice and Belief, 63 BCE–66 CE* (London: SCM, 1992), 225–27.

31. Ann Olga Koloski-Ostrow, *The Archaeology of Sanitation in Roman Italy: Toilets, Sewers, and Water Systems* (Chapel Hill: University of North Carolina Press, 2015), 42, 90.

32. On poverty and disease in the US, see Margaret Humphreys, *Malaria: Poverty, Race, and Public Health in the United States* (Baltimore: Johns Hopkins University Press, 2001).

33. Greg Kaufmann, "The Right's Cure for Poverty: Hard Work and Father Figures," *Nation*, June 20, 2019, www.thenation.com/article/poor-peoples-campaign-budget-house-hearing/. Theoharis has articulated her views on Jesus and poverty at length in her *Always with Us? What Jesus Really Said about the Poor* (Grand Rapids, MI: Eerdmans, 2017).

34. Julie Zauzmer, "Christians Are More Than Twice as Likely

to Blame a Person's Poverty on Lack of Effort," *Washington Post*, August 3, 2017, www.washingtonpost.com/news/acts-of-faith/p/2017/08/03/christians-are-more-than-twice-as-likely-to-blame-a-persons-poverty-on-lack-of-effort/.

35. Republican Christians often turn to another New Testament text, 2 Thess. 3:10 ("Anyone unwilling to work should not eat"), to support their opposition to welfare. As Werline has shown, this exhortation was intended for a community that became carried away with "fanatical fervor" for a rapidly approaching end-time. The letter sought to instruct believers that they should stop shirking their regular activities because the new age might not arrive so soon (Rodney A. Werline, "Work, Poverty, and Welfare," in *The Bible in Political Debate: What Does It Really Say?*, ed. Frances Flannery and Rodney A. Werline [London: Bloomsbury, 2016], 75–78).

36. Joel Osteen, *It's Your Time: Activate Your Faith, Achieve Your Dreams, and Increase in God's Favor* (New York: Howard, 2010), 45–46.

37. Tom Porter, "Joel Osteen: Televangelist Whose Church Closed during Hurricane Harvey Tells Victims Not to Have 'Poor Me' Attitude," *Newsweek*, September 4, 2017, www.newsweek.com/joel-osteen-televangelist-whose-church-closed-during-hurricane-harvey-tells-659302.

38. Luke 4:16–30, quoting Isa. 58:6; 61:1–2.

39. Lev. 25:8–55. See Jonathan Kaplan, "The Credibility of Liberty: The Plausibility of the Jubilee Legislation of Leviticus 25 in Ancient Israel and Judah," *Catholic Biblical Quarterly* 81 (2019): 183–203.

40. John Sietze Bergsma, *The Jubilee from Leviticus to Qumran: A History of Interpretation* (Leiden: Brill, 2007), 190–203.

41. E.g., Lev. 1:3–4; 22:20–21.

42. Gildas H. Hamel, *Poverty and Charity in Roman Palestine, First Three Centuries C.E.* (Berkeley: University of California Press, 1990), 164–211.

43. Luke 16:19–31.

44. Mark 10:46–52; Acts 3:1–10. See also John 9:1–12.

45. Luke 4:18; 7:22; 14:13, 21; 16:19–31.

46. Luke 10:25–37; 16:19–31; 19:1–10.

47. There are certain points in the Gospel of Luke at which Jesus commends someone for giving some surplus wealth to the poor (19:8), others at which he requires a person to sell "all that you own" (14:33; 18:22), and others at which Jesus commends giving alms according to what one can afford to give (21:3). See also Luke 11:41; 12:33; Acts 9:36; 10:2, 4, 31. For discussion of these and other complications in Luke's social ethics, see Halvor Moxnes, *The Economy of the Kingdom: Social Conflict and Economic Relations in Luke's Gospel* (Philadelphia: Fortress, 1988); James A. Metzger, *Consumption and Wealth in Luke's Travel Narrative* (Leiden: Brill, 2007); Christopher M. Hays, *Luke's Wealth Ethics: A Study in Their Coherence and Character* (Tübingen: Mohr Siebeck, 2010).

48. Luke 6:34–35, 38; 17:7–8.

49. Sabine R. Huebner, *Papyri and the Social World of the New Testament* (Cambridge: Cambridge University Press, 2019), 65–86; David A. Fiensy, *Christian Origins and the Ancient Economy* (Eugene, OR: Cascade, 2014), 5–55.

50. Mark 6:3; Matt. 13:55. See Chris Keith, *Jesus against the Scribal Elite: The Origins of the Conflict* (Ada, MI: Baker Academic, 2014), chap. 3.

51. John S. Kloppenborg, *Q, the Earliest Gospel: An Introduction to the Original Stories and Sayings of Jesus* (Louisville, KY: Westminster John Knox, 2008). This book includes a handy translation of the Q material. The existence of Q is part of the "Two Source Hypothesis" in which Mark and Q are the two main sources used independently by Matthew and Luke. While this theory is upheld by a majority of scholars, it has also received important criticisms (e.g., Mark Goodacre, *The Case against Q: Studies in Markan Priority and the Synoptic Problem* [Harrisburg, PA: Trinity, 2002]). Kloppenborg responds to the most significant critiques in chap. 1 of *Q, the Earliest Gospel*.

52. Q 6:20; 10:7; 11:3–4; 16:13 (my translations; the versification of Q follows Luke).

53. See Tony Keddie, *Revelations of Ideology: Apocalyptic Class Politics in Early Roman Palestine* (Leiden: Brill, 2018), 234–42.

54. In Mark, the main teaching on poverty is the story of the rich man who didn't wish to sell his possessions to follow Jesus, which includes the "eye of the needle" saying (Mark 10:17–31; compare Matt.

19:16–30; Luke 18:18–30). Mark's Jesus emphasizes that following him entails material rewards in both the present age and the age to come (Mark 10:30). Of the canonical gospels, John is the least interested in poverty as a theme; its most relevant story is Jesus healing a blind beggar (9:1–12), but it is presented as support for a broader theme of Jesus healing spiritual blindness (e.g., 9:35–41).

55. François Bovon, *Luke 1: A Commentary on the Gospel of Luke 1:1–9:50* (Minneapolis, MN: Fortress, 2002), 11.

56. In Acts 2:42–45; 4:32–37, Luke "portrays systematic economic sharing as a quaint artifact of an idealized past" (Steven J. Friesen, "Injustice or God's Will: Early Christian Explanations of Poverty," in *Wealth and Poverty in Early Church and Society,* ed. Susan R. Holman [Grand Rapids, MI: Baker, 2008], 27). The following narratives in Acts 5:1–11; 6:1–7 divulge Luke's criticism of systematic communal sharing.

57. Matt. 6:12, 14.

58. Compare Matt. 6:19–21; 13:44. See Nathan Eubank, *Wages of Cross-Bearing and Debt of Sin: The Economy of Heaven in Matthew's Gospel* (Berlin: De Gruyter, 2013). Matthew's treatment of almsgiving as a means of atonement and a path to salvation is an elaboration of themes found in Jewish texts and also becomes an influential paradigm for understanding charity in early Christianity. To be clear, Luke shares this theme (e.g., 12:33; 18:22) but goes to much greater lengths to emphasize the plight of the poor and the corruptive power of greed. See further Garrison, *Redemptive Almsgiving;* David J. Downs, *Alms: Charity, Reward, and Atonement in Early Christianity* (Waco, TX: Baylor University Press, 2016). On theological dimensions of Luke's understanding of charity, see Anthony Giambrone, *Sacramental Charity, Creditor Christology, and the Economy of Salvation in Luke's Gospel* (Tübingen: Mohr Siebeck, 2017).

59. Anderson, *Charity,* esp. 20–22.

60. Notably, Luke's distinctive version of the story of the woman's anointing doesn't mention the costs of the ointment and includes an interchange between Jesus and a Pharisee in which Jesus endorses the cancellation of debts (7:36–50). John's version of this story includes the accusation that the money for the ointment could have been given to the poor, but it is the traitor Judas who makes the accusation (12:1–8), rather than some of those present, as in Mark, or the disciples, as in

Matthew. John clarifies that Judas questioned this cost "not because he cared about the poor, but because he was a thief" (12:6), but then proceeds to give the same saying ("You always have the poor") as Matthew without Mark's qualification.

61. Robert Myles, *The Homeless Jesus in the Gospel of Matthew* (Sheffield: Sheffield Phoenix, 2014).

62. Quoted in Alison Collis Greene, "The Welfare of Faith," in *Religion in the Age of Obama*, ed. Juan M. Floyd-Thomas and Anthony B. Pinn (New York: Bloomsbury, 2018), 75.

63. Quoted in Greene, "Welfare of Faith," 75.

64. Quoted in Inderpal Grewal, *Saving the Security State: Exceptional Citizens in Twenty-First-Century America* (Durham, NC: Duke University Press, 2017), 94.

65. Abe Sauer, "Our Government-Funded Mission to Make Haiti Christian: Your Tax Dollars, Billy Graham's Son, Monsanto, and Sarah Palin," *Awl*, January 20, 2011, www.theawl.com/2011/01/our-government-funded-mission-to-make-haiti-christian-your-tax-dollars-billy-grahams-son/.

66. Grewal, *Security State*, 95.

67. David Gonzalez, "U.S. Aids Conversion-Minded Quake Relief in El Salvador," *New York Times*, March 5, 2001, www.nytimes.com/2001/03/05/world/us-aids-conversion-minded-quake-relief-in-el-salvador.html.

68. Gregorio Bettiza, *Finding Faith in Foreign Policy: Religion and American Diplomacy in a Postsecular World* (Oxford: Oxford University Press, 2019), 125.

69. Laurie Goodstein, "Billy Graham Warned against Embracing a President. His Son Has Gone Another Way," *New York Times*, February 26, 2018, www.nytimes.com/2018/02/26/us/billy-graham-franklin-graham-trump.html.

70. Lew Daly, *God and the Welfare State* (Cambridge, MA: MIT Press, 2006); John P. Bartkowski and Helen A. Regis, *Charitable Choices: Religion, Race, and Poverty in the Post-welfare Era* (New York: New York University Press, 2003). Obama renamed the office as the "White House Office of Faith-Based and Neighborhood Partnerships." Under Trump, the White House version of the office appears to have languished, but other

federal offices' "faith-based initiatives" actively pursue partnerships with religious organizations.

71. Grewal, *Security State,* 100.

72. Grewal, *Security State,* 101.

73. Grewal, *Security State,* 99–109; Robert P. Weiss, "Charitable Choice as Neoliberal Social Welfare Strategy," *Social Justice* 28 (2001): 35–53.

74. Nancy Jean Davis and Robert V. Robinson, *Claiming Society for God: Religious Movements and Social Welfare in Egypt, Israel, Italy, and the United States* (Bloomington: Indiana University Press, 2012), 113–42.

75. See further Philip F. Esler, *Community and Gospel in Luke-Acts: The Social and Political Motivations of Lucan Theology* (Cambridge: Cambridge University Press, 1989), 164–200.

76. Luke 10:34–35.

77. Acts 27:3; 1 Tim. 3:5.

78. Sviatoslav Dmitriev, *City Government in Hellenistic and Roman Asia Minor* (Oxford: Oxford University Press, 2005), 119–21.

79. Sirach 50:25–26; Josephus, *Jewish Antiquities* 9.288–91; 11:306–12; 13:74–77. On Jewish-Samaritan relations in antiquity, see Gary N. Knoppers, *Jews and Samaritans: The Origins and History of Their Early Relations* (Oxford: Oxford University Press, 2013). For ethnic stereotyping of Samaritans by Jews and Jewish followers of Christ, see Stewart Penwell, *Jesus the Samaritan: Ethnic Labeling in the Gospel of John* (Leiden: Brill, 2019).

80. Richard Bauckham, "The Scrupulous Priest and the Good Samaritan: Jesus' Parabolic Interpretation of the Law of Moses," *New Testament Studies* 44 (1998): 475–89.

81. Although Luke's story of the Samaritan parable does not appear in the other gospels, Luke incorporated into it Jesus's "Greatest Commandment" teaching from Mark 12:28–34.

82. Bauckham, "Scrupulous Priest."

83. Matthew S. Rindge, "Good Samaritan (Luke 10:25–37)," Bible Odyssey, www.bibleodyssey.org:443/en/passages/main-articles/good-samaritan.

84. Luke 17:18.

85. Tony Keddie, "Who Is My Neighbor? Ethnic Boundaries and the Samaritan Other in Luke 10:25–37," *Biblical Interpretation* 28 (2020): 246–71.

86. Martin Luther King Jr., "A Time to Break the Silence" (sermon delivered at Riverside Church in New York on April 4, 1967) in *A Testament of Hope: The Essential Writings and Speeches of Martin Luther King, Jr.*, ed. James M. Washington (New York: HarperCollins, 1986).

7. CHURCH AND STATE

1. Bruce Barton, *The Man Nobody Knows: A Discovery of the Real Jesus* (1925; repr., Chicago: Ivan R. Dee, 2000). See also the illustrated scenes Barton published as a series in *Good Housekeeping,* which were collected as *The Man of Galilee: Twelve Scenes from the Life of Christ* (New York: Competition, 1928). On the influence of Barton's Jesus, see Leo P. Ribuffo, "Jesus Christ as Business Statesman: Bruce Barton and the Selling of Corporate Capitalism," *American Quarterly* 33 (1981): 206–31; Erin A. Smith, *What Would Jesus Read? Popular Religious Books and Everyday Life in Twentieth-Century America* (Chapel Hill: University of North Carolina Press, 2015), chap. 4.

2. Jeff Sharlet, *The Family: The Secret Fundamentalism at the Heart of American Power* (New York: HarperCollins, 2008), 133.

3. Richard M. Fried, *The Man Everybody Knew: Bruce Barton and the Making of Modern America* (Chicago: Ivan R. Dee, 2005).

4. Barton, *Man Nobody Knows,* 4, 20–21.

5. *IEph* 17–19, ed. H. Engelmanm et al., *Die Inschriften von Ephesos* (Bonn, 1979–84), quoted and translated in Katherine A. Shaner, *Enslaved Leadership in Early Christianity* (Oxford: Oxford University Press, 2018), 33.

6. Edward A. Zelinsky reveals the deep entanglement of church and state in *Taxing the Church: Religion, Exemptions, Entanglement, and the Constitution* (Oxford: Oxford University Press, 2017).

7. Cicero, *Against Verres* 2.5.34, discussed by Brent Nongbri in *Before Religion: A History of a Modern Concept* (New Haven, CT: Yale University Press, 2013), 28.

8. Among others: Nongbri, *Before Religion;* Carlin A. Barton and Daniel Boyarin, *Imagine No Religion: How Modern Abstractions Hide Ancient Realities* (New York: Fordham University Press, 2016).

9. Beate Dignas, *Economy of the Sacred in Hellenistic and Roman Asia Minor* (Oxford: Oxford University Press, 2002).

10. Stanley K. Stowers, "The Religion of Plant and Animal Offerings versus the Religion of Meanings, Essences, and Textual Mysteries," in *Ancient Mediterranean Sacrifice,* ed. Jennifer Wright Knust and Zsuzsanna Várhelyi (Oxford: Oxford University Press, 2011), 35–56; Daniel C. Ullucci, *The Christian Rejection of Animal Sacrifice* (Oxford: Oxford University Press, 2012), 24–30.

11. Shaner, *Enslaved Leadership,* 34.

12. Josephus, *Jewish Antiquities* 16.163–65. Augustus's 12 BCE decree affirmed precedents set by Julius Caesar. See Miriam Pucci Ben Zeev, *Jewish Rights in the Roman World: The Greek and Roman Documents Quoted by Josephus Flavius* (Tübingen: Mohr Siebeck, 1998), 235–56.

13. *Digest* 48.13.7 (Ulpian). See my "Beyond the 'Den of Robbers': The Dialectics of Sacred and Profane Finances in Early Roman Jerusalem," in *The Dialectics of Religion in the Roman World,* ed. Francesca Mazzilli and Dies van der Linde (forthcoming).

14. Martin Goodman, "The Pilgrimage Economy of Jerusalem in the Second Temple Period," in *Jerusalem: Its Sanctity and Centrality to Judaism, Christianity, and Islam,* ed. Lee I. Levine (New York: Continuum, 1999), 69–76; Hayim Lapin, "Feeding the Jerusalem Temple: Cult, Hinterland, and Economy in First-Century Palestine," *Journal of Ancient Judaism* 8 (2017): 410–53.

15. See Tony Keddie, *Class and Power in Roman Palestine: The Socioeconomic Setting of Judaism and Christian Origins* (Cambridge: Cambridge University Press, 2019), 176–88.

16. Josephus, *Jewish Antiquities* 18.3.

17. For a full discussion of the evidence for the arguments in this section, see my *Class and Power,* chap. 4.

18. For overviews of the Roman economy, see Walter Scheidel, ed., *The Cambridge Companion to the Roman Economy* (Cambridge: Cambridge University Press, 2012); Peter F. Bang, *The Roman Bazaar: A Comparative Study of Trade and Markets in a Tributary Empire* (Cambridge: Cambridge University Press, 2008).

19. Russell Moore, "Hobby Lobby Ruling Is a Win for Separation of Church and State," *Time,* June 30, 2014, https://time.com/2942651/hobby-lobby-church-state/.

20. Ralph Drollinger, "Understanding the Separation of Church and State," Capitol Ministries, July 10, 2017, https://capmin.org/understanding-separation-church-state/.

21. Jeffrey Goldberg, "The Rick Warren Interview: No Compromise with Evil," *Atlantic*, August 15, 2008, www.theatlantic.com/daily-dish/archive/2008/08/how-pernicious-is-rick-warren/212933/.

22. Stephen McDowell, *Rendering to Caesar the Things That Are God's: Statism: The Golden Calf of the Modern World* (Charlottesville, VA: Providence, 2009), 3. See Sarah Pulliam Bailey, "This Christian Guide to the Nation's Capital Vows to Tell You What Other Tours Won't," *Washington Post*, May 15, 2018, www.washingtonpost.com/news/acts-of-faith/wp/2018/05/15/this-christian-guide-to-the-nations-capital-vows-to-tell-you-what-other-tours-wont/.

23. Christopher B. Zeichmann, "The Date of Mark's Gospel Apart from the Temple and Rumors of War: The Taxation Episode (12:13–17) as Evidence," *Catholic Biblical Quarterly* 79 (2017): 429–30.

24. Fabian E. Udoh, *To Caesar What Is Caesar's: Tribute, Taxes and Imperial Administration in Early Roman Palestine (63 B.C.E.–70 C.E.)* (Providence, RI: Brown Judaic Studies, 2005), 223–28; Zeichmann, "Date of Mark's Gospel," 431. I have argued in *Class and Power* (122–33) that Judaeans *probably* did pay head taxes to Rome, but there is insufficient evidence to decide one way or the other.

25. Kenneth Lönnqvist, "The Date of Introduction of Denarii to Roman Judaea and the Decapolis Region," *ARAM* 23 (2011): 307–18; Danny Syon, *Small Change in Hellenistic-Roman Galilee: The Evidence from Numismatic Site Finds as a Tool for Historical Reconstruction* (Jerusalem: Israel Numismatic Society, 2015), 212–15; Zeichmann, "Date of Mark's Gospel," 428–29.

26. See, among others, Christopher B. Zeichmann, "Loanwords or Code-Switching? Latin Transliteration and the Setting of Mark's Composition," *Journal of the Jesus Movement in Its Jewish Setting* 4 (2017): 42–64; John S. Kloppenborg, "*Evocatio Deorum* and the Date of Mark," *Journal of Biblical Literature* 124, no. 3 (2005): 419–50; Stephen Simon Kimondo, *The Gospel of Mark and the Roman-Jewish War of 66–70 CE: Jesus' Story as a Contrast to the Events of the War* (Eugene, OR: Pickwick, 2018).

27. L. Michael White, *From Jesus to Christianity: How Four Generations of Visionaries and Storytellers Created the New Testament and Christian Faith* (San Francisco: Harper San Francisco, 2004), 235–38.

28. See Tony Keddie, "Iudaea Capta vs. Mother Zion: The Flavian Discourse on Judaeans and Its Delegitimation in 4 Ezra," *Journal for the Study of Judaism* 49 (2018): 498–550; Marius Heemstra, *The* Fiscus Judaicus *and the Parting of the Ways* (Tübingen: Mohr Siebeck, 2010).

29. Suetonius, *Lives of the Caesars* 12.2–3 (Domitian), trans. Catharine Edwards (Oxford: Oxford University Press, 2008), 288.

30. My translation. See Martin D. Goodman, "Nerva, the *Fiscus Judaicus* and Jewish Identity," *Journal of Roman Studies* 79 (1989): 40–44.

31. Warren Carter, "Paying the Tax to Rome as Subversive Praxis: Matthew 17.24–27," *Journal for the Study of the New Testament* 22 (2000): 3–31.

32. It is worth noting that John is the only gospel that doesn't relate Jesus's teaching on head taxes. Arguably, John's avoidance of this topic is consistent with his distinct attempt to differentiate Christ followers from "the Jews." See J. Andrew Overman, "The First Revolt and Flavian Politics," in *The First Jewish Revolt: Archaeology, History, and Ideology*, ed. Andrea M. Berlin and J. Andrew Overman (London: Routledge, 2002), 218–19.

33. Bruce W. Winter, *Divine Honours for the Caesars: The First Christians' Responses* (Grand Rapids, MI: Eerdmans, 2015); Steven J. Friesen, *Imperial Cults and the Apocalypse of John: Reading Revelation in the Ruins* (Oxford: Oxford University Press, 2001); Monika Bernett, "Roman Imperial Cult in the Galilee: Structures, Functions, and Dynamics," in *Religion, Ethnicity, and Identity in Ancient Galilee: A Region in Transition*, ed. Jürgen Zangenberg, Harold W. Attridge, and Dale B. Martin (Tübingen: Mohr Siebeck, 2007), 337–56.

34. Dio Cassius, *Roman History* 65.7.2; Martial, *Epigrams* 7.55; 11.94. See Zeichmann, "Date of Mark's Gospel," 436; Christopher B. Zeichmann, "Martial and the *fiscus Iudaicus* Once More," *Journal for the Study of the Pseudepigrapha* 25 (2015): 111–17. Like the gospels, Josephus subversively dodges the issue of Jupiter as recipient, saying only that the new tax ordered "each of them to bring two drachmas every year into the Capitol" (*Jewish War* 7.218). See Heemstra, *Fiscus Judaicus*, 10.

35. E. P. Sanders provides an important critique of these anti-Jewish interpretations in *Jesus and Judaism* (London: SCM, 1985), 61–70.

36. Mark 11:15–19; Matt. 21:12–17; Luke 19:45–48; John 2:13–22. I have defended the arguments in this section at greater length in my essay "Beyond the 'Den of Robbers.'"

37. Isa. 56:7; Jer. 7:11. The quotation is from Luke 19:46, but is similar in Mark and Matthew. Mark 11:17, the earliest version, includes the phrase "for all the nations." Luke and Matthew (21:13) omitted this phrase and changed the tense of Mark's perfect-tense verb.

38. Ps. 69:9; Zech. 14:21; John 2:16.

39. Neh. 10:32. See also my discussion of Temple taxes in *Class and Power*, 188–95.

40. Jodi Magness, *The Archaeology of Qumran and the Dead Sea Scrolls* (Grand Rapids, MI: Eerdmans, 2002), 190.

41. Peter Richardson, *Building Jewish in the Roman East* (Waco, TX: Baylor University Press, 2004), 241–52. While Jews would often have paid their Temple taxes in this coinage because it was predominant in Jerusalem at the time, there was no requirement to pay the tax in Tyrian coins, as is sometimes assumed. See further Donald T. Ariel and Jean-Philippe Fontanille, *The Coins of Herod: A Modern Analysis and Die Classification* (Leiden: Brill, 2012), 38–40.

42. Richard Bauckham, "Jesus' Demonstration in the Temple," in *Law and Religion: Essays on the Place of the Law in Israel and Early Christianity*, ed. Barnabas Lindars (Cambridge: Clarke, 1988), 72–89.

43. With regard to animals sold for sacrifice, Mark and Matthew mention only doves, offerings given by the poor. John adds people selling cattle and sheep to those Jesus drove out, perhaps implying a broader critique of the sale of animals for sacrifice at the Temple.

44. Bill O'Reilly and Martin Dugard, *Killing Jesus: A History* (New York: Holt, 2013), 122. Notably, when the Roman governor Pilate tried to seize funds from the Temple treasury, he nearly caused a revolt (Josephus, *Jewish War* 2.175; *Jewish Antiquities* 18.60).

45. Psalms of Solomon 8:11.

46. Kenneth Atkinson, "The 'Three Nets of Belial' in the Dead Sea Scrolls: A Pre-Qumran Tradition," *Qumran Chronicle* 26 (2018): 23–38.

47. Testament of Moses 7:4–8 (my trans.). See my *Revelations of Ideology*, chap. 5.

48. Paula Fredriksen, *Jesus of Nazareth, King of the Jews: A Jewish Life and the Emergence of Christianity* (New York: Vintage, 2012), 233.

49. John 11:38–57.

50. See, among others, Peter Richardson and Douglas R. Edwards, "Jesus and Palestinian Social Protest: Archaeological and Literary Perspectives," in *Handbook of Early Christianity: Social Science Approaches*, ed. Anthony J. Blasi et al. (Walnut Creek, CA: Altamira, 2002), 247–66; John S. Kloppenborg, "Unsocial Bandits," in *A Wandering Galilean: Essays in Honour of Seán Freyne*, ed. Zuleika Rodgers, Margaret Daly-Denton, and Anne Fitzpatrick Mckinley (Leiden: Brill, 2009), 451–84.

51. Seth Schwartz, *Josephus and Judaean Politics* (Leiden: Brill, 1990), 58–109.

52. Mark 15:27, 32; Matt. 27:38, 44; cf. Luke 23:33, 39–43.

8. PROTECTION FROM INVADERS

1. Michael Hiltzik, "Just before a Shooter Killed 20 in El Paso, the NRA Celebrated Looser Texas Gun Laws," *Los Angeles Times,* August 4, 2019, www.latimes.com/business/story/2019-08-04/nra-celebrated-looser-texas-gun-laws-before-el-paso-shooting. A federal law that took effect on March 26, 2019, did, however, ban bump stocks nationwide.

2. Yasmeen Abutaleb, "What's inside the Hate-Filled Manifesto Linked to the Alleged El Paso Shooter," *Washington Post,* August 4, 2019, www.washingtonpost.com/politics/2019/08/04/whats-inside-hate-filled-manifesto-linked-el-paso-shooter/. The manifesto is excerpted in Laura Italiano, "Sick Manifesto Linked to Walmart Shooting Suspect Blames 'Hispanic Invasion,'" *New York Post,* August 3, 2019, https://nypost.com/2019/08/03/sick-manifesto-linked-to-walmart-shooting-suspect-blames-hispanic-invasion/. Note: the manifestos of white nationalists are rarely published by the mainstream media. I think it is important, however, to use these sources to analyze their ideologies and their intersections with wider political trends. Therefore, I have cited

shooters' manifestos from sources that I consider less reliable, though notably they are not affiliated with the Far Right.

3. Kevin Breuninger, "Trump Suggests Tying 'Strong Background Checks' to Immigration Reform after Two Mass Shootings," CNBC, August 5, 2019, www.cnbc.com/2019/08/05/trump-suggests-tying-background-checks-to-immigration-bill-after-mass-shootings.html.

4. Roxanne Dunbar-Ortiz, *Loaded: A Disarming History of the Second Amendment* (San Francisco: City Lights, 2018). See also Scott Melzer, *Gun Crusaders: The NRA's Culture War* (New York: New York University Press, 2012).

5. Dunbar-Ortiz, *Loaded*, 33–37.

6. Eugene Scott, "Why Ted Cruz Was Making a Biblical Case for Gun Rights after the Odessa Shooting," *Washington Post*, September 4, 2019. www.washingtonpost.com/politics/2019/09/04/why-ted-cruz-was-making-biblical-case-gun-rights-after-odessa-shooting/.

7. Seneca the Younger, *Epistles* 14.9, quoted in Lincoln H. Blumell, "Beware of Bandits! Banditry and Land Travel in the Roman Empire," *Journeys* 8 (2007): 10.

8. See Brent D. Shaw, "Bandits in the Roman Empire," in *Studies in Ancient Greek and Roman Society*, ed. Robin Osborne (Cambridge: Cambridge University Press, 2004), 326–74; Thomas Grünewald, *Bandits in the Roman Empire: Myth and Reality*, trans. John Drinkwater (London: Routledge, 2004).

9. Ari Z. Bryen, *Violence in Roman Egypt: A Study in Legal Interpretation* (Philadelphia: University of Pennsylvania Press, 2013), 105.

10. Bryen, *Violence in Roman Egypt*, 114.

11. One possible exception is the Jewish philosopher Philo of Alexandria's claim that the Roman governor in Egypt responded to an accusation that Jews were rebels by having their houses searched for arms, which weren't there. As part of his defense of these Jews, Philo disparaged indigenous Egyptians by noting that, when their homes had been searched for arms at an earlier date, it took a literal fleet of ships to carry away all of their arms (*Flaccus* 83–95). In this much-embellished account, however, Philo is not speaking of bandits but of accusations of Jewish sedition during a period of Jewish persecution in

Alexandria. Philo's account also reflects the rivalry between Jews and Egyptians in Alexandria, where both were marginalized.

12. "2014 Crime in the United States," FBI, Uniform Crime Reporting, 2014, https://ucr.fbi.gov/crime-in-the-u.s/2014/crime-in-the-u.s.-2014/tables/expanded-homicide-data/expanded_homicide_data_table_6_murder_race_and_sex_of_vicitm_by_race_and_sex_of_offender_2014.xls; Jon Greenberg, "Trump's Pants on Fire Tweet That Blacks Killed 81% of White Homicide Victims," Politifact, November 23, 2015, www.politifact.com/truth-o-meter/statements/2015/nov/23/donald-trump/trump-tweet-blacks-white-homicide-victims/.

13. David Neiwert, "Vast Majority of Most Crimes Are Committed by a Person of the Same Race as the Victim, Bureau of Justice Statistics Reports," Southern Poverty Law Center, October 23, 2017, www.splcenter.org/hatewatch/2017/10/23/white-supremacists-favorite-myths-about-black-crime-rates-take-another-hit-bjs-study.

14. See Katheryn Russell-Brown, *The Color of Crime,* 2nd ed. (New York: New York University Press, 2009).

15. P. A. Brunt, "Did Imperial Rome Disarm Her Subjects?," *Phoenix* 29 (1975): 260–70; Christopher J. Fuhrmann, *Policing the Roman Empire: Soldiers, Administration, and Public Order* (New York: Oxford University Press, 2012), 51–52.

16. Galen, *On Anatomical Procedures* 1.2, quoted in Blumell, "Beware of Bandits," 11.

17. Josephus, *Jewish War* 2.125, quoted in Blumell, "Beware of Bandits," 11.

18. Grünewald, *Bandits,* chap. 5.

19. See Shaw, "Bandits"; Grünewald, *Bandits;* John S. Kloppenborg, "Unsocial Bandits," in *A Wandering Galilean: Essays in Honour of Seán Freyne,* ed. Zuleika Rodgers, Margaret Daly-Denton, and Anne Fitzpatrick Mckinley (Leiden: Brill, 2009), 451–84.

20. Blumell, "Beware of Bandits," 12–15; Fuhrmann, *Policing the Roman Empire,* chap. 8.

21. Christopher B. Zeichmann, *The Roman Army and the New Testament* (Lanham, MD: Lexington/Fortress, 2018); Ian P. Haynes, *Blood of the Provinces: The Roman Auxilia and the Making of Provincial Society from*

Augustus to the Severans (Oxford: Oxford University Press, 2013); Fuhrmann, *Policing the Roman Empire,* chaps. 6–7.

22. Dale B. Martin, "Jesus in Jerusalem: Armed and Not Dangerous," *Journal for the Study of the New Testament* 37 (2014): 3–24; F. Gerald Downing, "Dale Martin's Swords for Jesus: Shaky Evidence?," *Journal for the Study of the New Testament* 37, no. 3 (2015): 326–33; Dale B. Martin, "Response to Downing and Fredriksen," *Journal for the Study of the New Testament* 37 (2015): 334–45.

23. Martin, "Jesus in Jerusalem."

24. Grünewald, *Bandits,* chap. 5.

25. For a range of views on ethnic prejudice and racism (or "protoracism") in Roman antiquity, see Benjamin Isaac, *The Invention of Racism in Classical Antiquity* (Princeton, NJ: Princeton University Press, 2004); Denise Kimber Buell, *Why This New Race: Ethnic Reasoning in Early Christianity* (New York: Columbia University Press, 2008); Laura Nasrallah and Elisabeth Schüssler Fiorenza, eds., *Prejudice and Christian Beginnings: Investigating Race, Gender, and Ethnicity in Early Christian Studies* (Minneapolis, MN: Fortress, 2009).

26. A. N. Sherwin-White, *The Roman Citizenship* (Oxford: Clarendon, 1980).

27. On provincial and district border tolls, see my *Class and Power in Roman Palestine: The Socioeconomic Setting of Judaism and Christian Origins* (Cambridge: Cambridge University Press, 2019), 133–35, and the literature cited there.

28. Timothy Luckritz Marquis, *Transient Apostle: Paul, Travel, and the Rhetoric of Empire* (New Haven, CT: Yale University Press, 2013); Cavan Concannon, "Economic Aspects of Intercity Travel among the Pauline Assemblies," in *Paul and Economics s: A Handbook,* ed. Thomas R. Blanton IV and Raymond Pickett (Minneapolis, MN: Fortress, 2017), 333–60.

29. Hector Avalos, "Diasporas 'R' Us: Attitudes toward Immigrants in the Bible," in *The Bible in Political Debate: What Does It Really Say?,* ed. Frances Flannery and Rodney A. Werline (London: Bloomsbury, 2016), 33–46.

30. 1 Pet. 1:1; 2:11; 4:17. See John H. Elliott, *A Home for the Homeless: A Social-Scientific Criticism of 1 Peter, Its Situation and Strategy* (Eugene, OR: Wipf and Stock, 2005).

31. E.g., Heb. 11:13–16. See Benjamin H. Dunning, *Aliens and Sojourners: Self as Other in Early Christianity* (Philadelphia: University of Pennsylvania Press, 2012), chap. 2. See further Matthew Thiessen, "Hebrews and the End of the Exodus," *Novum Testamentum* 49 (2007): 353–69, on the persistence of the Exodus in Hebrews.

32. Joseph A. Marchal, *The Politics of Heaven: Women, Gender, and Empire in the Study of Paul* (Minneapolis, MN: Fortress, 2008), chap. 2.

33. Ed Mazza, "Fox News Cohosts: Jesus Wasn't a Refugee, His Family Just Wanted to Pay Their Taxes," *HuffPost,* February 1, 2017, www.huffingtonpost.ca/entry/fox-news-refugee-jesus_n_589176d9e4b0c9 0eff010786.

34. Carol Kuruvilla, "Trump's Spiritual Adviser: Sure, Jesus Was a Refugee, but He Didn't Do Anything Illegal," *HuffPost,* July 11, 2018, www.huffingtonpost.ca/entry/trump-spiritual-adviser-jesus-refugee-paula-white_n_5b4638bce4b0bc69a783160a.

35. Matt. 2:5–7 cites as "the prophet" a modification of Mic. 5:2 based on 2 Sam. 5:2 and other intertexts. Luke 2:4 implies a similar tradition as the source for this gospel's account of the birth in Bethlehem. John mentions Bethlehem as the place that the Davidic Messiah comes from in 7:42 but does not supply a birth narrative like those in Matthew and Luke.

36. Among others: Raymond E. Brown, *The Birth of the Messiah: A Commentary on the Infancy Narratives in Matthew and Luke* (New York: Doubleday, 1977); L. Michael White, *From Jesus to Christianity: How Four Generations of Visionaries and Storytellers Created the New Testament and Christian Faith* (San Francisco: Harper San Francisco, 2004), 32–35. The accuracy of Luke's description of the census remains much debated. For a sophisticated recent defense of the accuracy of Luke, see Sabine R. Huebner, *Papyri and the Social World of the New Testament* (New York: Cambridge University Press, 2019), chap. 3. I agree with Huebner that Luke wouldn't have described the census in a way that his audience would have considered implausible, and thus that Luke implied that Joseph owned land in Bethlehem, but I reject her claim that Luke had accurate information about a census under Herod.

37. Psalms of Solomon 17:11; Testament of Moses 6:4; Josephus, *Jewish Antiquities* 15.50–56; 16.392–94; 17.182–87.

38. Macrobius, *Saturnalia* 2.4.11.

39. Matt. 5:17; see also 7:12; 11:13; 22:40. Compare this to the different understanding of the era of the Law and the Prophets as ending with John the Baptist in Luke 16:16–17.

40. Dale C. Allison Jr., *The New Moses: A Matthean Typology* (Eugene, OR: Wipf and Stock, 2013).

41. Dave Armstrong, "Borders and the Bible," *National Catholic Register,* January 14, 2019, www.ncregister.com/blog/darmstrong/borders-and-the-bible.

42. In Mark 3:19b–30, Luke's source, armor is not mentioned but instead the strong man is tied up. Similarly, however, the strong man represents Satan. The parable is an allusion to Isa. 49:26, where God ("the Strong One of Jacob") rescues captives from a strong tyrant. Matt. 12:22–32 preserves Mark's binding and does not mention armor. See Elizabeth E. Shively, *Apocalyptic Imagination in the Gospel of Mark: The Literary and Theological Role of Mark 3:22–30* (Berlin: De Gruyter, 2012).

43. Tara Isabella Burton, "The Racist History of the Bible Verse the White House Uses to Justify Separating Families," *Vox,* June 15, 2018, www.vox.com/2018/6/15/17467818/bible-verse-white-house-immigration-racism-romans-13.

44. Ralph Drollinger, "What the Bible Says about our Illegal Immigration Problem," Capitol Ministries, February 18, 2019, https://capmin.org/bible-says-illegal-immigration-problem/. The italics on "foreign" are Drollinger's, although he also puts the word in bold.

45. Angela Denker, *Red State Christians: Understanding the Voters Who Elected Donald Trump* (Minneapolis, MN: Fortress, 2019), 61.

46. Katie Reilly, "Here Are All the Times Donald Trump Insulted Mexico," *Time,* August 31, 2016, https://time.com/4473972/donald-trump-mexico-meeting-insult/; Ben Zimmer, "Where Does Trump's 'Invasion' Rhetoric Come From?," *Atlantic,* August 6, 2019, www.theatlantic.com/entertainment/archive/2019/08/trump-immigrant-invasion-language-origins/595579/; Jessica Schulberg, "The NRA Has Long Urged Americans to Arm Themselves against an Immigrant Invasion," *HuffPost,* August 6, 2019, www.huffingtonpost.ca/entry/nra-el-paso-shooting-anti-immigrant_n_5d49b2d8e4b0d291ed07a824.

47. Nolan D. McCaskill, "Trump's Favorite Bible Verse: 'Eye for an Eye,'" *Politico*, April 14, 2016, www.politico.com/blogs/2016-gop-primary-live-updates-and-results/2016/04/trump-favorite-bible-verse-221954; Breuninger, "Trump Suggests."

48. Melzer, *Gun Crusaders*.

49. Jill Lepore, "Battleground America: One Nation, under the Gun," *New Yorker*, April 16, 2012, www.newyorker.com/magazine/2012/04/23/battleground-america.

50. Melzer, *Gun Crusaders*, 35–42; Michael Waldman, *The Second Amendment: A Biography* (New York: Simon and Schuster, 2015), 87–102.

51. Jessica Dawson, "Shall Not Be Infringed: How the NRA Used Religious Language to Transform the Meaning of the Second Amendment," *Palgrave Communications* 5, no. 1 (2019): 1–13.

52. Brad Plumer, "How the U.S. Gun Industry Became So Lucrative," *Washington Post*, December 19, 2012, www.washingtonpost.com/news/wonk/wp/2012/12/19/seven-facts-about-the-u-s-gun-industry/.

53. Plumer, "How the US Gun Industry," 7–8; Melzer, *Gun Crusaders*, 14.

54. Brandon Withrow, "Does Jesus Want Gun-Toting Christians," *Daily Beast*, April 28, 2018, www.thedailybeast.com/does-jesus-want-gun-toting-christians. Another influential but deeply simplistic biblical justification for gun rights based on this passage is Wayne A. Grudem, *Politics According to the Bible: A Comprehensive Resource for Understanding Modern Political Issues in Light of Scripture* (Grand Rapids, MI: Zondervan, 2010), 201–3.

55. John Piper, "Why I Disagree with Jerry Falwell Jr. on Christians and Guns," *Washington Post*, December 22, 2015, www.washingtonpost.com/news/acts-of-faith/wp/2015/12/23/john-piper-why-i-disagree-with-jerry-falwell-jr-on-christians-and-guns/.

56. T. Rees Shapiro, "Gun-Friendly Liberty University to Open On-Campus Shooting Range," *Washington Post*, December 15, 2016, www.washingtonpost.com/news/grade-point/wp/2016/12/15/gun-friendly-liberty-university-to-open-on-campus-shooting-range/.

57. Mark 14:43–52; Matt. 26:47–56; Luke 22:47–53; John 18:1–11.

58. Ernst Bammel, "The Revolution Theory from Reimarus to Brandon," in *Jesus and the Politics of His Day*, ed. Ernst Bammel and

C.F.D. Moule (Cambridge: Cambridge University Press, 1984), 11–68. Reza Aslan's *Zealot: The Life and Times of Jesus of Nazareth* (New York: Random House, 2013) has recently reinvigorated this debate among scholars. See the essays in *Journal for the Study of the New Testament* 37 (2015).

59. Paula Fredriksen, "Arms and The Man: A Response to Dale Martin's 'Jesus in Jerusalem: Armed and Not Dangerous,'" *Journal for the Study of the New Testament* 37 (2015): 312–25.

60. Luke probably knew the same tradition (from the Q source) that Jesus would bring a sword at the end-times, but he rewrote this saying so that Jesus would bring "division" instead of a sword (Luke 12:49–53). See also Martin's remarks in his "Response to Downing and Fredriksen."

61. The New Testament gospels do, nonetheless, relate certain traditions that portray Jesus as violent. At the very least, these call into question any assumption that Jesus was purely "nonviolent." See Hector Avalos, *The Bad Jesus: The Ethics of New Testament Ethics* (Sheffield: Sheffield Phoenix, 2015), chap. 4.

62. See my "How a Bill O'Reilly Bestseller Helps Explain the Anti-Semitism behind the Poway Shooting," Religion Dispatches (Rewire.News), May 13, 2019, https://rewire.news/religion-dispatches/2019/05/13/how-a-bill-oreilly-bestseller-helps-explain-the-anti-semitism-behind-the-poway-shooting/.

63. "Manifesto of Poway Synagogue Shooter," *San Diego 411*, April 27, 2019, http://sandiegoca411.com/manifesto-of-poway-synagogue-shooter/ (my italics).

9. THE END OF THE WORLD

1. "The 25 Most Influential Evangelicals in America: Tim and Beverly LaHaye," *Time*, February 7, 2005, http://content.time.com/time/specials/packages/article/0,28804,1993235_1993243_1993291,00.html. Amy Johnson Frykholm provides an excellent analysis of the influence of the Left Behind series on American culture in *Rapture Culture: Left Behind in Evangelical America* (Oxford: Oxford University Press, 2004).

2. Tim F. LaHaye and Edward E. Hindson, *Global Warning: Are We on the Brink of World War III?* (Eugene, OR: Harvest House, 2007), 30–31.

3. LaHaye and Hindson, *Global Warning*, 32–38.

4. LaHaye and Hindson, *Global Warning*, 136.

5. Josephus, *Jewish War* 6.283–86.

6. For historical introductions to ancient apocalyptic literature, see John J. Collins, *The Apocalyptic Imagination: An Introduction to Jewish Apocalyptic Literature,* 3rd ed. (Grand Rapids, MI: Eerdmans, 2016); Greg Carey, *Ultimate Things: An Introduction to Jewish and Christian Apocalyptic Literature* (St. Louis, MO: Chalice, 2005).

7. Collins, *Apocalyptic Imagination*, chap. 3.

8. Carey, *Ultimate Things*, 6–11.

9. Stephen D. O'Leary, *Arguing the Apocalypse: A Theory of Millennial Rhetoric* (Oxford: Oxford University Press, 1994); Tony Keddie, *Revelations of Ideology: Apocalyptic Class Politics in Early Roman Palestine* (Leiden: Brill, 2018), 73–86.

10. Stephen L. Cook, "Apocalyptic Prophecy," in *The Oxford Handbook of Apocalyptic Literature,* ed. John J. Collins (Oxford: Oxford University Press, 2014), 19–35.

11. Alexandria Frisch, *The Danielic Discourse on Empire in Second Temple Literature* (Leiden: Brill, 2017); Anathea Portier-Young, *Apocalypse against Empire: Theologies of Resistance in Early Judaism* (Grand Rapids, MI: Eerdmans, 2011).

12. See Keddie, *Revelations of Ideology,* 77–79, and the literature cited there.

13. Some of the issues in the scholarly debate are discussed in Bart D. Ehrman, *Jesus: Apocalyptic Prophet of the New Millennium* (New York: Oxford University Press, 2000); Robert J. Miller, ed., *The Apocalyptic Jesus: A Debate* (Santa Rosa, CA: Polebridge, 2001).

14. Mark 4:31–32; Matt. 13:31–32; Luke 13:8–9.

15. Collins, *Apocalyptic Imagination*, 268.

16. E.g., Psalms of Solomon 17–18. See Barbara R. Rossing, *The Rapture Exposed: The Message of Hope in the Book of Revelation* (New York: Basic Books, 2007), 174–77.

17. Rossing, *Rapture Exposed*, chap. 2.

18. Donald H. Akenson, *Discovering the End of Time: Irish Evangelicals in the Age of Daniel O'Connell* (Montreal: McGill-Queen's Press, 2016).

19. Donald H. Akenson, *Exporting the Rapture: John Nelson Darby and the Victorian Conquest of North-American Evangelicalism* (Oxford: Oxford University Press, 2018); Matthew Avery Sutton, *American Apocalypse: A History of Modern Evangelicalism* (Cambridge, MA: Harvard University Press, 2014), chap. 1; Paul S. Boyer, *When Time Shall Be No More: Prophecy Belief in Modern American Culture* (Cambridge, MA: Belknap Press, 1992), chap. 3; George M. Marsden, *Fundamentalism and American Culture*, 2nd ed. (Oxford: Oxford University Press, 2006), 48–62.

20. Marsden, *Fundamentalism and American Culture*, 66–68. Under the influence of the political tactics of premillennialists like Tim LaHaye and the leaders of the Moral Majority, late twentieth-century premillennialists started to make alliances with postmillennialists and thus express interest in political action (see Michelle Goldberg, *Kingdom Coming: The Rise of Christian Nationalism* [New York: Norton, 2006], 39).

21. Robin Globus Veldman, *The Gospel of Climate Skepticism: Why Evangelical Christians Oppose Action on Climate Change* (Berkeley: University of California Press, 2019).

22. Joseph J. Romm, *Climate Change: What Everyone Needs to Know* (Oxford: Oxford University Press, 2016), 9, 189.

23. Intergovernmental Panel on Climate Change (IPCC), "Special Report on the Ocean and Cryosphere in a Changing Climate," 2019, www.ipcc.ch/srocc/home/.

24. Bulletin of the Atomic Scientists, "Current Time," https://thebulletin.org/doomsday-clock/current-time/.

25. Frances L. Flannery, *Understanding Apocalyptic Terrorism: Countering the Radical Mindset* (London: Routledge, 2015), 208.

26. Rossing, *Rapture Exposed*, 2.

27. Pew Research Center, "Religion and Views on Climate and Energy Issues," October 22, 2015, www.pewresearch.org/science/2015/10/22/religion-and-views-on-climate-and-energy-issues/. See also the survey results showing that climate denial is much more common among Republicans; Cary Funk and Brian Kennedy, "How Americans See Climate Change in 5 Charts," Pew Research Center, April 19, 2019,

www.pewresearch.org/fact-tank/2019/04/19/how-americans-see-climate-change-in-5-charts/.

28. Veldman, *Gospel of Climate Skepticism,* chap. 4; Antony Alumkal, *Paranoid Science: The Christian Right's War on Reality* (New York: New York University Press, 2017), chap. 4.

29. Katharine K. Wilkinson, *Between God and Green: How Evangelicals Are Cultivating a Middle Ground on Climate Change* (New York: Oxford University Press, 2012). On the use of biblical verses in Christian debates over climate change, see Frances Flannery, "Senators, Snowballs, and Scripture: The Bible and Climate Change," in *The Bible in Political Debate: What Does It Really Say?,* ed. Frances Flannery and Rodney A. Werline (London: Bloomsbury, 2016), 61–74.

30. Cornwall Alliance, "The Cornwall Declaration on Environmental Stewardship," 2000, https://cornwallalliance.org/landmark-documents/the-cornwall-declaration-on-environmental-stewardship/. See Wilkinson, *Between God and Green,* 66–69; Alumkal, *Paranoid Science,* 162–66.

31. Alumkal, *Paranoid Science,* 162.

32. See Wilkinson, *Between God and Green,* chap. 1 on Evangelical climate care and the Evangelical Climate Initiative.

33. Alumkal, *Paranoid Science,* 175.

34. Quoted in Susan Friend Harding, *The Book of Jerry Falwell: Fundamentalist Language and Politics* (Princeton, NJ: Princeton University Press, 2000), 244.

35. See, among others, Adela Yarbro Collins, *Crisis and Catharsis: The Power of the Apocalypse* (Philadelphia: Westminster, 1984); Leonard L. Thompson, *The Book of Revelation: Apocalypse and Empire* (Oxford: Oxford University Press, 1990); Harry O. Maier, *Apocalypse Recalled: The Book of Revelation after Christendom* (Minneapolis, MN: Fortress, 2002); Steven J. Friesen, *Imperial Cults and the Apocalypse of John: Reading Revelation in the Ruins* (Oxford: Oxford University Press, 2001). The following discussion is indebted to these important studies.

36. Rev. 12:18–13:10.

37. David E. Aune, *Revelation 6–16* (Nashville, TN: Nelson, 1998), 770–72.

38. Friesen, *Imperial Cults,* 136–37.

39. *Sibylline Oracles* 5:28–34, 93–100, 137–49.

40. Rev. 13:11–18. This beast is described as a "beast that rose out of the earth" (13:11). I refer to it as the "Land Beast" to differentiate it from the other beast that rose out of the sea.

41. Friesen, *Imperial Cults,* 195–96.

42. E.g., Rossing, *Rapture Exposed,* 147–50; Micah D. Kiel, *Apocalyptic Ecology: The Book of Revelation, the Earth, and the Future* (Collegeville, PA: Liturgical Press, 2017).

43. John J. Collins, *What Are Biblical Values? What the Bible Says on Key Ethical Issues* (New Haven, CT: Yale University Press, 2019), 123.

44. Kiel, *Apocalyptic Ecology,* 65–88. See also J. Nelson Kraybill, *Imperial Cult and Commerce in John's Apocalypse* (Sheffield: Sheffield Academic Press, 1996).

45. Brigitte Kahl, "Gaia, Polis, and *Ekklēsia* at the Miletus Market Gate: An Eco-Critical Reimagination of Revelation 12:16," in *The First Urban Churches 1: Methodological Foundations,* ed. James R. Harrison and L.L. Welborn (Atlanta, GA: SBL, 2015), 111–50; Barbara R. Rossing, "Alas for Earth! Lament and Resistance in Revelation 12," in *The Earth Story in the New Testament,* ed. Norman C. Habel and Vicky Balabanski (Sheffield: Sheffield Academic Press, 2002), 180–92. See also Harry O. Maier, "There's a New World Coming! Reading the Apocalypse in the Shadow of the Canadian Rockies," in Habel and Balabanski, *Earth Story,* 166–79.

46. Yaniv Belhassen and Jonathan Ebel, "Tourism, Faith and Politics in the Holy Land: An Ideological Analysis of Evangelical Pilgrimage," *Current Issues in Tourism* 12 (2009): 359–78.

47. On Zion traditions in the Hebrew Bible, see Christl Maier, *Daughter Zion, Mother Zion: Gender, Space, and the Sacred Ancient Israel* (Minneapolis, MN: Fortress, 2008). On later interpretations of these traditions, see Aaron Sherwood, *Paul and the Restoration of Humanity in Light of Ancient Jewish Traditions* (Leiden: Brill, 2012).

48. Those who believe Petra is the site where Jews will hide out during the tribulation base this interpretation on Zech. 13:9; 14:5; Isa. 63:1; Dan. 11:41.

49. Harding, *Book of Jerry Falwell*, 229.

50. Harding, *Book of Jerry Falwell*.

51. Sutton, *American Apocalypse*, 20.

52. This motivation is considered among other factors in Stephen Spector, *Evangelicals and Israel: The Story of American Christian Zionism* (New York: Oxford University Press, 2009).

53. John Hagee, *Jerusalem Countdown* (Lake Mary, FL: FrontLine, 2006).

54. Sanford Nowlin, "Apocalypse Now: Why Pastor John Hagee Has Never Been More Politically Powerful—or Terrifying," *San Antonio Current,* September 10, 2019, www.sacurrent.com/the-daily/archives/2019/09/10/apocalypse-now-why-pastor-john-hagee-has-never-been-more-politically-powerful-or-terrifying.

55. Alissa Wise, "I'm a Rabbi, and I'm Done with Trump Using My People to Cover for His Racism," *Newsweek,* July 23, 2019, www.newsweek.com/rabbi-trump-anti-semitism-1450667.

56. For critical analysis of CUFI's apocalyptic rhetoric, see Sean Durbin, *Righteous Gentiles: Religion, Identity, and Myth in John Hagee's Christians United for Israel* (Leiden: Brill, 2018).

57. Judy Maltz, "Inside the Evangelical Money Flowing into the West Bank," *Haaretz,* December 9, 2018, www.haaretz.com/israel-news/.premium.MAGAZINE-inside-the-evangelical-money-flowing-into-the-west-bank-1.6723443.

58. John Fea, *Believe Me: The Evangelical Road to Donald Trump* (Grand Rapids, MI: Eerdmans, 2018), 143–45.

59. Gus Bova, "Under Trump, Islamophobic Pastor John Hagee's Star Rises Again," *Texas Observer,* August 9, 2018, www.texasobserver.org/trump-pastor-john-hagee-texas-jerusalem/.

60. "Full Transcript of Pence's Knesset Speech," *Jerusalem Post,* January 22, 2018, www.jpost.com/Israel-News/Full-transcript-of-Pences-Knesset-speech-539476. The Christian Right's apocalyptic influencers are often careful to demonize Muslims' end-times fantasies, as understood through their own fundamentalist interpretive lens, without admitting that their own end-times fantasies operate on the same logic; LaHaye and Hindson, *Global Warning,* 39–44, 88–100; Hagee, *Jerusalem Countdown,* 67–82.

61. On the settlements, see the important essays in Ariel Handel, Marco Allegra, and Erez Maggor, eds., *Normalizing Occupation: The Politics of Everyday Life in the West Bank Settlements* (Bloomington: Indiana University Press, 2017).

62. Jessica Schulberg, "The Minnesota Congresswoman Who Can Criticize Israel," *HuffPost,* October 11, 2019, www.huffingtonpost.ca/entry/betty-mccollum-minnesota-israeli-palestinian_n_5d926349e4boe9e760514c1f?ri18n=true.

63. Wise, "I'm a Rabbi."

64. Wise, "I'm a Rabbi."

65. Wise, "I'm a Rabbi."

66. See, among others, Judith Lieu, *Christian Identity in the Jewish and Graeco-Roman World* (Oxford: Oxford University Press, 2004); Adam H. Becker and Annette Yoshiko Reed, eds., *The Ways That Never Parted: Jews and Christians in Late Antiquity and the Early Middle Ages* (Minneapolis, MN: Fortress, 2007).

67. Elaine Pagels, *Revelations: Visions, Prophecy, and Politics in the Book of Revelation* (New York: Viking, 2012). See also Paul B. Duff, *Who Rides the Beast? Prophetic Rivalry and the Rhetoric of Crisis in the Churches of the Apocalypse* (Oxford: Oxford University Press, 2001); John W. Marshall, *Parables of War: Reading John's Jewish Apocalypse* (Waterloo: Wilfrid Laurier University Press, 2001); David Frankfurter, "Jews or Not? Reconstructing the 'Other' in Rev 2:9 and 3:9," *Harvard Theological Review* 94 (2002): 403–25.

68. Gen. 9:4–6; see also Lev. 17:8–18:30. These laws were developed in later Jewish literature, and especially in the rabbinic writings. See Markus Bockmuehl, *Jewish Law in Gentile Churches: Halakhah and the Beginning of Christian Public Ethics* (Edinburgh: T&T Clark, 2000), chap. 7; Christine Hayes, *What's Divine about Divine Law? Early Perspectives* (Princeton, NJ: Princeton University Press, 2017), 354–70.

69. Rom. 9–11; Gal. 6:16.

70. Cavan W. Concannon, *"When You Were Gentiles": Specters of Ethnicity in Roman Corinth and Paul's Corinthian Correspondence* (New Haven, CT: Yale University Press, 2014), chap. 4.

71. Lev. 18:1–30 (18:19 on menstruation). Paul does, however, require Gentiles to follow at least some of these sexual purity laws in 1 Cor.

5–7. See further Bockmuehl, *Jewish Law;* Peter J. Tomson, *Paul and the Jewish Law: Halakha in the Letters of the Apostle to the Gentiles* (Minneapolis, MN: Fortress, 1990).

72. Pagels, *Revelations,* 54–55.

AFTERWORD

1. Ed Pilkington, "'Truth Isn't Truth': Giuliani Trumps 'Alternative Facts' with New Orwellian Outburst," *Guardian,* August 19, 2018, www.theguardian.com/us-news/2018/aug/19/truth-isnt-truth-rudy-giuliani-trump-alternative-facts-orwellian.

2. Hector Avalos, *The Bad Jesus: The Ethics of New Testament Ethics* (Sheffield: Sheffield Phoenix, 2015).

Suggestions for Further Reading

The bibliography on topics addressed in this book is as enormous as a megachurch but often far less accessible. In the endnotes, I have provided references to scholarly books, mostly in English, that range from the widely accessible to the very technical. Here, however, I wish to highlight some resources that might be of particular interest to a nonspecialist who wishes to pursue certain topics in this book further.

First, I recommend reading the biblical texts in one of the following scholarly study Bibles (both of which use the New Revised Standard Version translation): Michael D. Coogan, ed., *The New Oxford Annotated Bible: New Revised Standard Version with the Apocrypha: An Ecumenical Study Bible* (Oxford: Oxford University Press, 2018); Harold W. Attridge, ed., *The HarperCollins Study Bible: Fully Revised and Updated* (New York: HarperCollins, 2006). Both of these books were prepared by teams of leading scholars. They provide useful introductions, maps, and notes on alternative translation choices and issues pertaining to historical context and interpretation.

An excellent new resource for historical research on the Bible is Bible Odyssey, the Society of Biblical Literature's online platform for short, accessible, peer-reviewed articles by biblical scholars on a wide and rapidly expanding range of topics: www.bibleodyssey.org.

Readers looking for historical introductions to the New Testament texts might begin by consulting the following textbooks: Bart D. Ehrman, *The New Testament: A Historical Introduction to the Early Christian Writings* (Oxford: Oxford University Press, 2004); L. Michael White, *From Jesus to Christianity: How Four Generations of Visionaries and Storytellers Created the New Testament and Christian Faith* (San Francisco: Harper San Francisco, 2004). Each of these authors has also written engaging books on the differences between the gospels: Ehrman, *Jesus, Interrupted: Revealing the Hidden Contradictions in the Bible (And Why We Don't Know about Them)* (New York: Harper Collins, 2009); White, *Scripting Jesus: The Gospels in Rewrite* (New York: HarperOne, 2010).

Those seeking to understand how historically informed interpretations of the New Testament may be enriched by critical engagement with contemporary social justice issues are encouraged to consult Mitzi J. Smith and Yung Suk Kim's *Toward Decentering the New Testament: A Reintroduction* (Eugene, OR: Cascade Books, 2018), a textbook that prioritizes the voices and concerns of minoritized communities.

Scholarly quests to recover the historical Jesus have left a long paper trail. A reliable guide to the main issues and the history of research is Helen K. Bond, *The Historical Jesus: A Guide for the Perplexed* (London: Bloomsbury, 2012).

New Testament scholars are continuing to experience their "come to Jesus" moment with regard to Jesus's Jewishness. It is one thing to concede that Jesus and the earliest people who wrote about him were Jewish, but another to recognize that they were genuinely and unremittingly Jewish. Paula Fredriksen has written two excellent books on the Jewishness of Jesus and the gospels: *Jesus of Nazareth, King of the Jews: A Jewish Life and the Emergence of Christianity* (New York: Vintage, 2012) and *When Christians Were Jews: The First Generation* (New Haven, CT: Yale University Press, 2018). Readers might also wish to consult the introductions and notes in Amy-Jill Levine and Marc Z. Brettler, eds., *The Jewish Annotated New Testament* (Oxford: Oxford University Press, 2011).

On the New Testament world, in all of its social, political, cultural, and economic complexity, Wayne A. Meeks's widely influential study is a great starting point: *The First Urban Christians: The Social World of the Apostle Paul*, 2nd ed. (New Haven, CT: Yale University Press, 2003). For more recent perspectives, one might refer to the essays in Dietmar Neufeld and Richard E. DeMaris, eds., *Understanding the Social World of the New Testament* (London: Routledge, 2009).

The socioeconomic situation in Judaea/Palestine, in particular, at the time of Christian origins is addressed succinctly in Samuel L. Adams, *Social and Economic Life in Second Temple Judea* (Louisville, KY: Westminster John Knox, 2014), and in a more detailed manner in Ekkehard Stegemann and Wolfgang Stegemann, *The Jesus Movement: A Social History of Its First Century*, translated by O.C. Dean (Minneapolis, MN: Fortress, 1999), and my own *Class and Power in Roman Palestine: The Socioeconomic Setting of Judaism and Christian Origins* (Cambridge: Cambridge University Press, 2019).

For a handy introduction to social relations and daily life in the Roman Empire, see Robert Knapp, *Invisible Romans* (Cambridge, MA: Harvard University Press, 2011). A more comprehensive resource on the social history of the Roman Empire is Peter Garnsey and Richard P. Saller, *The Roman Empire: Economy, Society and Culture*, 2nd ed. (Oakland: University of California Press, 2015). Harry O. Maier's *New Testament Christianity in the Roman World* (Oxford: Oxford University Press, 2018) does a splendid job of showing how the New Testament texts are products of the culture and society of the Roman Empire.

A reader interested in further study of Judaism at the time of Christian origins will find much of interest in James C. VanderKam's textbook, *An Introduction to Early Judaism* (Grand Rapids, MI: Eerdmans, 2001), as well as Shaye Cohen's more narrative-based overview, *From the Maccabees to the Mishnah*, 3rd ed. (Louisville, KY: Westminster John Knox, 2014).

There is an unfortunate lack of scholarly literature on the political abuses of biblical texts. For a starting point on some of the key issues, see Frances Flannery and Rodney A. Werline, eds., *The Bible in Political Debate: What Does It Really Say?* (London: Bloomsbury, 2016). For an exceptionally judicious historical-critical exploration of the biblical basis of modern Christian ethics, see John J. Collins, *What Are Biblical Values? What the Bible Says on Key Ethical Issues* (New Haven, CT: Yale University Press, 2019).

Turning now to more recent history, Roland Boer and Christina Petterson's *Idols of Nations: Biblical Myth at the Origins of Capitalism* (Minneapolis, MN: Fortress, 2014) makes important inroads by examining the cross-fertilization of Protestant and capitalist ideologies in early modern Europe.

On the myth of America's providential founding as a Christian nation, see Steven K. Green's *Inventing a Christian America: The Myth of the Religious Founding* (Oxford: Oxford University Press, 2015) and Amanda Porterfield's *Conceived in Doubt: Religion and Politics in the New American Nation* (Chicago: University of Chicago Press, 2010). John Fea offers more of a middle-ground approach that, nonetheless, rightly emphasizes complexity: *Was America Founded as a Christian Nation? A Historical Introduction*, rev. ed. (Louisville, KY: Westminster John Knox, 2016).

Those interested in the political history of Christianity in the US might wish to read influential studies such as George M. Marsden's *Fundamentalism and American Culture*, rev. ed. (Oxford: Oxford University Press, 2006) and John T. McGreevy's *Catholicism and American Freedom: A History* (New York: Norton, 2003). Or they might wish to begin with more recent works on Evangelicalism, in particular Matthew Avery Sutton, *American Apocalypse: A History of Modern Evangelicalism* (Cambridge, MA: Harvard University Press, 2014); Frances FitzGerald, *The Evangelicals: The Struggle to Shape America* (New York: Simon and Schuster, 2017); and Steven P. Miller, *The Age of Evangelicalism: America's Born-Again Years* (Oxford: Oxford University Press, 2014).

Daniel K. Williams provides a page-turning overview of the rise of the Christian Right in *God's Own Party: The Making of the Christian Right* (Oxford: Oxford University Press, 2010). For a close analysis of the role of corporations in this history, Kevin M. Kruse's *One Nation under God: How Corporate America Invented Christian America* (New York: Basic, 2015) is required reading. For further insights into these crucial historical developments, see Kim Phillips-Fein's *Invisible Hands: The Businessmen's Crusade against the New Deal* (New York: Norton, 2009) and Darren E. Grem's *The Blessings of Business: How Corporations Shaped Conservative Christianity* (Oxford: Oxford University Press, 2016). In *The Spiritual-Industrial Complex: America's Religious Battle against Communism in the Early Cold War* (Oxford: Oxford University Press, 2011), Jonathan P. Herzog further exposes the anticommunist dimension of the rise of the Right. And in *Family Values and the Rise of the Christian Right* (Philadelphia: University of Pennsylvania Press, 2015), Seth Dowland traces the early history of the Culture Wars.

On the shifting politics and rhetoric of the Christian Right since the Great Recession, two important studies that reward a close reading are Theda Skocpol and Vanessa Williamson's *The Tea Party and the Remaking of Republican Conservatism,* 2nd ed. (Oxford: Oxford University Press, 2016) and Bryan T. Gervais and Irwin L. Morris's *Reactionary Republicanism: How the Tea Party in the House Paved the Way for Trump's Victory* (Oxford: Oxford University Press, 2018).

Finally, the go-to book on the politics of the Christian Right in the Trump era is John Fea's *Believe Me: The Evangelical Road to Donald Trump* (Grand Rapids, MI: Eerdmans, 2018). Other books that illuminate the motivations for allegiance to Trump among the Christian Right include Stephen Mansfield's *Choosing Donald Trump: God, Anger, Hope, and Why Christian Conservatives Supported Him* (Grand Rapids, MI: Baker, 2017) and Angela Denker's *Red State Christians: Understanding the Voters Who Elected Donald Trump* (Minneapolis, MN: Fortress, 2019). Much more will surely be written on this topic in the years to come.

Index

Abbott, Greg, 216
abortion: Christian Right on, 96;
  Drollinger on, 127; Evangelicals'
  opposition to, 135–36, 147–48; as
  murder in early Christian texts,
  149, 308n51; NT silence on, 150,
  164; Republican influencers on,
  149; Republican Jesus as
  opposed to, 26, 50; in Roman
  Empire, 140, 142; Samaritan's
  Purse's agenda against, 183; Tea
  Party movement and, 107;
  Trump on, 148. *See also* fetal
  personhood
Acts of the Apostles, 16, 150, 177, 181,
  186, 261, 311nn84,90
Adams, John, 73
almsgiving, 169, 180–81, 190, 191,
  317n47, 318n58. *See also* charity
androgyny, 161 fig.14, 161–63, 241.
  See also eunuchs
anti-Semitism: Christian Right
  and, 259–60; Christian Zionism
  on, 258–59, 265; in *Killing Jesus*,

33, 39, 43; Poway Synagogue
  Shooting, 235–36, 237; white
  nationalism and, 39
Arabs: in *Killing Jesus*, 43; racist
  view of in *Killing Jesus* (O'Reilly
  and Dugard), 280–81n61
Archelaus (son of Herod I), 225–26
Arminianism, 60–61, 63–69, 75,
  116–17, 174
Arminius, Jacob, 59–60
Armstrong, Dave, 227–28
Augustine of Hippo, 55, 60, 106,
  267
Augustus, Caesar, 322n12
Avalos, Hector, 269

Babatha, 138–39
Bachmann, Michele, 109, 110–12,
  113, 126
Baden, Joel, 129, 302n82
bandits, 206–14, 218–20, 231–34,
  327n11
Bannon, Steve, 108
Barber, William, 173–74, 177

Founded in 1893,
UNIVERSITY OF CALIFORNIA PRESS
publishes bold, progressive books and journals
on topics in the arts, humanities, social sciences,
and natural sciences—with a focus on social
justice issues—that inspire thought and action
among readers worldwide.

The UC PRESS FOUNDATION
raises funds to uphold the press's vital role
as an independent, nonprofit publisher, and
receives philanthropic support from a wide
range of individuals and institutions—and from
committed readers like you. To learn more, visit
ucpress.edu/supportus.